An Ecology
of the Spirit

An Ecology of the Spirit

RELIGIOUS REFLECTION AND ENVIRONMENTAL CONSCIOUSNESS

EDITED BY

Michael Barnes

THE ANNUAL PUBLICATION OF THE
COLLEGE THEOLOGY SOCIETY
1990
VOLUME 36

UNIVERSITY
PRESS OF
AMERICA

Lanham • New York • London

ISSN 0276-2064
ISBN 0–8191–8960–X (pbk. : alk. paper)
ISBN 0–8191–8959–6 (cloth : alk. paper)

 The paper used in this publication meets the minimum requirements of
American National Standard for Information Sciences—Permanence
of Paper for Printed Library Materials, ANSI Z39.48–1984.

TABLE OF CONTENTS

PREFACE

The essays here were presented at the 1990 Annual Meeting of the College Theology Society at Loyola University of New Orleans. The theme of the meeting was "Theology in an Ecological Perspective." Thanks are due to Dan Sheridan as the local coordinator who made everything run smoothly, to Terry Tilley as national convention director who selected plenary speakers and organized the all the sessions, to Mary Lea Schneider as president of the society and the board of directors who select the themes and locations.

The Religious Studies Department of the University of Dayton contributed greatly to the work of this volume. Joanne Beirise gave proper format to the papers and typed them onto computer disk, with the help of Shannon Ayrey along with Lisa Boone, Melissa Thomson, and Nancy Wagner. As the extensive help from this staff attests, thanks are due to Tom Martin, chair of Religious Studies, for generously making this help available. The first-draft proofreading was done by graduate student Mary Jo Milillo; second-draft proofing, reference work, and knowledgeable advice came from the very able Joyce Karl, also a graduate student.

INTRODUCTION

THE TASK OF THIS VOLUME

Michael H. Barnes

The engineer approaches the ecology to modify the interaction of forces, earth and air and fire and water. The citizen cares about how easy it is to breathe, about beauty lost, about the health of the children. The politician worries about conflicting interests and costs. The religious scholar or theologian tries to place all these concerns within a larger vision of nature and person and God.

The ecologically minded theologian may perceive the divine sacramentally present within the flow of nature. But a general belief in the immanence of God, by power and presence and majesty, as one expression had it, has not always produced ecological consciousness. The same person who practiced finding the presence of God in all things might yet have sought God in order to finally escape from this world. Even a Teilhard de Chardin, whose mystical visions of an evolving creation as a presence of the divine Logos, still hoped eventually to transcend materiality.[1] Christian theology was formed under the strong influence of an otherworldly asceticism. The task for all forms of religious thought in this generation is to form the language that allows people to perceive their own origins and participation in the flow of God's creation.

Ecologically concerned theologians do not all agree on how to interpret creation. For some, nature is an subordinate reality to be controlled by people for their own benefit. For others, nature is a home which we cherish and keep tidy. Others perceive nature to be an overall process superior as a whole to any of its parts, including even the human part. Still others stand before nature as a source of grace, as a gift to which we must be open.

Disagreements arise partly because of differences in temperament. They arise also because in spite of decades of thought and writing by Thomas Berry,[2] Paul Santmire,[3] John Cobb,[4] and others, for most religious thinkers

---

[1]Pierre Teilhard de Chardin, *Hymn of the Universe* or *The Divine Milieu* (Harper and Row, 1961 and 1965 respectively).

[2]Thomas Berry, *The Dream of the Earth* (San Francisco: Sierra Club Books, 1988).

[3]Paul Santmire, *The Travail of Nature: The Ambiguous Ecological Promise of Christian Theology* (Philadelphia: Fortress, 1985).

[4]See John B. Cobb, *Is It too Late? A Theology of Ecology* (Beverly Hills, CA: Bruce,

ecological consciousness is still in formation, still defining itself in relation to specific issues. Ecological aspects of feminism, creation spirituality, sacramental presence, ethics of nature, scripture and tradition, nature and grace are all still developing. It is the growth of an ecology of the spirit.

It is we humans who do ecological thought, develop ecological consciousness, make choices about attitudes and actions. The shared thoughts and choices that constitute human cultures and traditions are the historical manifestation of the human spirit. The cultures and traditions are in turn the spirit-forming forces that guide each new person in history. The job of ecological theology is to articulate the symbols that can locate this spirit in the cosmos as a whole, in the environment of our planet, and in the social ecology that can nurture or diminish each one of us.

For the Christian this ecology of the human spirit is also an ecology of the Spirit, which seeks to locate cosmos, earth environment, society, and self in relation to ultimate value and beauty and truth. This is a difficult theological task that is in its early stages. This volume of essays is a contribution to that work.

The Topics of the Essays

The first part of this volume presents some general approaches to the relation of Christianity to ecological thought. Paul Santmire leads off with a quick survey of themes in Christian tradition that promote or inhibit concern for the environment. Santmire insists that Lynn White's famous thesis, that Christian tradition instilled disregard for the earth, is at best only half right.[5] There is more than one pattern in the history of Christian thought. It includes those who affirmed the earth as well as those who denied it, those who loved and praised it as well as those who sought to escape from it. Santmire's 1985 book *The Travail of Nature* describes these options in detail in the words of Christians from Irenaeus to Teilhard. He seeks a realistic balance between fallenness and fulfillment, appreciative of the kinds of affirmation of nature made by writers like Matthew Fox, but cautious about dreams of ecological bliss without the costs imposed by life's limitations and evils.

John Haught has written theological works on creation, such as his 1984 *The Cosmic Adventure*. In his essay here he begins by locating the source of our anthropocentrism in a feeling of homelessness: "Anthropocentrism is our way of responding to the feeling of not really belonging to the earth and the cosmos." Walker Percy defined us as the only truly alien creature in the entire cosmos, Haught notes. It is better, he thinks, to describe us as the universe

---

1972); and sections of Herman E. Daley and John B. Cobb, *For the Common Good: Redirecting the Economy toward Community, the Environment, and a Sustaining Future* (Boston: Beacon Press, 1989).

[5]Lynn White, Jr., "The Historical Roots of Our Ecologic Crisis," *Science*, Mar.10, 1967, Vol. 155, #3767, 1203-1207.

creating symbols of itself. Where Bultmann tried to make Christian faith an act of freedom that separates us from the threat of unfree nature, Haught reintegrates human life into the adventuresome universe.

The second part of the volume is based on two plenary presentations at the CTS national convention for 1990, by Rosemary Reuther[6] and by Matthew Fox[7] with responses by Jay B. McDaniel[8] and J. Patout Burns. Reuther and Fox look at ecological themes from two distinctive perspectives, the one ecofeminism and the other creation-centered spirituality. Reuther applies her research and reflections on the history of patriarchal attitudes in order to draw the outlines of a different way of perceiving relationships, among people, between people and the environment, and with God, all in a comprehensive ecosystem which is guided by values of cooperation rather than competition and nurturance rather than dominance. Fox pronounces similar ideas, in phrases familiar to his readers, calling for a sense of participation like to that of mysticism, rather than the alienation of the human through false images of a judgmental God and a fallen cosmos.

McDaniel provokes further reflection by four questions to Reuther, seeking from her ecofeminism an affirmation of animal rights, acceptance of other cultural visions like that of shamanism, attention to the fact of a tragic aspect to nature, and a way of speaking of God as interdependent with creation. Burns summarizes the major themes Fox has developed in his various writings and confronts them with a sharp challenge to Fox to show that they are really consonant with the scriptural roots which Fox claims for them. In Fox's theology, says Burns, what is distinctively human and divine are both swallowed up in the cosmic ocean.

The third part of the volume presents historical research into the traditions that have formed our current culture and consciousnesses. Dennis Hamm reflects on Luke's attitudes towards creation. He teases out of Paul's speech on the Areopagus in Acts and from the parable of the Rich Fool in Luke an implicit theology, one that tips all the conflicting opinions in eco-consciousness, whether anthropocentric or biocentric or cosmocentric, into a Christian theocentric context.

---

[6]For more of her thought on ecofeminism see her article "Toward an Ecological-Feminist Theology of Nature," in Judith Plant, ed, *Healing the Wounds: The Promise of Ecofeminism* (Philadelphia: New Society Publications, 1989). Some of her ideas are foreshadowed in the last chapter of her book *New Woman, New Earth: Sexist Ideologies and Human Liberation* (New York: Seabury, 1975).

[7]Similar ideas can be found at greater length in his recent book *The Coming of the Cosmic Christ: The Healing of Mother Earth and The Birth of a Global Renaissance* (San Francisco: Harper and Row, 1988).

[8]He presents many ecological reflections in his two recent books, *Of God and Pelicans: A Theology of Reverence for Life* (Louisville: Westminster/John Knox, 1989); and *Earth, Sky, Gods, and Mortals: Developing an Ecological Spirituality* (Mystic, CT: Twenty-Third Publications, 1990).

Maureen Tilley delights us with stories of how early Christians thought of animals and insects. Early Christianity did not articulate a particular form of eco-consciousness, Tilley tells us. But in an assembly of stories and analysis she shows how the confluence of Greco-Roman culture, Judaic traditions, and early Christian writings flowed into stories of ascetics and martyrs as well as into theological reflections.

John Barciauskas analyzes the fifteenth century ideas of Meister Eckhart, digging to find the roots of this mysticism planted in an earthly soil. The results of this excavation are ambivalent, says Barciauskas. While Eckhart offers a vision of a community of beings in the divine essence, he still seeks a God who transcends a hierarchically structured anthropocentric universe.

The fourth part of the volume contains two works on ecological spirituality, including under this heading the development of attitudes, habits, values, and practices, that become the inner life of the person and guide the person in relations to God, others, and the world. Traditional spirituality tended to be somewhat otherworldly and individualistic, providing ways for the solitary believer to find God beyond earthly attachment. The spirituality outlined in this part of the volume is an ecological one.

Eugene Bianchi explores human psychic structures in relation to the ecological matrix. His work is ambitious, ranging widely over themes old and new, East and West, primitive and modern, literary and scientific, seeking resources for counseling and therapy. It is a two-way process, Bianchi says. The many ecologically relevant symbols of various religions, of ecofeminism, and of naturalism, can nourish the spirit. The person who draws life from these sources will in turn participate in a mood and style of life that nurtures the ecology.

Dorothy Jacko builds upon sacramental themes in Eduard Schillebeeckx's works. She notes that recent spirituality has shifted from a prior vertical orientation in which the individual sought a transcendent God to a horizontal one in which the divine is discovered immanent in others and creation. Jacko argues that even though human liberation takes precedence in Schillebeeckx's perspective over other concerns of his, he nonetheless grounds his complex thought in his theology of creation in a way that embraces all aspects of the cosmos in a relational and non-hierarchical spirituality.

In the fifth part of this volume two essays on ethics outline aspects of a general approach. There are innumerable very specific ethical issues concerning the environment: the trade-off between economic development to help the poor and the cost to the environment; the level of cleanliness of the air balanced against the dislocation of people when jobs are lost because of changes in fuels or modes of power generation; the risk of nuclear pollution against the need to decrease the use of fossil fuels. Behind these specific issues, however, are larger questions of the nature of ethical judgments and of the most basic values to be followed in making any ethical judgments. The two essays in this section address these more fundamental topics.

James Donahue, in a work as broadly ambitious as Bianchi's, surveys major elements in contemporary moral discourse that are related to an ecological awareness. He urges us to exercise human moral responsibility in accord with the belief that all life constitutes the arena of God's creation and activity. He seeks to guide people to reconfigure their choices imaginatively, as he walks the reader through the options of communitarian vs liberal, universalist vs. particularist, narrative vs. theoretical, and classical vs revisionist perspectives.

William French retrieves from traditional Catholic natural law ethics the theme of the common good, to extend it to all life forms. An ethics of rights, even of animal rights, grants rights to the solitary individual. The individual in a community of life in a larger cosmos should be the new context, French argues. He reviews a recent "greening" of papal opinion, from Pius XII to John Paul II, and seeks to shift from an anthropocentric heritage in scripture, Stoic thought, and Aquinas to that of the good of the order of the universe.

The sixth part calls the reader out of Western religious awareness into a small sampling of other religious approaches. It is not just Western religion that has been ambivalent towards or even sometimes disdainful of creation. The traditions which originated in India also have shared in a great world rejection, a declaration that this universe is a fundamentally mistaken or even illusory form of existence. Yet in both Japanese Buddhism and in current Jain and Hindu thought in India people have found resources in their own traditions to justify a positive concern for the environment and connect that concern positively with religious consciousness.

William Grosnick describes a conflict in Japanese religious history between the Buddhist doctrine of no-self (no individual soul or spirit) and the indigenous belief in spirits, even of trees and grasses. From a form of Chinese Buddhism came a middle path, which could include even nonsentient beings in a universal and inclusive struggle for Enlightenment. Popular religious imagination in particular, finding form less in orthodox theology than in the Noh dramas, has been open to a sacred unity of all things.

Christopher Chapple gives first-hand reports of efforts in India to change lifestyles, education, and modes of action to counteract the violence to the environment caused by economic development in that huge nation. Chapple writes hopefully that the ancient culture of India can provide symbols and patterns to overcome the evident threats of pollution, but the facts he cites also return the reader to an awareness of those limits and evils of which Santmire wants to remind us.

Finally, two pieces of a literary nature. Ecological consciousness can be formed by reflecting on the broad issues, the large picture. But our inner habits are probably more often built out of many small occasions. To discover a need to protect a few flowers surviving among the rocks; to see life's larger struggle in the journey of an aging animal limping towards its own death: it is in such moments that our awareness takes its shape.

Fred McCleod gives us such a moment, in the story that Anne Morrow Lindbergh tells about finding her whole life in a few seashells. It can speak beautifully for itself. Sally Kenel provides a final summary of some themes, reviewing them as part of a general metaphor of creation as God's body. Such a metaphor can create new theologies or at least revise old ones.

The Power and Limitations of Theological Reflections

The special competence of Christian theologians is to search the sources of Christian thought, to reflect on human experiences, values, and knowledge, and to elicit from this themes to guide life patterns. There is a great deal of that in this volume. Theologians, however, are not usually also economists, agronomists, botanists, chemists, meteorologists, and medical researchers. So some issues of great relevance to the ecology are not analyzed here.

The earth will always have some ecological order. It need not be one favorable for human life. The most recent ice ages constricted human living space; another ice age could do that again. An extra heating of the earth caused by a greenhouse effect could also harm the human habitat, even while the planet would find its own new balance.

Of all the things that we humans do to make the environment threatening to ourselves, the basic one may weel be to have too many of us. To extract from the earth's potential enough food, medical resources, basic sanitation, simple education, and a few luxuries like books to read, to provide for every person on this earth at least what the United States government would now classify as the poverty level for U.S. citizens, would require an enormous increase in the use of energy. We now worry about the greenhouse effect, about burning jungle forests for room and fuel and food production, about overloading the oceans and the air with chemicals. Population growth makes every one of these problems worse.

It would be possible to minimize these population-caused problems somewhat by accepting a high level of misery for the poor of the earth, still the earth's great majority, while the one billion of us or so that live in relative comfort can continue to battle ecological dangers to our comfort and standard of living. But the other four billion would like to have most of their children live past the age of ten, would like to have enough shoes and sewers to prevent infestations of intestinal parasites from draining energy from the limbs and minds of their children, would like to send their children to schools to learn to read and write, would like to have the techniques and resources to provide themselves and their children with sufficient food and shelter to live long and happy lives. When all five billion people on this earth have achieved that minimum, the burden on the environment can be far worse than it is now. But soon there will be six billion of us. A current estimate is that by the year 2050 there will be ten billion. The economic development needs of the poor should be at the top of the list of human concerns, I believe. Balancing this with concern for the ecology will be difficult.

It is important, I believe, not to be lulled into a sense of satisfaction by the many positive insights and perspectives and values that the theological imagination at work in this volume can provide. We may draw inspiration and a sense of direction from theological resources. But it will be crucial to the future that we not forget that inspiration and a sense of direction are inadequate by themselves. They may comfort the individual who prefers sweet visions without hard truths, but they will help save the environment only when they are connected to very precise information and accurate analysis of the interaction of all the actual forces at work in the intersection of natural processes and human activity.

This requires great expertise in such matters as the interplay of agricultural methods and technologies, in various climates in a world structure of trade and tariffs and subsidies, with different population growth rates under different types of political economies. But part of the process of caring for the planet is to revise basic images and expectations, to implant in our culture certain attitudes. Theological and religious reflections are part of that work. They will serve best if they produce an ecology of the spirit that supports honest and full analyses, difficult decisions, and enduring effort.

Sociobiologists portray the problem faced by the genes of living organisms. The genes program the organism to behave in such a way as to survive and reproduce and pass on copies of the genes. But the life of any organism is much too complex for the genes to be able to give specific instructions to the organism on how to handle successfully every situation in life. So the genes instead provide a two-aspect set of instructions. One aspect is to give a few general instinctual responses. A rabbit that perceives a potential threat is programmed first to freeze, then to flee, and finally to fight. This program increases the chance that the rabbit will survive most threatening situations. The other aspect of the genetic instructions is a program on how to learn. A rabbit learns through experience about areas where there are frequent threats and little food and comes to avoid those areas.

There are analogies to this in our ecological problem today. We cannot foresee every situation that will arrive. So we must give ourselves a general program, one of caution, concern, and calculation. We must first be cautious about what effects we may have on the environment. When we act we must do so with concern that the ecological balances not be upset in any irreparable way. With this caution and care we can then calculate the precise actions to take. Such general rules are necessary, but they are not enough. The other major requirement is to use our ability to learn from our successes and our mistakes.

It is not prose paragraphs like these, however, that can best express and maintain the general rules and the results of our learning. It is rather through vivid images and striking stories that we humans set our minds and hearts on a certain path of life. Well-told stories of caution, concern, and careful calculation will most effectively imprint on the human psyche the attitudes to carry with us when we look at the grasslands and hear the reports about the forests. So we need to collect and reflect on images of life. The essays here do that work, bringing ideas from ecofeminism and nature poetry and tales of the animals and insects, all to refocus our vision.

We humans have an advantage over genes in the way we give instructions to ourselves and future generations. The genes simply produce a set of instinctual programs that rule behavior. The genes are rigidly dogmatic in their instructions. The rabbit cannot reprogram its genes; it can only obey. But when we human persons tell stories and invent images we are also able to remind ourselves that they are our stories and images, produced by us deliberately and able to be changed by us also. This is important in order to avoid ecological dogmatism.

It will always be difficult to maintain a balance between taking our ecological stories and images very seriously, and remembering that we sometimes will have to change those stories. Stories work most powerfully when they take on the appearance of utterly reliable truth, dogmatically certain. We need powerful stories to produce the caution and concern and calculation needed, to draw people to make the commitments needed. But if there is any error in the story, any instructions which unknown to us now will someday become more harmful than helpful, we need to have the freedom to change those stories and revise the images they contain. So we must also undercut the power of the stories to at least some small degree by reminding ourselves that they are our stories and not simply the dogmatic truth. Our own images and thoughts must be as carefully balanced in the long run as the ecology itself. The ecological spirit we need must itself have an ecological balance and flexibility. As the ecology evolves, so must our thoughts, images, and stories about it. The task of this volume is to provide resources for this.

Part One

THE INFLUENCE OF CHRISTIANITY

ON ECOLOGICAL CONSCIOUSNESS

IS CHRISTIANITY ECOLOGICALLY BANKRUPT?
THE VIEW FROM ASYLUM HILL

H. Paul Santmire

When Henry David Thoreau established his residence in Walden, he made a mythic statement which has echoed throughout the caverns of American cultural and religious history ever since. Reinforced in our time by the voices of many sensitive souls, who stand in dread before the face of our global ecological crisis, that Thoreauvian echo has now become an uproar.[1]

What we hear, from many different places, is this: Christianity is ecologically bankrupt. Christianity is predicated on a profound bias against the earth. Christianity heats up history over against nature. Christianity may not have *caused* the modern environmental crisis, as some believe, but, in any case, to invoke its traditions in our situation of ecological crisis would be like trying to put out the fire by reaching for the kerosene.[2]

Today's situation of global ecological crisis, we are told, requires something else. It requires a religious worldview that cools down history, that shows us how to commune with the earth rather than dominate the earth. It requires us to be tutored anew by eccentric teachers such as Henry David Thoreau or by indigenous interpreters of primal religions, who have kept alive a sense of the healing powers of nature. Better, then, repair to the cooling milieu of some Walden, where the experience of communion with nature is still alive, and begin to construct our religious worldview, all over again.

In fact, however, our theological situation today is much more complex than these advocates of the Thoreauvian vision generally seem to realize. We may be losing much if we decide to follow the shamans of the primal religious traditions or their fellow travelers, such as Thoreau. Indeed, it may be the case that the kerygmatic and dogmatic traditions of Christianity are better equipped to guide the faithful in this global, ecological era than the much-heralded primal religious traditions themselves.

---

[1]For a balanced description of the urgency of the environmental crisis, see *Keeping and Healing the Creation*, a Resource Paper Prepared by the Presbyterian Eco-Justice Task Force (Louisville: Presbyterian Church [USA], 1989) 1-42.

[2]I explore this kind of criticism of Christianity at some length in my introduction to *The Travail of Nature: The Ambiguous Ecological Promise of Christian Theology* (Philadelphia: Fortress Press, 1985) chap. 1.

To explore this possibility, I propose to look briefly at the thought of Thoreau, and then review the teachings of Matthew Fox, perhaps the most illustrious and the most illustrative spokesperson for the primal traditions in the contemporary American theological milieu.[3] I will conclude with some reflections about what I consider to be the rich but ambiguous resources of the kerygmatic and dogmatic traditions of Christianity. All this I propose to say not from the vantage point of Walden, but Asylum Hill, a locale which I will identify as these explorations unfold.

Thoreau and the Wilderness Ideal

Thoreau was a complex thinker whose ideas touch the reader's ear with symphonic force. I want to highlight two major themes of his thought.[4] The first definitely predominates over the second in his most renowned work, *Walden,* and others like it, such as *Cape Cod.* Call this *the mythos of wild nature.* It is predicated on a radical rejection of urban life, on the one hand, and on a thoroughgoing affirmation of the healing powers of the wilderness, on the other.

"The city does not *think* much," Thoreau once observed. "On any moral question, I would rather have the opinion of Boxboro than of Boston and New York put together."[5] In nature alone, Thoreau says, not in the "pomp and parade" of the town, the individual may "walk with the Builder of the Universe." "Our village life," he explains, "would stagnate if it were not for the unexplored forests and meadows which surround it. We need the tonic of wilderness. . . . We can never have enough of nature. We must be refreshed by the sight of its inexhaustible vigor, its vast and titanic features. . . ."[6]

The Book of Nature was surely Thoreau's most celebrated teacher, not the Book of the Scriptures. Throughout *Walden* he keeps a courteous silence, for the most part, concerning the biblical claims of Christianity. He does

---

[3]If space permitted, a similar approach to the works of the widely read Catholic "geologian," Thomas Berry, would also be revealing. More sophisticated in his analysis and more cautious in his conclusions than Matthew Fox, Berry nonetheless draws the same kind of conclusions predicated on the same kind of analysis. See Thomas Berry, *The Dream of the Earth* (San Francisco: Sierra Club Books, 1988). Also the contributions of Protestant process theologians would have to be considered and carefully evaluated in this context, from the same perspective. See, for example, Jay B. McDaniel, *Of God and Pelicans: A Theology of Reverence for Life* (Louisville: Westminster/John Knox Press, 1989), and the literature that he cites. For a thoughtful analysis of the place of thinkers such as Fox and Berry in the context of recent Catholic theology, see William C. French, "Subject-centered and Creation-centered Paradigms in Recent Catholic Thought," *Journal of Religion* 70.1 (Jan. 1990): 48-72.

[4]Here I take up an analysis of Thoreau that I first proposed in H. Paul Santmire, *Brother Earth: Nature, God, and Ecology in a time of Crisis* (New York: Thomas Nelson, 1970) ch. 1.

[5]Henry David Thoreau, "Slavery in Massachusetts," *The Writings of Henry David Thoreau: Cape Cod and Miscellanies* (New York: Houghton Mifflin, 1906) 396.

[6]Henry David Thoreau, *Walden* (New York: W. W. Norton Company, 1951) 350.

allude positively, on occasion, to the writings of Asian sages. But his most inspired teacher, by his own witness, remains the Book of Nature.

Nature for him is a salutary teacher of humility and finitude. "We need to witness our own limits transgressed," he observes, "and some pasturing freely where we never wander." Nature is also a salutary teacher of simplicity and virtue. "I am convinced," he writes, "that if all . . . were to live as simply as I did [at Walden Pond], thieving and robbery would be unknown."[7] Nature was the existential substance of his life. Nature was for him, in this sense, the veritable expression of the Divine.

At the same time, Thoreau felt hemmed in by what he called "the dirty institutions" of humans, by their pressures on him "to belong to their desperate odd fellow society."[8] This led him to look ever more passionately beyond civilization to the wilderness. He wistfully concludes his account of his journey to Cape Cod at its easternmost shore, at the sea, at the very edge of what he calls "Naked Nature": "A man may stand there and put all America behind him."[9] Such, in outline, is the mythos of wild nature in Thoreau's thought.

Woven in with this mythos is a second prominent theme to which I also wish to call attention, *the ethos of individual freedom.* This theme comes to the fore especially in his discussion, "Slavery in Massachusetts," and in his essays on John Brown. Here we see Thoreau the man of great moral passion, concerned with freedom for all, even to the point of being disenchanted with his love for wild nature.

"Who can be serene," Thoreau asks, "in a country where both the rulers and the ruled are without principle?" "The remembrance of my country," he glumly concludes, "spoils my walk."[10] So he resolutely calls the state of Massachusetts to task for failing to free its slaves while directing its political attention elsewhere. "Show me a free state, and a court truly of justice," he writes, "and I will fight for them, if need be, but show me Massachusetts, and I refuse her my allegiance, and express contempt for her courts."[11] In the same spirit he gave his support to the raid of John Brown to free the slaves.

Thoreau's mythic statement, enacted in his life and his writings, has been assessed in many ways. For now we must be content with a few general observations. Operative in his life and his thought, as various interpreters have suggested, is that deeply rooted American theological image of the New Adam in the new Garden, and within that image is the romantic ideal of the noble savage.[12] *This is a theology of origins, par excellence.* The idea was that here,

---

[7]Thoreau, *Walden* 337f., 191.

[8]Thoreau 90.

[9]Thoreau, *Cape Cod* (New York: Thomas Y. Crowell Company, 1961) 319.

[10]Thoreau, *Writings* 407.

[11]Thoreau 404.

[12]See R. B. Y. Lewis, *The American Adam: Innocence, Tragedy, and Tradition in the Nineteenth Century* (Chicago: The University of Chicago Press, 1955).

in this new land, in communion with the wilderness, individuals could be free from the constraints of the decadent institutions of Europe. They could go back to the beginning. They could recreate history.

Note, however, what this theology of origins leaves behind. First, it is predicated on a profoundly anti-urban bias. The classical motif of the *polis* and the biblical motif of the City of God suffer a grand eclipse. Instead, the new Adam in the Garden comes to the fore, along with the image of certain kinds of intimate societies, "garden clubs" they might be called, such as the kind that Thoreau enjoyed with Emerson and his friends. We are left mainly with the image of the heroic individual alone, with a few like-minded souls, contemplating the wilderness.

With this went a thoroughgoing denial of the significance of peaceful participative action for the sake of greater justice in society, the kind of democratic politics that was championed by both the Jeffersonian and the Madisonian traditions in America. For Thoreau, the socio-political options for the individual tended to be two: on the one hand to withdraw from the corruptions of society altogether to some sacrosanct literary, if not geographical, Walden; on the other hand to attack the injustices of society head on with either radical individual disobedience, as Thoreau himself did when he refused to pay his taxes and was sent to jail, or with sectarian violence, as John Brown did at Harpers Ferry.

One further question suggests itself in this respect. With this theology of origins, what becomes of "radical evil," that reality which that great champion of enlightened thinking, Immanuel Kant, so powerfully but so paradoxically identified? Is it really true that the great corruptions of this world can be so singularly identified with the corrupt institutions of European society or, more generally, with "civilization" itself? Was Thoreau himself truly free of those corruptions when he went to Walden, or did he perchance carry them with him in his own heart? And did he perchance carry them with him, ironically, all the more as he tried to leave them behind in the city? I will return to such questions presently.

The Writings of Matthew Fox

Matthew Fox writes in an entirely different context, but with a strikingly similar outcome.[13] The issue is no longer the artificiality of European culture and its denials of individual freedom. Now the issue is the perniciousness of what Fox calls the fall-redemption theology of the West, and the possible destruction of the human species, whether by environmental catastrophe or thermonuclear holocaust, if the influence of that dualistic fall-redemption

---

[13]For a balanced presentation and evaluation of Fox's program, see Wayne G. Boulton, "The Thoroughly Modern Mysticism of Matthew Fox," *Christian Century* 107.14 (April 25, 1990): 428-32.

theology continues to hold sway.

The original sin, as Fox sees it, is for all intents and purposes the traditional Christian doctrine of original sin itself, as that doctrine has allegedly shaped the history of Western culture. In this sense, for Fox, a *bad idea*, namely theological dualism, is the root of all evil, rather than bad institutions, as in the case of Thoreau. So Fox writes:

> I believe that an exaggerated doctrine of original sin, one that is employed as a starting point for spirituality, plays kindly into the hands of empire-builders, slavemasters, and partriarchial society in general. It divides and thereby conquers, pitting one's spirit, one's political vocation against one's personal needs, people against earth, animals, and nature in general. By doing this it so convolutes people, so confuses and preoccupies them that deeper questions about community, justice, and celebrations never come to the fore.[14]

The great perpetrator of this bad idea, in Fox's view, was St. Augustine, who allegedly had no positive regard for nature, whose thought from beginning to end was, allegedly, rife with sexual dualism and an other-worldly, spiritualizing eschatology.

Fox proposes to sweep away the dominance of this allegedly pernicious fall-redemption theology, and to put in its place something else: a theology of original blessing and a theology of the coming Cosmic Christ. Fox wants to return as it were, to the era of the Garden, before the fall, much as Thoreau sought to establish the world of a New Adam at the edge of the wilderness, prior to the inroads and the corruptions of civilization.

In this context, Fox believes, we can discover a new understanding of Jesus Christ. We can now encounter Christ as the eternal Ground of creation, as the Cosmic Christ or Cosmic Wisdom. Fox invokes a kind of logos christology at this point, reminiscent of some early Christian thinkers. He is, in this respect, much more concerned with the *logos asarkos,* the eternal Word, mystically understood as creatively immanent in all things--traditionally called the *logos spermatikos*--rather than the present in Jesus of Nazareth. Fox does hold that the *logos ensarkos* is very much an expression, the clearest and most powerful expression for us, of the *logos asarkos.*

Fox announces his theological agenda, accordingly:

> What is needed . . . is a spiritual vision that prays, celebrates, and lives out the reality of the Cosmic Christ who lives and breathes in Jesus and in *all* God's children, in all the prophets of religion everywhere, in all the creatures of the universe.[15]

---

[14]Matthew Fox, *Original Blessing: A Primer in Creation Spirituality* (Santa Fe, New Mexico: Bear and Company, 1983) 54.

[15]Matthew Fox, *The Coming of the Cosmic Christ: The Healing of Mother Earth and the Birth of a Global Renaissance* (New York: Harper and Row, 1988) 7.

Fox thus seeks to strip away what he considers to be the false theological constructions of so-called fall-redemption theology, in order to reveal the original blessings of God in the whole created order, through the marvelous activity and wondrous manifestations of the eternal Logos of God. Fox refers to this vision of ultimate origins restored as his "living cosmology."

Note that the particular salvific function of Jesus of Nazareth in this schema is to serve as the revealer or the teacher or the exemplar. Call this a *Christus Exemplar* soteriology. Jesus of Nazareth's role, as the mediator of salvation, is to reveal the universal functioning of the Cosmic Christ, manifest and operative everywhere, at all times and in all places, and in so doing to call us all to a greater awareness of the workings of the Cosmic Christ everywhere. Thus Fox characteristically describes the role of Jesus in the Eucharist: "Like wisdom, the perfect hostess (Prov. 91, 92) he reveals in a banquet context the mysteries of our origin and of God."[16] Jesus, for Fox, is primarily understood as the New Adam[17], who functions as "a poet, a storyteller, and artist," a kind of shaman figure who serves as "an awakener to the sacrament of the cosmos."[18] The Cross, then, in the tradition of Abelard, is seen by Fox mainly as a *symbol* of self-giving, as a revelation of the process that all the faithful must go through.[19] The historical Jesus remains mainly "a model and a teacher of letting go."[20]

For Fox, moreover, this particular historical Jesus, who is the revealer of the Cosmic Christ or Cosmic Wisdom, discloses to us, as we follow in his footsteps, that *we are also Divine,* born of God, as Jesus of Nazareth was. In this way, Fox suggests, we "awake to our divinity."[21] Jesus' divinity, in this sense, is the prototype and exemplar of our own divinity.

As we thus awake to our divinity, according to Fox, our eyes are also opened and we see God in all things. Like St. Francis, Fox insists, aware of our divinity we can lead an "enchanted existence," which is our salvation. Or, in the words of Meister Eckhart, which Fox quotes: "This then is salvation; to marvel at the beauty of created things and praise the beautiful providence of their Creator."[22]

It virtually goes without saying, then, that this Foxian theology of origins or original blessing must be in emphasis, if not totally in content, a theology of *realized* eschatology. What else could it be, since Fox predicates everything on his protological vision of the Divine creativity through the eternal Logos. Here and now, Fox suggests characteristically, not in the End Time, as Paul

---

[16]Fox, *Original Blessing* 123.
[17]Fox 123.
[18]Fox 239.
[19]Fox 166.
[20]Fox 169.
[21]Fox 235.
[22]Fox 120f.

maintains in I Corinthians 15:28 when he says that God *will be* all in all, but here and now: God *is* "all in all."[23] Jesus' theology, accordingly, as Fox sees it, is "*a kingdom come theology,* a proclaiming of Good News and even Better News than creation had ever heard before, the news that humanity could, after all, learn here and now to enjoy creation rightly."[24]

On the basis of such mystical intuitions, Fox anticipates the dawning of a global renaissance in our time, as the subtitle of his book *The Coming of the Cosmic Christ* indicates.[25] This kind of anticipation is not unlike the medieval speculations of Joachim, who projected a new age of the Spirit, when the sacramental ordinances of the Church would no longer be the singular mediators of salvation. Accordingly, Fox envisions the emergence of an ever increasing number of mystics and artists, shamans and gardeners, dancers and lovers, around the globe, as harbingers of the new age. Such individuals themselves will be, as it were, exemplars of *the* Exemplar, Jesus Christ. In this sense, for Fox, as for Joachim, a new kind of universal priesthood will emerge to initiate this global renaissance. "The creation tradition," Fox explains, "is essentially nonclerical because it recognizes existence, life itself, as the primary sacrament. This sacrament requires awareness and wakefulness, not ordination, to bring about its proper distribution and to elicit the sacrament from children and adults, workers, artists, lovers, citizens."[26]

To this end, Fox lifts up the image of the noble savage at the conclusion of his exposition, envisioning a new kind of spiritual education for all, not unlike Thoreau's prescription of a Walden-immersion experience for all. "Sweat lodges," Fox concludes, "ought to become a regular feature on the campuses of every high school, college, and university, as well as every seminary, church, and synagogue."[27] Such is the overall shape of Fox's theology of original blessing and the coming Cosmic Christ.

On Not Avoiding the Challenge of the Human City

It would perhaps seem disingenuous to say of this sweeping mystical theology that it all rings true. But it does. Fox's critique of some of the spiritualizing, anthropocentric excesses of the received theology of the West is telling, in many respects. The same is true of his critique of the theological tradition's patriarchal excesses and its marked rejection, on occasion, of creation spirituality in the West, particularly among the mystics. Fox's reflections are highly suggestive and serve as a corrective to those readings of Christian traditions that focus on kerygmatic and dogmatic motifs alone.

---

[23]Fox 106.
[24]Fox 125. (Emphasis added.)
[25]See also Fox, *Original Blessing* 162.
[26]Fox 275.
[27]Fox, *Cosmic Christ* 239.

But the ring of truth, in this case, is not the whole truth. This Foxian truth, indeed, taken by itself, resonates all too disquietingly with the anti-urban, romantic individualism of the Thoreauvian tradition. Fox leaves us in the sweat lodge, not in the struggling inner-city parish. This I find highly problematic, both as one who has been a pioneer in the field of ecological theology for more than twenty-five years, and as one who has struggled with questions of urban justice for still longer.

What Good News does Fox's mystical theology really offer for an inner city neighborhood like Asylum Hill, located in the fourth poorest city of the United States? What does he have to say to the AFDC mother in Asylum Hill who falls short on every initiative she undertakes to better her life and the well being of her family? What word of hope does he have to speak to the prospective teenage mother in Asylum Hill, who unknowingly awaits the ravages of an infant mortality rate that is higher than some Third World countries? What does he have to say to the unemployed, alienated African-American males, who hang out at Sigourney Park, many of them suffering from the delayed stress syndrome of Vietnam?

The message of Walden may speak to an elite, largely affluent few. What does it have to say to the impoverished urban masses around this globe, who must struggle every day for their bread, often against overwhelming odds?

It appears, regrettably, that Matthew Fox's strategy is to shoot the bearer of bad news, in this case the theologians of the so-called fall-redemption tradition, such as Augustine. Soberly, however, the real problem is not a bad idea and its influence, namely original sin. The real problem is rather *the finally undeniable reality of radical evil itself,* to which the doctrine of original sin, in various ways, has historically--and sometimes inadequately--born witness.[28]

Few among the masses who live in the Asylum Hills of this globe, most of whose citizens are impoverished and powerless, would for a moment deny the reality of radical evil. Only intellectuals, once removed, would even feel called upon to have to argue for it, pointing to Dachau and Buchenwald, Hiroshima and Nagasaki, apartheid and genocide, raping and battering, millions of malnourished and starving children, and the threat of global nuclear or environmental catastrophe.

Nor would it take a Martin Luther to convince powerless and impoverished residents of neighborhoods such as Asylum Hill of the bondage of the will or the reign of the principalities and powers of death and destruction in this world. It all may look different from the top of the Sierras

---

[28]Fox seems to be overreacting to the biologizing of original sin that sometimes has characterized theological manuals. He seems unaware of modern reconstructions of the doctrine, above all the influential contributions of Reinhold Niebuhr, for example, his magisterial *The Nature and Destiny of Man: A Christian Interpretation* (New York: Charles Scribner's Sons, 1955).

or from the bosom of some Walden, but radical evil looks starkly real and starkly inescapable from the vantage point of Asylum Hill. The problem, really, is not the idea of original sin. The problem, really, is the fact of original sin. As Reinhold Niebuhr used to say, this would seem to be the one Christian Belief that is empirically verifiable.

The fact of original sin as Fox describes it, however, tends to be domesticated. Fox can catalog the works of the demonic in our history, but as he envisions human suffering it tends to be swept up quickly into the experience of cosmic redemption. It tends to become an occasion for mystical participation in the dark side of the cosmos, rather than an occasion to struggle with alien powers that wreak havoc in this world, come what may.[29] Likewise, although Fox talks frequently about "justice-making," he chiefly seems to be thinking about a revolution of consciousness that is going to transform the world, not unlike the idea of "Consciousness III," proposed by Charles Reich in *The Greening of America* during the heyday of the sixties. In Fox's work we encounter little attention to the often stalemated, anguished struggles of the oppressed, that can sometimes last for decades, even longer, and then, with some regularity, still be lost.[30]

The Christian masses throughout the ages, in contrast, have lived and died with the bitter reality of struggle. Struggle against overwhelming odds has been their daily bread. This is why they have turned again and again to the figure of the Crucified, and all the more desperately struggled, in this instance, to make sense out of this apparently senseless, but nevertheless atoning death.

Historically, the vocation of Jesus Christ has been interpreted in at least three ways, as Gustav Aulen showed.[31] Matthew Fox seems to appreciate only one of these ways, which clearly *does* have roots in the Scriptures and which came to its classical expression in the teaching Abelard, the *Christus Exemplar* theology of the Atonement. But the faithful throughout the ages, not just the theologians, have again and again turned to other approaches to the Atonement also, in liturgical and martyriological praxis, as well as in theological reflection and mystical meditation, indicated by the expressions *Christus Victor* and *Christus Victim.*

This is the experiential matrix of the *Christus Victor* motif among the faithful throughout the ages. Given the reign of the principalities and powers

---

[29]See *Original Blessing* 151ff.

[30]Charles Reich, *The Greening of America* (New York: Random House, 1970) Cf. Boulton 432, regarding Fox's programs for social and personal transformation: "Creation and redemption are brought so close together in Fox's work that his programs for social transformation are almost inevitably simplistic. And in his call for personal transformation ("a resurrection of the human psyche") he can sound faintly like a Robert Schuller of the left."

[31]Gustav Aulen, *Christus Victor: A Historical Study of the Three Main Types of the Idea of the Atonement.* Trans. A. G. Herbert (New York: MacMillan, 1967).

of death in this world, a profound struggle had to be won by God at some particular point. Otherwise death would still remain the final victor. We could not have won that struggle ourselves, moreover, nor could we simply have been *taught* how to win it ourselves. We mortals surely do not have that capacity.

This, likewise, is the experiential matrix of the *Christus Victim* motif among the faithful throughout the ages. Given the radical breach between us and God, an immeasurable price had to be paid by God at some particular point. Otherwise our estrangement from our Creator could not have been healed. We could not have paid that immeasurable price ourselves, nor could we simply have been *taught* how to pay it ourselves. We sinful mortals surely do not have that capacity.

To write off these experientially-rooted fall-redemption motifs, however much they might be beyond our rational ken, and to do so as cavalierly as Fox does, is to show an innocence born of some protected cloister, certainly not the cruciform world of Asylum Hill or the miserable hovels of the downtrodden Christian masses throughout the ages.

The faithful who live and groan for liberation in Asylum Hill live and groan in a world of struggle, and so they find empowerment in the figure of *Christus Victor*. The faithful who live and groan for liberation in Asylum Hill live and groan in a world that they find alienated from God, and so they find healing in the figure of *Christus Victim*. This is why they demand that the Church minister the historical Eucharist to them, and not something else. This is why some sweat lodge experience or a life of leisure devoted to artistic creativity, were it to be presented to them, would appear baffling or even bizarre.

Further, the faithful in Asylum Hill are all too aware of their own mortality and their own sinfulness to make any sense at all out of the claim that they themselves, not just the Christ of their salvation, are somehow divine. They do not want to be told that they are divine. They do want to hear that they have been delivered and that they have been forgiven, so that they can than engage in the struggles for justice in this world, liberated from hopelessness and freed from the burden of their own alienation.

Cosmic Christology must be, assuredly, an urgent theme for contemporary theology, precisely for some of the reasons Fox has articulated. Joseph Sittler made that point with resounding clarity in his World Council of Churches address in New Delhi in 1961.[32] But a cosmic christology must be predicated, as Sittler knew so well, and as Jurgen Moltmann has forcefully reminded us, on a theology of the crucified God.[33] Otherwise we will end up with a so-

---

[32]Joseph Sittler, *Called to Unity* (Philadelphia: Muhlberg Press, 1962).

[33] Jurgen Moltmann, *The Crucified God: The Cross of Christ as the Foundation and Criticism of Christian Theology*. Trans. R. A. Wilson and John Bowden (New York: SCM Press, 1974). This work is then the foundation for Moltmann's comprehensive and balanced essay

called savior whose salvation is commensurate neither with the powers of evil nor with our alienation from God. The Gospels, after all, are basically passion stories with introductions. We ought not to forget that exegetical fact in our zeal to get to the cosmic christologies of Ephesians and Colossians.

In a certain sense the shadow of the Cross falls upon the entire cosmos, not just on us, as the whole creation groans in travail under the principalities and powers of death. For, creation itself longs for liberation, as Paul proclaims in Romans 8. For all its harmony and its healing power, indeed, nature can sometimes be a capricious friend: when the roar of the lion reigns in the night, when the tornados or the volcanos block out the midday sun. Thoreau finally discovered this alien face of nature when he journeyed to Maine's great northern peak, Mount Katahdin, in the springtime and encountered the black flies. Wordsworth might have discovered the same insight had he been around long enough to read Aldous Huxley's striking essay, "Wordsworth in the Tropics." This is why the biblical prophets longed for a new day for the whole creation, for cosmic history as well as for human history, a day when the lamb would finally lie down with the lion.

Interestingly enough, the Bible begins with the Garden and ends not with the Garden but with the redeemed City, in the midst of a renewed creation. Biblical theology is not a theology of origins alone, but a theology of cosmic history oriented to the final manifestation of a glorified City of God and a glorified Cosmos of God. In between, moreover, the biblical narrative allows us to hear the shrieking laments of human fratricide and the groaning cacophonies of cosmic violence, from Cain and Abel to Noah and Job, and it comes to rest in godforsaken silence along the way, in the agony of Golgotha.

Protology is not the ending but the beginning for the Bible. Original blessing is not the ending, but the beginning for the Bible. Eschatology as a yet-to-be-fully-realized dawning of a new heavens and a new earth, in the midst of which the New Jerusalem is to be situated this is the driving biblical vision: but there is always what Kaesmann has called that "eschatological reservation," the witness to the Cross, as *the* sign of "God with us" in our struggle to hope and to love in the midst of this oppressed and alienated world which God creates and blesses as good.

The question then remains whether this traditional eschatological theology of the Cross, which witnesses so necessarily to a *Christus Victor* and a *Christus Victim* as well as to a *Christus Exemplar,* is also equipped to speak to the ecological issues which trouble us so profoundly in these times. Are the kerygmatic and dogmatic traditions of Christianity, which attest catholicity in their theologies of the Atonement, also capable of attesting catholicity in their theology of the cosmos? I believe that, sensitively read and rightly construed,

---

which addresses many of the themes that are of concern to Matthew Fox. Moltmann, *God in Creation: A New Theology of Creation and the Spirit of God*. Trans. Margaret Kohl (New York: SCM Press, 1985).

they are. I want to conclude now with some observations that will indicate how a biblically inspired, traditionally conversant, narrative of creation, fall, redemption, and fulfillment can be historically viable and ecologically relevant theological project in our time.

St. Augustine and Creation

There is perhaps no more illustrative way to focus these concluding observations than by turning to the figure who is the arch-demon in Matthew Fox's theological Hades, St. Augustine. The Augustine who emerges in Fox's two major works is largely a caricature, an introspective, sex-obsessed cleric, who hates the created world and wants to subject all to the authority of the church. The historical Augustine was, in fact, a much more complex, much more ambiguous, and much more instructive figure, as I have shown in my study, *The Travail of Nature.*[34] There I argued, on the basis of a study of Augustine's theological development, that his mature theology represents a flowering of the ecological promise of Christian theology, which later was to be practically expressed in the life of St. Francis.

To read Augustine right, it is helpful to consider the metaphorical assumptions of his thinking. Augustine drew on three "root metaphors," which I have described in some detail in aforementioned study. I have called them the metaphor of ascent, the metaphor of fecundity, and the metaphor of migration to the good land.[35]

According to the first, the metaphor of ascent, the mind moves, as it were, from the base of a mountain toward the heights, traversing various orders of being until it reaches the pure ethereal regions of the naked sun in the heavens above. In classical metaphysics this was expressed in terms of a great chain of being, rising from the Many at the totally material nadir, through various forms of material and spiritual being, to the totally spiritual all-transcending One at the apex.

According to the second, the metaphor of fecundity, the mind moves, as it were, circuitously from the apex to the nadir, contemplating many orders of being descending from the overflowing One at the apex to the richly manifold Many at the nadir. In classical metaphysics this was expressed with the image of a great chain of being, again, but this time not in terms of the transcendent Good high above, but now in terms of Overflowing Goodness, extending outward and downward to all things.

According to the third, the metaphor of migration to a good land, the mind moves with a pilgrim community from a situation of duress, through times of testing, toward what is envisioned as a promised land: in biblical terms, a land of abundance flowing with milk and honey. In biblical thought,

---

[34]Santmire, *Brother Earth,* chap. 4.
[35]See Santmire, chap. 2.

this metaphor was influential not only in terms of Israel's wilderness wandering, but also in a more apocalyptic context, with the vision of the people of God being gathered from exile at Mount Zion in the End Times, together with all the nations, in the midst of a totally renewed cosmos.

I have shown that as far as his understanding of the material cosmos was concerned, Augustine moved from (A) an early stage when the metaphor of ascent totally dominated his thinking, mainly during his Manichean period, through a (B) stage when the metaphor of fecundity, following Plotinus, began to shape his thought more thoroughly, to (C) his mature thought when the influence of both the metaphor of fecundity and the metaphor of migration to a good land coalesced in his thought, in terms of a vision of a glorious cosmic history of God.

If anything, in his mature thought Augustine overreacted to his Manichean past in celebrating the goodness of the earth. Notably, he even came to the point, as Margaret Miles has shown, where he began to bring himself to overcome some of his deepest alienation from matter, toward his own body and his own sexuality.[36]

That Augustine was *later* read more in terms of his early thought than his mature thought, may well be true. That in those early years he made what might seem to us to be outrageous statements about the solitude of the soul and the corruption of matter is surely true. But to read his thought solely in terms of that early anti-nature bias and his fascination with the so-called "introspective conscience" is to lay blame at his door, which more properly should be laid at the door of his less visionary and less biblically inspired disciples.

In his mature thought, we encounter a majestic, universal vision of cosmic history, predicated on the then traditional idea of the six days of creation. This is the little known, universal cosmic context of his otherwise celebrated theology of history, which focuses on the narrative of the City of God. The thought of God's overflowing goodness and immanence in nature shapes Augustine's mature understanding of cosmic history. He also envisions nature itself as a kind of universal process, unfolding through time, according to his doctrine of the so-called "seminal reasons." Further, he insists, over against the Manichees and some other more mainstream theologians, such as Origen, that the material order has *not* fallen. On the contrary, in its manifoldness and in its own history with God, in Augustine's eyes, the material cosmos as we know it to this day is resplendent with God's glory, as from the first day of creation. It portrays, fittingly, the beautiful providence of the all-transcending, but all-nurturing Creator. So Augustine states characteristically:

> How can I tell you of the rest of creation, with all its beauty and utility, which the divine goodness has given to man to please his eyes and serve his purposes,

---

[36]Margaret Miles, *Augustine on the Body* (Missoula, Montana: Scholars Press, 1979).

condemned though he is, and hurled into these labors and miseries? Shall I speak of the manifold and various loveliness of sky, and earth, and sea; of the plentiful supply and wonderful qualities of the light; of sun, moon, and stars; of the shade of trees; of the colors and perfume of flowers; of the multitude of birds, all differing in plumage and in song; of the variety of animals, of which the smallest in size are often the most wonderful, of the works of ants and bees astonishing us more than the huge bodies of whales? Shall I speak of the sea, which itself is so grand a spectacle, when it arrays itself as it were in vestures of various colors, now running through every shade of green, and again becoming purple or blue? Is it not delightful to look at in the storm, and experience the soothing complacency which it inspires, by suggesting that we ourselves are not tossed and shipwrecked? What shall I say of the numberless kinds of foods to alleviate hunger, and the variety of seasonings to stimulate the appetite which are scattered everywhere by nature, and for which we are not indebted to the art of cookery? How many natural appliances are there for preserving and restoring health? How graceful is the alteration of day and night! How pleasant the breezes that cool the air! How abundant the supply of clothing furnished us by trees and animals! Can we enumerate all these blessings we enjoy?[37]

With this vision of the infinite blessings of the Creator in the cosmos, Augustine also teaches what can be called a contemplative idea of human dominion over the earth. His thought is not that humans are called to dominate the earth, but that by their knowing they are called to contemplate and give thanks for the wonders of the earth, as no other creatures are called to do in precisely that way. He also stresses that many creatures are brought into being by God, with no human utility implied whatsoever, but solely for the sake of enhancing the beauty of the whole created order.

All this he finally brings together with an all-comprehending vision of cosmic renewal in the End Times. He depicts that coming Day of universal fulfillment, as it is envisioned in the Book of Revelation, not just the consummation of the City of God, but the consummation of the entire cosmos.

Such is the grand sweep of Augustine's theology of cosmic history. Notably, he projects this grand vision from the context of the city of this world, the *civitas terrena*. While Augustine is fascinated with the theology of origins, and never forsakes that theology in his mature thought, he takes his stand existentially not in the Garden, but in the midst of the brokenness of the human *polis*. So in addition to his celebration of the universal goodness of cosmic history, Augustine is also driven to trace a theology of fall and redemption, a theology which speaks to the realities of death and estrangement in human experience, a theology which addresses the particular human condition, as we find ourselves "condemned," as he says, and "hurled into these labors and miseries."

---

[37]Augustine, *City of God* 22-24.

This is not to suggest that everything Augustine ever said or did is to go uncriticized. He never fully overcame his early androcentric bias of his patriarchal understanding of society. His theology of human history, though visionary in many respects, lacks a coherent infrastructure of penultimate meanings as Langdon Gilkey has shown.[38] His hierarchical vision of the church and his tendency to identify it with the Kingdom of God, also seems to be highly problematic. In addition, his tendency to view evil in terms of privation of the good, rather than in the more active biblical terms of principalities and powers, must also be challenged, along with the somewhat less-than fully biblical soteriology that accompanies that understanding of evil. He tended also to biologize the theology of original sin, for which he has been appropriately criticized by many, above all Reinhold Niebuhr.[39] But the point here is not to argue that Augustine somehow transcended his sinful mortality or the limitations of his own historical particularity. The point rather is to show that this pivotal theologian, the *Doctor Gratiae*, historically speaking perhaps the singlemost important "father" in the Christian West, is at once the author of a highly suggestive theology of cosmic history: right in the mainstream, as it were, of the kerygmatic and dogmatic traditions of Christianity.

A contemporary theology of nature can certainly seek to go beyond his constructions. His grand cosmic theology can stand to be developed much more explicitly than he does in terms of the cosmic christologies of Colossians and Ephesians, and with more explicit treatment of the *Christus Victor* and *Christus Victim* themes. Other concerns of importance to us due to our situation, such as the preservation of species and the rights of all creatures, would also have to be given explicit attention.

But we have seen enough of this Augustinian theology of the City of God and the Cosmos of God to be able to say that those who would claim that the kerygmatic and dogmatic traditions of Christianity are ecologically bankrupt should take another, more careful look: in light of the catholicity of these traditions as they come to expression in terms of the Atonement, and, as in Augustine's case especially, the vision of the city and the cosmos as partners in the unfolding universal history of God. That, at least, is the view from Asylum Hill.[40]

---

[38] Langdon Gilkey, *Reaping the Whirlwind: Christian Interpretation of History* (New York: Seabury, 1976).

[39]Niebuhr, *Nature*.

[40]For a brief, constructive statement of this position, see especially my essay, "The Future of the Cosmos and the Renewal of the Church's Life with Nature," in *Cosmos and Creation: Theology and Science in Consonance*, ed. Ted Peters (Nashville: Abingdon Press, 1989), chap. 9. along side of my early programmatic study, *Brother Earth*, and my longer historical study, *The Travail of Nature*, both cited.

RELIGION AND THE ORIGINS OF THE ENVIRONMENTAL CRISIS

John F. Haught

Several important scholars have traced the origins of our environmental crisis to thinking and acting associated with religion, and especially with biblical religion.[1] The charge that religion in some way lies at the roots of our neglect of and hostility toward nature is problematic to anyone who participates in a religious tradition today. If it is merely an incidental or peripheral ingredient of religion that leads us to the abuse of nature, then we could in principle dispense with this component without throwing away the faith in its entirety. But if it turns out that it is something central to a religious outlook that promotes our negative attitudes toward the environment, then this might be sufficient reason for our forsaking such a tradition altogether. If we considered our particular faith tradition *essentially* racist or sexist, we would have to abandon it on ethical grounds. Likewise today we would be obliged to hand in our religious membership cards if our creeds turned out to be in some way *inextricably* connected with a negative attitude toward the natural environment.

One of the central aspects of many religions is their teaching that authentic existence is "homeless," that pilgrimage, sojourning and rootlessness define our lives in this world. Is it possible that these apparently essential attributes of religious existence also give rise to a carelessness about our natural homeland, the earth? It appears quite likely that the origins of our environmental crisis lie, in part at least, in a deeply entrenched suspicion by humans that the cosmos is not really our home. The feeling of cosmic homelessness is, to a great extent at least, apparently "religious" in origin. We have translated the indispensable ideal of spiritual homelessness into an environmentally unacceptable *cosmic* homelessness. Thus an uncritical identification of religious with cosmic homelessness makes nature a victim of the human need for self-transcendence. In those cultures and historical periods where religious homelessness is idealized, a sense of alienation from nature is often a likely accompaniment.

But if religious or spiritual homelessness logically and *inevitably* entails a cosmic homelessness, then religious existence becomes ethically problematic

---

[1]Lynn White, Jr., "The Historical Roots of our Ecologic Crisis," *Science* 155, #3767: 1203-07 (Mar.10, 1967). See also the articles by and about Thomas Berry collected in *Cross Currents* XXXVII, No.'s 2 & 3 (1988): 178-239.

from the point of view of environmental concern. In the following, therefore, I shall discuss some of the environmental implications of the religious ideal of homelessness. At the same time I shall be addressing the question whether religious homelessness *necessarily* requires or promotes an attitude or cosmic homelessness.

Often anthropocentrism is fingered as the root cause of environmental degradation. Placing an exaggerated emphasis on the human dimension seems to rob the rest of nature of any intrinsic worth. The pursuant impression that nature is perhaps only instrumentally valuable to us leaves it open to our abuse. Perhaps, though, our anthropocentric tendencies are themselves secondary to a more fundamental impression that we are "lost in the cosmos" (to use the title of a recent book by the late novelist and critic, Walker Percy). Exaggerating our own importance may be an understandable reaction to the prior conviction that we are exiles from any value-bestowing universe. When we feel that we don't really "belong" somewhere, we are vulnerable to the feeling of shame. So we seek to counter this stigma by way of a groundless self-inflation. Anthropocentrism is our way of responding to the feeling of not really belonging to the earth and the cosmos.

Thus a frontal attack on our anthropocentric tendencies, which is how so much contemporary environmental advocacy begins, will hardly be effective unless we simultaneously address the embarrassing feeling of cosmic exile to which anthropocentrism is an understandable response. As long as we feel that we are not really at home in the natural world, or that we do not really belong to it, can we ever seriously care for it? Of course, evolutionary theory instructs us that our species (as well as other forms of life) would probably not be here at all if the earth had been in every sense a *perfectly* congenial habitat for living beings. At least some degree of misfit with respect to the natural environment is what challenges life to evolve into new forms. Even so, however, each living species can survive only because it is borne abreast of the more pervasive "caringness" provided by the physical, chemical and biotic processes that make up the cosmos. We too rely for our existence upon a complex set of intercooperative dimensions of nature. Thus it would seem that only those ways of thinking which allow us to look upon nature as *in some sense* a nurturing and sustaining "home" can be environmentally wholesome.

But this axiom immediately raises a serious question about the environmental worth of some of the world's religious traditions, including Christianity. For do they not, especially in their mystical leanings, teach us that we *should* feel dislocated from our natural (as well as cultural) environment? It is true, of course, that religious sacramentalism logically requires that the natural basis of our symbols remain intact. It is especially in its sacramental aspects that religion seems at home with nature and shows that it has a vested interest in our preservation of the earthly environment. If we lose the environment, we forfeit along with it the sense of mystery that originally becomes transparent to religious people through a sacramentalism rooted in the natural world. But in some of religion's mystical, apophatic, and transformative or activist developments it has fostered a normative feeling of rootlessness and detachment from nature that has at times suppressed the sacramental emphasis. In promoting a spiritual homelessness it has, perhaps unwittingly, instilled in its devotees an impression that they do not "really" belong to the cosmos. In that case the origins of our environmental crisis do seem to have a "religious" component.

Religions idealize homelessness. The prophetic traditions, for example, go back to Abraham whose God called him to move from his ancestral home toward an unknown but promising future. And even though the theme of "the Land" is prominent in Judaism, the period of wandering without a home is glorified by the prophets as the time when Israel had its great opportunity for authentic faith. In the New Testament the Son of Man, born in a stable, has "nowhere to lay his head." In such traditional Christian spirituality we are said to be only pilgrims on earth. One of its ideals for example, is to be a knight-errant for the faith. How many Christian hymns have the theme that this world is not our home? And if we turn to the East we observe that Hinduism sets forth as an exemplar of piety the *sannyasin* one who becomes homeless for the sake of more intense union with the divine. And the Buddha's Great Renunciation required that he abandon wife, child and home.

Examples could be multiplied. Clearly according to the religions homelessness is our most authentic state of being. Unless we are somewhat uncomfortable with "the world" or "this present age," which often seems to include the natural environment, we will hardly experience any incentive to break free of the shackles of immediacy. Only a continually "going beyond" present actuality brings liberation/fulfillment/salvation. For many religious people, both East and West, the need to transcend "the world" is interpreted as the command to sever the human completely from the natural.

The biblical focus on history as the locus of redemption interrupts in a dramatic way any easy domesticity with respect to the purely natural world. The prophets considered it to be regressive piety for people to seek refuge from the terrors of history by returning to the regularities of nature. Biblical religion overlaid numerous "natural" sacraments with historic meaning. Is this already a subtle demotion of nature? Is it possible that the exilic motif in biblical and other religions requires our moving beyond what seems to be the ensnarements of the physical cosmos?

To repeat, it is especially in its sacramentalism that religion is environmentally important. Through its sacramentalism religion can ground a positive attitude toward nature. But in addition to sacramentalism religion also has mystical, apophatic and activist tendencies that sometimes lose touch with the sacramental links through which religion is primordially connected with nature. When the mystical, silent and active aspects are divorced from the sacramental (as often happens) it becomes easy to interpret the religious requirement of homelessness as though it demands a *cosmic* exile as well.

When sacramentalism is suppressed, religion makes the natural world a victim of our religious attempts to implement the ideal of spiritual homelessness. When religion abandons its sacramental mystique of nature, it is likely to become incompatible with any serious environmental ethic, with any sensitivity towards nature. If the religious journey requires our feeling disconnected from or lost in the cosmos, then spiritual teachings will continue to foster the very posture that provokes an environmentally unhealthy anthropocentrism as a defensive reaction.[2]

Yet those of us who embrace the teachings of religious traditions cannot simply abandon their disturbing ideas about the fundamental homelessness or our being. Religious existence surely *does* require that we not accommodate ourselves too comfortably to any present actuality. This would be called "idolatry." Incidentally, it is not that religions are absolutely opposed to "home." Rather they resist our settling for something as home which is really not an adequate domicile for our seemingly infinite restlessness. Religions promote homelessness not as an end in itself but as a necessary moment in the quest for our true "home." But how often is this "true home" located in some setting quite divorced from earth and the physical universe? Such a location of our ultimate destiny may give rise to an escapism that carelessly leaves the cosmos behind.

Fortunately, though, the confusion of religious with cosmic homelessness is avoidable. We can, at least in principle, preserve the lofty ideal of religious homelessness without its requiring the environmentally unhealthy conviction that we are essentially only sojourners in the world of nature. Developments in both theology and science make this adjustment possible today. We may now even interpret religious homelessness in a way that situates us firmly within the natural world. I shall develop this proposal later, but before doing so let me review some influential interpretations of both science and religion that seem to resist any such integration.

Scientism and Materialism

Our sense of being exiles from nature originates in myths and other forms of thought according to which we humans are only accidentally present to, but essentially absent from, the cosmos. The roots of this attitude go back to ancient forms of religious dualism. In modern times, though, it is not just religion but also the dominant assumptions of scientific epistemology and cosmology that have justified our sense of estrangement from the natural world. Scientism and its offshoot, scientific materialism, have given unprecedented intellectual support to the belief that we do not really belong to the cosmos.

---

[2]It might be more accurate to say, therefore, that the origins of the environmental crisis lie not in religion so much as in the *disintegration* of religion.

For example, scientism (according to which only the methods of science can yield true knowledge of reality) puritanically segregates the human knower from nature. By isolating the knowing subject from the object-world, scientism repudiates the ecological vision according to which all entities in the cosmos are somehow interrelated and interdependent. In scientism the knowing subject is no longer considered to be a part of the scientifically known universe. In order to be appropriately disinterested and therefore "objective" about the world, the scientific subject is set apart from nature. And even though in other respects science tells us that humans are part of the cosmos, that we are materially continuous with it, a scientistic epistemology excuses us, cognitively speaking, from the universe. As Michael Polanyi has observed, scientism constructs a picture of the universe in which we ourselves are absent.[3]

What Alfred North Whitehead calls "scientific materialism" also contributes to the modern sense of cosmic exile. Materialism reduces all reality to "matter", often as conceived along the line of the abstractions made by classical physics. It flows out of several questionable assumptions going back to the seventeenth century, chief among them the belief that "primary qualities" (such as mass, momentum, shape and position) are the most concrete aspects of nature. Unlike secondary qualities (color, taste, sound, smell, texture) which require the presence of a perceiving subject, primary qualities are allegedly "out there" in the world in a permanent sort of way. They are said to have an "objective" character independent of any participation by an observer. While secondary qualities seem to be our own creations, primary qualities are held to be objectively "real". This distinction of primary from secondary qualities initially seems quite harmless. But, if we adhere to it too strictly, it eventually leads us also to locate ethical values and religious symbols within the same insubstantial arena as that occupied by secondary qualities. Value, beauty, importance and purpose will seem, therefore, to depend for their reality exclusively on our own creative subjectivity. (Thus they are sometimes called "tertiary" qualities.) Following the assumption that abstract primary qualities are ontologically fundamental and concrete, modern thought from mechanism to existentialism has made us out to be the lonely and cosmically rootless authors not only of secondary qualities but also of all values and meanings.

Such an assumption obviously robs nature of any importance it might have apart from us. It allows nature at most only an instrumental significance, namely, as the stuff to be shaped into our own projects. It exiles us from the cosmos. It constructs a peculiar cosmology in which primacy of being is given to the colorless, valueless and humanly uninteresting aspects of nature, while the world of color and value originates in the insubstantial realm of subjective

---

[3]Michael Polanyi, *Personal Knowledge* (New York: Harper Torchbooks, 1964) 142.

caprice. In this cosmological set-up there is a seemingly unbridgeable gulf between the perceiving and valuing human subject "in here" and in the "real," material, and valueless world of primary qualities "out there." This means nothing less than that we are cosmically homeless, strangers to the cold indifference of the allegedly objective natural world of primary qualities.

Those who adopt the assumptions of scientific materialism sometimes allow that we may usefully entertain the illusion that we have overcome this exile. Through the psychological mechanism of "projection" we are permitted to paint over the neutrality of nature with our own imaginative, artistic, poetic and religious creations. These fictions may momentarily give us the impression that the universe is hospitable. However, if we follow with logical rigor the assumptions of materialism, we are eventually compelled to acknowledge that underneath all our projections lie only the inherently valueless and meaningless "primary" qualities discovered by classical physics. If these are the fundamental constituents of the "real" world, then we shall forever remain exiles from it. We will still be "lost in the cosmos."

Since they do not allow for any vital interrelationship of the human subject with nature, scientism and materialism cannot support a truly ecological vision. Ironically the proponents of scientism and materialism are themselves often vigorous supporters of environmental causes. But their explicit doctrines about nature, if they are thought out consistently, can only lead to an attitude of cosmic homelessness. In the final analysis a thoroughgoing scientism and materialism would logically justify our disregard for an environment that seemingly fails to nurture our estranged subjectivity. There is little hope for our recovering the feeling of truly belonging to the cosmos as long as our culture and universities continue to harbor (as they indeed still do) these by now worn-out assumptions. Until we completely revise our contemporary scientific cosmologies we will not be able to shake the persistent suspicion that the "real" world is radically different from our projections. We shall continue to caress the conviction that we are without a home in a valueless universe lurking beneath our perceptions and projections.

But can we improve on this modern view of a valueless universe, one that makes us seem, in our search for value and transcendent meaning, to be so out of place on such terrain? Recently a number of notable and worthy cosmological alternatives have been provided, though departments of science and philosophy are still suspicious of many of them.

Earlier in this century, for example, Alfred North Whitehead convincingly demonstrated that the primary qualities taken as fundamental by materialism are really not so "primary" after all. Rather they are themselves mathematical abstractions that have been logically mistaken for concrete reality.[4] Moreover,

---

[4]See Alfred North Whitehead, *Modes of Thought* (New York: The Free Press, 1968): 123: "The degeneracy of mankind is distinguished from its uprise by the dominance of chill abstractions, divorced from aesthetic content."

recent developments in science have overthrown the assumptions of classical physics that gave ontological priority to them. In contrast with the scientism that had absolutized Newtonian physics, relativity physics and quantum physics have shown us that the scientific observer is no longer an exile from, but an integral participant in, the universe.

Contrary to the cosmic pessimism based on classical mechanics, recent astrophysics indicates how hospitable the material universe has always been to our eventual arrival here. The initial conditions and fundamental physical constants that determine the structure of the universe are remarkably suited to the emergence of life. We must be careful not to build a whole theology on something so precarious as the so-called "anthropic principle." But we may at least be heartened by the conclusion, even in its uncontroversial "weak" version, that life and mind would not have appeared at all unless the physical nature of the universe had from its very beginning fifteen billion years ago fallen within the very narrow range of numerical possibilities suitable for life's eventual coming. Matter has not given birth to life as grudgingly as we used to think. Nor, apparently, is the universe indifferent to our being here.

If we compare all these observations to the cosmic pessimism of the nineteenth and much of the twentieth century, it is a remarkable breakthrough in cosmology, and one with considerable environmental implications. Even physics, the science that formerly seemed to exile us forever from nature, now concludes that we do belong here after all.

In spite of such developments in science and the philosophy of nature, however, much of our intellectual culture today continues to cling to the classical assumptions on which scientism and materialism are based. Philosophy, psychology and even literary criticism commonly suspect that the symbols and myths that might reconcile us to the earth, have only a derivative, projective or humanly "constructed" character. Symbolic expression, whether of poetry, art or religion, seems to be as ontologically thin as Galileo's and Locke's secondary qualities.

Walker Percy, for example, thought that it is precisely our ability to signify through symbols that shows us to be strangers in the cosmos, "Man," he said, " . . . is the only alien creature, as far as we know, in the entire Cosmos."[5] In Percy's theory of semantics our capacity to point by way of signifiers to referents beyond those signifiers (and I assume these would include the symbols of religion as well) implies that our symbolizing subjectivity must exist *outside* of the cosmos. A very important dimension of our being (the symbolizing self) occupies a totally different kind of terrain from that of nature. Percy doubted that we would have the freedom to signify one thing by way of another unless the signifying self somehow stands freely beyond the natural environment.

---

[5]Walker Percy, *Lost in the Cosmos: The Last Self-Help Book* (New York: Washington Square Press, 1984) 8.

Percy's rather gnostic way of explaining, and also justifying, our cosmic homelessness is very tempting. Like most dualistic views it has a tidiness about it that appeals to the puritanical mind-set of modern scientism and literary criticism, as well as to much traditional spirituality. But I think it is fundamentally mistaken. If its dis-incarnate character were thought out quite seriously and consistently, it would eventually prove to be environmentally disastrous as well.

Why could we not learn instead to look at our symbolic activity in a more cosmological fashion? At the same time that (psychologically speaking) it is certainly our own creative production, our symbolizing is also the expression of a more primordial creativity, that of the universe itself. Our humanly symbolic activity is, in a very literal sense, a self-disclosure of the cosmos rather than something that originates outside of that cosmos. Our symbolic life is *the cosmos itself* seeking adventurously, through us, to expand and intensify its own being. Our symbols do not require, as a condition of their referential capacity, any alienation of ourselves from the universe. More fundamentally, our subjective symbols are expressions *of* the universe (subjective genitive). Our religious symbols are the means through which the cosmos itself gropes toward a mystery.

As long as we think of our signifying activity as though it were the activity of strangers occupying or standing outside an alien universe, our symbols will not deeply take hold of us or motivate us. Most important, however, they will fail to reconcile us to the cosmos. For we will still suspect that they are nothing more than our own fickle projections. When we do so, we shall no longer be able to be grasped by them in any profound way. As an alternative to this suspicion, I would propose that we begin to think of our symbols, myths, metaphors and religions not simply as psychic creations (which in some sense they are, proximately speaking), but more fundamentally as the flowering forth of the universe itself. Theologically speaking these symbolic constructions are the universe's, and not just our own, response to the mystery that calls it and us into being. We need to outgrow our long held premonition that humanly symbolic creativity is groundless, ethereal gesturing of lonely subjects adrift on the surface of an uncaring universe. But we will not be able to envisage our symbolic creativity in this cosmological way until we have become convinced (as I suspect most of us still are not) that we *ourselves* are, in a very literal sense, a natural germination arising from the depths of the universe, and not aliens who have strayed here from some other world.

Theology and Cosmic Homelessness

It is not just scientism and materialism, however, that have taught us to accept on intellectual grounds a posture of cosmic homelessness. For modern theology as well has been pervasively influenced by some of the same assumptions which in other quarters have led to scientism and materialism.

Perhaps the most obvious place where the assumption of cosmic homelessness continue to influence theology is in existentialist forms of religious thought. Rudolf Bultmann, for example, turned to the philos*ophy of existentialism in order to rescue Christian faith from its being mistaken for an outdated cosmology. Christian faith, he declared, is really about freedom, not nature. By directing the focus of theology away from nature and toward the inward realm of existential subjectivity, he and his students established a very influential way of thinking about faith that provides much of value for hermeneutical theory, but few resources for the development of an environmentally helpful theology.

Furthermore, to a great extent existentialist theology uncritically embraces the materialist-mechanistic conception of nature whose overall negative environmental consequences were criticized earlier. By separating the realm of freedom sharply from the determinisms of nature, existentialism makes human subjectivity inherently alien to cosmic reality. Given the classical mechanistic notion that nature is rigorously determined, we can appreciate existentialism's vigorous attempt to salvage human freedom. In this respect, it has made valuable contributions, and I do not intend to be excessive in my criticism of it. But in order to rescue our freedom form the "world-machine" of classical mechanics existentialism requires a separate realm for this freedom, a domain clearly outside of nature. Thus it too exiles the core of our existence from the cosmos. Obviously a theology based on this dualism of nature and human existence cannot take the natural world seriously enough to ground a solid environmental ethic. Theologies that employ existentialist concepts, worthy as they are in other respects, are likely to perpetuate the sense of cosmic homelessness and the restrictive anthropocentrism that it inevitably evokes.

Such also seems to be the case, at times at least, even in the otherwise environmentally wholesome theology of Karl Rahner. Rahner helpfully emphasizes that human existence is "spirit in the world" (*Geist im Welt*), and his Christology situates the Christian mystery firmly within an evolutionary universe. But in at least one of his more recent essays he gives theological legitimacy to the feeling of being "lost in the cosmos." Perhaps he really means to say that we must feel lost in mystery, in which case we would have no objection. But like other existentialist thinkers (including Martin Heidegger), he interprets the essential feeling of "forlornness" in a way that alienates us from the cosmos. Science, he observes, has given us a fresh awareness of our smallness and apparent insignificance in the universe. But instead of allowing this insight of science to embed us even more firmly in the fabric of the cosmos, Rahner follows the kind of thinking we find in cosmic pessimists who dwell on the incongruity of humans finding themselves at all the cosmos. Awareness of the utter contingency of our existence in this immense universe, according to Rahner, can elevate us "above" the cosmos:

> Today, and more than ever in the future, human beings and Christians are also going to have to realize more clearly and more radically that their very *recognition* and *acceptance* of the fact of being lost in the cosmos actually raises them above it.[6]

In still more disturbing language, he adds:

> If people have to give up their feeling of being at home in the universe in exchange for a feeling of not being at home, *which reflects the character of their religious experience*, then this is at root a *legitimate* element of humankind's fate.[7]

I would suggest that our current environmental crisis requires that we subject to criticism any such theological language because it carelessly identifies religious experience with cosmic homelessness. We must seek new ways of affirming the former without requiring the latter.

In still other and more subtle ways contemporary theology persists in segregating human existence from the natural world. It does so especially where it has come under the spell of psychology and the social sciences. These human sciences themselves still often share the assumptions of materialism with its attendant cosmic homelessness. They tend to interpret religious symbolism (like other aspects of culture) as something done *on* the earth by our species, rather than as something the earth does through us. They view our symbolic expression as imaginative world-building, or world-construction, superimposed upon rather than flowing out of the natural realm. Accordingly, religion is often seen as nothing more than the product of human creativity.

An increasing number of theologians now envisage religion and theology simply as human construction. Probably the most obvious example is Harvard theologian, Gordon Kaufmann.[8] Even though Kaufmann was earlier quite critical of existentialist theology's dualism of mind and nature,[9] his recent theological publications are all built on the thesis that religious and theological ideas are nothing more than *human* constructs. He offers a very Kantian picture of religion and theology according to which the "noumenal" reality of God can in no way be represented or come to expression in our religious symbols or theological concepts (and therefore that revelation is an obsolete theological notion). Instead our religions and theologies must be accepted simply as our own *human* imaginings or constructs.

It cannot be denied that some very helpful insights into religion can be gained by viewing it from the point of view of its relative, historically conditioned, and socially constructed character.   But an unfortunate

---

[6]Karl Rahner, *Theological Investigations* XXI, trans. Hugh M. Riley (New York: Crossroad, 1988) 50.

[7]Rahner, *Investigations* 50. (Emphasis added.)

[8]See Gordon Kaufmann, *An Essay on Theological Method* (Missoula, Montana: Scholars Press, 1975).

[9]Gordon Kaufmann, *God the Problem* (Cambridge: Harvard University Press, 1972) 122.

reductionism occurs when our dizzying new awareness of the constructed character of religion becomes the dominant or exclusive way of looking at so complex a phenomenon. Such reductionism does seem to characterize Kaufmann's work. I think this is so partly because the cosmological assumptions underlying his theological program are not fundamentally different from those of scientism, materialism and existentialism. His rigorously Kantian segregation of an unavailable noumenal world from the available phenomenal one has not yet escaped the seventeenth century's questionable divorcing of primary qualities from the phenomenal, but fictitious, realm of secondary and tertiary qualities on the other. In both cases imaginative and creative human subjects are pictured as estranged from the "real" world, a world which they can approach only by covering it over with a perceptive or imaginative clothing of their own making that may have little or no relation to the underlying substratum itself. In Kaufmann's case religion and other forms of symbolic expression do not emanate from or reflect any ultimately real world, but are instead only exercises of the human imagination bounced off but not expressive of the noumenal realm. The symbols and ideas of religion are thus located ontologically in the same sphere as secondary (or tertiary) qualities. The origin of religious meaning is ascribed primarily to the human subject, since the "objective" world apparently lacks, or is reluctant to disclose, any possible inherent value or meaning.[10]

This kind of theology still suffers from a lack of an ecological sense of the continuity and interrelatedness between humans and the cosmos. If it were taken with complete consistency, it too would fail to ground an adequate environmental outlook. A theology shaped by ecological wisdom, on the other hand, would nest us and our religious symbolism more intimately in nature. It would propose that our religious world-construction is, more fundamentally speaking, a natural emergent from an already value-permeated universe which is home to us as well as our religions. Instead, however, much contemporary theology is still shaped by the dualistic, and therefore cosmically homeless, way of thinking such as we observe in the case of Kaufmann. It makes humans out to be primarily value-creating or meaning-projecting beings, and it sees the physical universe as little more than the stage upon which the creative and constructive human religious drama plays itself out. The cosmos itself lacks the intrinsic value or meaning that might nurture our religiousness. It is left up to us isolated subjects to provide such significance.

Certainly, as modern thought has helped us to realize, creativity is one of our main human attributes. But by over-emphasizing it the human sciences

---

[10]A lack of cosmic awareness is present also in much liberation theology. However, as an increasing number of theologians sympathetic to this perspective are now insisting, a socio-economic concern can no longer plausibly be separated from cosmic concern. Today a synthesis of concerns for the environment and human liberation has produced the neologism "eco-justice."

and the theologies based on them at times almost imply that there is no meaningful creativity going on in the universe outside of ourselves. Early in the modern age Cartesian dualism separated cognitional *subjectivity* from the cosmos, locating it in us humans alone. Whitehead has corrected this dualism through his "reformed subjectivist principle" which attributes subjectivity to every actual entity in the universe. In the past century, however, the temptation has been to wrest *creativity* from nature by placing it in us alone. This expulsion of creativity from nature contributes, no less than the earlier exorcism of experiential subjectivity.

The central anthropological image governing this modern approach is that of *homo faber*. One-sided pursuit of this image implies that authentic human existence is attained only in those moments when we are creating and are at the same time conscious of our creativity. The work-ethic, Marxism and some types of existentialism all contribute to the enshrinement of this icon. They judge to be inauthentic any ideas or attitudes that obscure awareness of our purely human productivity. The natural environment then appears as little more than material waiting to be turned into *homo faber*'s creations. If human subjectivity is authentic only in moments of grasping its own creativity, then nature will be seen as neutral stuff whose value is only instrumental to our creativity. Obsession with the *homo faber* image leads us to suppress the fact that our constructive potential is itself the outcome of a multi-layered cosmos, whose own emergent creativity has given birth to us long before we expropriated this creativity as our own exclusive franchise.

To the extent that Christian theology has come under the spell of existentialism, Marxism, and the humanistic social sciences, it too is vulnerable to the excesses pertaining to the *homo faber* image. Theology also at times gets carried away with the theme of human creativity and ignores the more foundational cosmic resourcefulness. It implicitly sanctions an excessive humanism with its devaluation of non-human nature. In doing so it continues to support the sense of cosmic homelessness that underlies our environmental crisis.

A Theology of Adventure

Now, to return to our main question: can we seriously care for nature while at the same time remaining faithful to the religious need to be continually restless until we rest in God? Can we accept the worthy ideal of religious homelessness without bringing along with it a feeling that we are lost in the cosmos? Or will the universe and the earth continue to be little more than the *terminus a quo* of our religious pilgrimage? Will nature, then, continue to be a victim of our religious sojourning?

Religions require that our lives not be embedded too comfortably in any domain short of the inexhaustible mystery which is the ultimate goal and horizon of our existence. Thus, for religions "home" in the fullest sense means nothing less than the incomprehensible "mystery" that invites us to enter more deeply into it. Therefore, fidelity to our traditions demands that we accept religious homelessness as an aspect of genuine spiritual life. But it would be ethically intolerable to interpret religious homelessness in a way that allows it to sanction an environmentally unhealthy *cosmic* homelessness.

So precisely how are we to connect a feeling of fully belonging to nature with the ideal of religious pilgrimage? How are we to prevent the religious journey from becoming a flight *from* the cosmos? This, I think, is one of the most important issues in contemporary spirituality.

Fortunately science can itself come to our aid as we seek to address this question. For scientific cosmology now instructs us that the universe itself is a restless adventure, one that coincides with and supports rather than always resists the spiritual self-transcendence enjoined by our traditions. It is our good fortune to live at a time in the intellectual history of the earth when we can envisage the cosmos itself as a grand story into which our religious journeying fits comfortably as one important chapter instead of being a whole new book with no connection to the cosmic narrative.

As we now know from science, nature itself has always been creatively restless. More and more explicitly the sciences are representing the cosmos itself as a *story*, or perhaps even better, as an adventure. Adventure, according to Whitehead's definition, is the aim toward novel forms of order, or toward increasingly wider beauty.[11] Viewed over the long haul, the universe appears to be an adventure toward increasingly intense versions of ordered novelty, toward a surpassing and always elusive beauty.

Thus, in a certain sense, we can now envisage the *entire* cosmos, and not just religion, as a pilgrimage, as a long story of "homeless" wandering. The cosmos is not a static point of departure for the religious journey; it is itself a journeying. The religious adventure may now be situated within a more comprehensive cosmic epic. The context and precondition for humanity's spiritual adventure is the universe's own inherent "instability." The cosmos therefore is a fellow traveler, not something we merely pass through and then leave behind on our voyage into mystery. Nature is a companion to spirituality, not a temptation to inertia. It appears to us as a constraint or prison only when our concepts of it abstract from the processive, creative, intersubjective and exploratory character of all physical reality. In religion's long search nature's evolutionary experiment reaches toward its own fulfillment. Many religious thinkers have been aware of this for some time, but we have not yet appreciated fully its environmental implications.

Holmes Rolston III writes that the most expressive metaphor for what science finds in nature today is no longer *law* but *story*.[12] There have always been narrative undercurrents in some aspects of scientific theory, but since the

---

[11]Alfred North Whitehead, *Adventures of Ideas* (New York: The Free Press, 1967) 265, 241-72.

[12]Holmes Rolston, *Science and Religion* (New York: Random House, 1987) 119.

time of Darwin science has become increasingly dramatic in its representations of what goes on in the natural world. Now our entire cosmos seems to have unfolded gradually and narratively in a fifteen billion year chronicle of adventure. Astronomer Fred Hoyle even calls it the most fascinating story ever told.

Another physicist, Brian Swimme, observes that at its most basic level, the universe is not so much matter or energy or information, but story.[13] And, like Thomas Berry, he proposes that this cosmic story is deep and extensive enough to embrace the story (or stories) of religion. The encompassing cosmic story may also now serve as a common narrative thread around which weave the results of our interreligious and intercultural encounters.[14]

Science did not take on this narrative countenance without a struggle. Swimme recalls how Albert Einstein himself turned away from the narrative implications of his own research. His mathematics indicated that the universe had a singular origin and that it then unfolded in a gradual manner, but he doctored his equations so that they would fit his predilection for a law-bound cosmos. It was only after Edwin Hubble convinced him that the red-shift phenomenon shows our universe to be expanding that Einstein admitted he had blundered.[15]

Nowadays it is common scientific knowledge that the galaxies, stars and planets have themselves evolved out of simpler configurations. They have come into being as part of an unimaginably complex cosmic story.

Swimme observes also that story forced its way still further into physics when in recent decades scientists discovered that even the fundamental interactions of the universe *evolved* into their present form. *The laws that govern the physical universe today, and that were thought to be immutable are themselves the results of developments over time.* We had assumed that the laws were fixed, absolute, eternal. Now we discover that even the laws tell their own story of the universe. That is, the Cosmic Story, rather than being simply governed by fixed underlying laws, draws these laws into its drama. [16]

I have suggested with Whitehead that we may even more aptly characterize the cosmic process as an *adventure* story.[17] The cosmos is itself a risk-taking, the chronicle of a struggle from simplicity toward more intensely ordered novelty and complexity. Like any adventure it is precarious because its reaching toward further complexity is not always rewarded. There are many regressive moments, episodes of chaos and simply flat periods of endless waiting in the story of the universe. In any narrative, though, there are going

---

[13]Brian Swimme, "The Cosmic Creation Story," in David Ray Griffin, ed., *The Reenchantment of Science* (Albany: SUNY Press, 1988) 47-56.

[14]Swimme 52.

[15]Swimme 50.

[16]Swimme 50.

[17]See my book, *The Cosmic Adventure* (New York: Paulist Press, 1984).

to be long spells of time in which nothing much happens. But the back-sliding and the stretches of tedium are clearly not the whole story. Viewed over the long run there has been much adventurous development in the cosmos so far.

Why did our species become so religious? Cosmologically speaking, it was not in order to escape the earth, or to construct imaginative schemes that would provide a fictitious sense of the caringness of our environment. Rather it came about to sustain and prolong the adventure that was already going on in the universe. Religions arose out of an inherently adventurous universe whose struggle toward novelty it now seeks to keep alive and extend further. The restlessness that propelled the cosmos on its fifteen billion year pilgrimage has not yet died out. At the present phase of evolution it continues to stir within the hearts of those who realize their destiny lies in surrendering themselves *and their world* to mystery.

Conclusion

The long search of religion is an extension of the *cosmic* struggle toward "perfection" (a term Whitehead employs to designate the widest possible harmony of contrasts, or beauty).[18] Thinking of religions as a prolongation of the cosmic adventure may prevent our disconnecting their summons to a life of homelessness from the cosmos which itself has always also been far away from "home." The theme of homelessness is so integral to our religious traditions that we cannot simply ignore it. Instead we may learn to appropriate it in a scientifically intelligent and an environmentally healthy way. Religious people uninformed by the findings of science can too easily interpret nature as though it were a restraint. They are often inclined to interpret our natural habitat as though it were holding us back from the spiritual journey. But now science itself teaches us that the universe is itself the primary subject of adventurous journeying. Religious searching is not opposed to, but instead expressive of, the adventurous nature of the universe itself. We need not, therefore, make our earthly environment a victim of religious homelessness. We and the earth and the universe, all together, still live in exile from our universal destiny, but not from one another. Thus we are not obligated to feel lost in the cosmos in order to embrace the homelessness that religion requires. This should make a difference in our evaluation of the environmental significance of our religious traditions.

---

[18]Whitehead, *Adventures of Ideas* 258.

Part Two

ECOFEMINISM

CREATION CENTERED SPIRITUALITY

AND RESPONSES

ECOFEMINISM:
SYMBOLIC AND SOCIAL CONNECTIONS OF THE OPPRESSION OF WOMEN AND THE DOMINATION OF NATURE

Rosemary Radford Ruether

What is Ecofeminism?

Ecofeminism represents the union of the radical ecology movement, or what has been called "deep ecology" and feminism. The word "ecology" emerges from the biological science of natural environmental systems. It examines how these natural communities function to sustain a healthy web of life and how they become disrupted, causing death to the plant and animal life. Human intervention is obviously one of the main causes of such disruption. Thus ecology emerged as a combined socio-economic and biological study in the late sixties to examine how human use of nature is causing pollution of soil, air and water, and destruction of the natural systems of plants and animals, threatening the base of life on which the human community itself depends.[1]

Deep ecology takes this study of social ecology another step. It examines the symbolic, psychological and ethical patterns of destructive relations of humans with nature and how to replace this with a life-affirming culture.[2]

Feminism is also a complex movement with many layers. It can be defined as just a limited movement within the liberal democratic societies for the full inclusion of women in political rights and economic access to employment. It can be defined more radically, however, in a socialist and liberation tradition, as a transformation of the patriarchal socio-economic system, in which male domination of women is the foundation of all socio-economic hierarchies.[3] Feminism, finally, can also be studied in terms of culture and consciousness, charting the symbolic, psychological and ethical connections of domination of women and male monopolization of resources and controlling power. This

---

[1]Paul R. Ehrlich, et al, *Human Ecology: Problems and Solutions* (San Francisco: W. H. Freeman, Co., 1973).

[2]Bill Devall and George Sessions, *Deep Ecology: Living as if Nature Mattered* (Salt Lake City: Peregrine Smith Books, 1985).

[3]Zillah Eisenstein, ed., *Capitalist Patriarchy and the Case for Socialist Feminism* (New York: Monthly Review Press, 1979).

third level of feminist analysis connects closely with deep ecology. Some would even say that feminism is the primary expression of deep ecology.[4]

Yet, although many feminists make a verbal connection between the domination of women and the domination of nature, the development of this connection in a broad historical, social, economic and cultural analysis is only just beginning. Most studies of ecofeminism, such as the essays in the book edited by Judith Plant, *Healing the Wounds: The Promise of Ecofeminism*, are brief and evocative, rather than comprehensive.[5]

Fuller exploration of ecofeminism goes beyond the expertise of any one person. It needs the cooperation of a team of historians of culture, natural scientists, and social economists who would all share a concern for the interconnection of domination of women and exploitation of nature. It needs visionaries to imagine how to construct a new socio-economic system and a new cultural consciousness that would support relations of mutuality, rather than competitive power. For this one needs poets, artists and liturgists, as well as revolutionary organizers, to incarnate more life-giving relationships in our cultural consciousness and social system.

Such a range of expertise certainly goes beyond my own competence. Although I am interested in continuing to gain working acquaintance with the natural and social sciences, my primary work lies in the area of history of culture. What I plan to do in this paper is to trace some symbolic connections of domination of women and domination of nature in Mediterranean and Western European culture. I will then explore briefly the alternative ethic and culture that might be envisioned, if we are to overcome these patterns of domination and destructive violence to women and to the natural world.

Pre-Hebraic Roots

Anthropological studies have suggested that the identification of women with nature and males with culture is both ancient and wide-spread.[6] This cultural pattern itself expresses a monopolizing of the definition of culture by males. The very word "nature" in this formula is part of the problem, because it defines nature as a reality below and separated from "man," rather than one nexus in which humanity itself is inseparably embedded. It is, in fact, human beings who cannot live apart from the rest of nature as our life-sustaining context, while the community of plants and animals both can and, for billions of years, did exist without humans. The concept of humans outside of nature

---

[4]For example, see Sharon Doribiago, "Mama Coyote Talks to the Boys," *Healing the Wounds: The Promise of Ecofeminism*, ed. Judith Plant (Philadelphia: New Society Publishers, 1989) 40-44.

[5]Plant 40-44.

[6]Sherry Ortner, "Is Female to Male as Nature is to Culture?" *Woman, Culture and Society*, ed. Michelle Z. Rosaldo and Louise Lamphere (Stanford, CA: Stanford University Press, 1974) 67-88.

is a cultural reversal of natural reality.

How did this reversal take place in our cultural consciousness? A key element of this identification of women with non-human nature lies in the early human social patterns in which women's reproductive role as childbearer was tied to making women the primary productive and maintenance workers. Women did most of the work associated with child care, food production and preparation, production of clothing, baskets and other artifacts of daily life, clean-up and waste-disposal.[7]

Although there is considerable cross-cultural variation, males generally took for themselves the work that was both more prestigious and more occasional, demanding bursts of energy, such as hunting larger animals, war and clearing fields, but allowing them more space for leisure. This is the primary social base for the male monopolization of culture, by which men reinforced their privileges of leisure, the superior prestige of their activities and the inferiority of the activities associated with women.

Perhaps, for much of human history, women ignored or discounted these male claims to superiority, being entirely too busy with the tasks of daily life, and expressing among themselves their assumptions about the obvious importance of their own work as the primary producers and reproducers.[8] But, by stages, this female consciousness and culture for the whole society, socialized both males and females into this male-defined point of view.

It is from the perspective of this male monopoly of culture that the work of women in maintaining the material basis of daily life is defined as an inferior realm. The material world itself is then seen as something separated from males and symbolically linked with women. The earth, as the place from which plant and animal life arises, became linked with the bodies of women from which babies emerge.

The development of plow agriculture and human slavery very likely took this connection of woman and nature another step. Both are seen to be a realm, not on which men depend, but which men dominate and rule over with coercive power. Wild animals which are hunted retain autonomy and freedom. Domesticated animals become an extension of the human family. But animals yoked and put to the plow, driven under the whip, are now in a new relation to humans. They are enslaved and coerced for their labor.

Plow agriculture generally involves a gender shift in food production. While women monopolize food gathering and gardening, men monopolize food production done with plow animals. This shift to men as agriculturalists brings a sense of land as owned by the male family head, passed down in a male line of descent, rather than communal land-holding and matrilineal

---

[7]See Marilyn French, "The Long View Back: Matricentry," *Beyond Power: On Women, Men and Morals* (New York: Summit Books, 1985) 25-64.

[8]Yolanda & Robert Murphy, *Women of the Forest* (New York: Columbia University Press, 1974) 111-41.

descent that is often found in hunting-gathering and gardening societies.[9]

The conquest and enslavement of other tribal groups created another category of humans, beneath the familiar community, owned by it, whose labor is coerced. Enslavement of other people often took the form of killing the males and enslaving the women and their children for labor and sexual service. Women's work becomes identified with slave work.[10] The women of the family are defined as a higher-type slave over a lower category of slaves drawn from conquered people. In patriarchal law possession of women, slaves, animals, and land all are symbolically and socially linked together. All are species of property and instruments of labor, owned and controlled by a male head of family as a ruling class.[11]

As we look at the mythologies of the Ancient Near Eastern, Hebrew, Greek and early Christian cultures, one can see a shifting symbolization of women and nature as spheres to be conquered, ruled over and, finally, repudiated altogether.

In the Babylonian Creation story, which goes back to the third millennium B.C., Marduk, the warrior champion of the gods of the city states, is seen as creating the cosmos by conquering the Mother Goddess Tiamat, pictured as a monstrous female animal. Marduk kills her, treads her body underfoot and then splits it in half, using one half to fashion the starry firmament of the skies, and the other half the earth below.[12] The elemental mother is literally turned into the matter out of which the cosmos is fashioned (not accidently, the words "mother" and "matter" have the same etymological root). She can be used as matter only by being killed; that is, by destroying her as "wild," autonomous life, making her life-giving body into "stuff" possessed and controlled by the architect of a male-defined cosmos.

The Hebraic World

The view of nature found in Hebrew Scripture has several cultural layers, but the overall tendency is to see the natural world, together with human society, as something created, shaped and controlled by God, a God imaged after the patriarchal ruling class. Under God, the patriarchal male is the steward and caretaker of nature, which remains a partly uncontrollable realm that can confront human society in destructive droughts and storms. These experiences of a nature that transcends human control, bringing destruction

---

[9]M. Kay Martin and Barbara Voorhies, *Female of the Species* (New York: Columbia University Press, 1975) 276-332.

[10]Gerda Lerner, *The Creation of Patriarchy* (New York: Oxford University Press, 1986), chapter 4.

[11]On the Roman family in late antiquity, see David Herligy, *Medieval Households* (Cambridge, MA: Harvard University Press, 1988) 1-28.

[12]"The Creation Epic," *Religion in the Ancient Near East*, ed. Isaac Mendelssohn (New York: Liberal Arts Press, 1955) 17-46.

to human work, are seen as divine judgments on the evils of human sin and unfaithfulness to God.[13]

God acts in the droughts and the storms to bring human work to naught, to punish humans for sin, but also to call humans (Israel) back to faithfulness to God. When Israel learns obedience to God, nature in turn will become benign and fruitful, a source of reliable blessings rather than unreliable destruction. Nature remains ultimately in God's hands, and only secondarily in male hands, in their role as servants of God,. Yet the image of God as a patriarchal male, and Israel as wife, son and servant of God, creates a basic analogy of woman and nature. God is the ultimate patriarchal Lord under whom the human patriarchal lord rules over woman, children, slaves and land.

The image of God as single, male and transcendent, prior to nature, also shifts the symbolic relation of male consciousness to material life. Marduk was a young male god, who was produced out of a process of theogony and cosmogony. He conquers and shapes the cosmos out of the body of an older Goddess that existed prior to himself, within which he himself stands. The Hebrew God exists above and prior to the cosmos, shaping it out of a chaos that is under his control. Genesis 2 gives us a parallel view of the male, not as the child of woman, but as the source of woman. She arises out of him, with the help of the male God, and is handed over to him as her Master.[14]

The Greek World

In Greek philosophical myth the link between mother and matter is made explicit. Plato in his creation myth, the *Timaeus*, speaks of primal unformed matter as the receptacle and "nurse."[15] He imagines a disembodied male mind as divine architect or Demiurgos, shaping this matter into the cosmos by fashioning it after the intellectual blueprint of the Eternal Ideas. These Ideas exist in an immaterial and transcendent world of Mind, separate from and above the material stuff that he is fashioning into the visible cosmos.

The World Soul is also created by the Demiurgos by mixing together dynamics of antithetical relations (the Same and the Other). This world soul is infused into the body of the cosmos in order to make it move in harmonic motion. The remnants of this world soul are divided into bits to create the souls of humans. These souls are first placed in the stars, so that human souls will gain knowledge of the eternal ideas. Then the souls are sown in earthly human bodies. The soul is to govern the unruly passions that arise from body.

---

[13]For example, Isa. 24.

[14]Phyllis Trible views the story of Eve's creation from Adam as essentially egalitarian, "Depatriarchalizing in Biblical Interpretation," *Journal of the American Academy of Religion* 41.1 (1973): 29-48. For an alternative view from the Jewish tradition, see Theodor Reik, *The Creation of Woman* (New York: McGraw-Hill, 1960).

[15]B. Jowett, ed., *Timaeus* (49), by Plato, vol. 2 of *The Dialogues of Plato* (New York: Random House, 1937) 29.

If the soul succeeds in this task, it will return at death to its native star and there live a life of leisured contemplation. If not, the soul will be reincarnated into the body of a woman or an animal. It will then have to work its way back into the form of an (elite) male and finally escape from bodily reincarnation altogether, to return to its original disincarnate form in the starry realm above.[16] Plato takes for granted an ontological hierarchy of being, the immaterial intellectual world over material cosmos, and, within this ontological hierarchy, the descending hierarchy of male, female, and animal.

In the Greco-Roman era, a sense of pessimism about the possibility of blessing and well-being within the bodily, historical world deepened in Eastern Mediterranean culture, expressing itself in apocalypticism and gnosticism. In apocalypticism God intervenes in history to destroy the present sinful and finite world of human society and nature and to create a new heaven and earth freed from sin and death.[17] Gnostic mystical philosophies chart the path to salvation by way of withdrawal of the soul from the body and its passions and its return to an immaterial realm outside of and above the visible cosmos.[18]

Christianity

Early Christianity was shaped by both the Hebraic and Greek traditions, including their alienated forms in apocalypticism and gnosticism. Second century Christianity struggled against gnosticism, reaffirming the Hebraic view of nature and body as God's good creation. The second-century Christian theologian Irenaeus sought to combat gnostic anticosmism and to synthesize apocalypticism and Hebraic creationalism. He imaged the whole cosmos as a bodying forth of the Word and Spirit of God, as the sacramental embodiment of the invisible God.

Sin arises through a human denial of this relation to God. But salvific grace, dispensed progressively through the Hebrew and Christian revelations, allows humanity to heal its relation to God. The cosmos, in turn, grows into being a blessed and immortalized manifestation of the divine Word and Spirit which is its grounds of being.[19]

However, Greek and Latin Christianity, increasingly influenced by neo-Platonism, found this materialism distasteful. They deeply imbibed the platonic eschatology of the escape of the soul from the body and its return to a transcendent world outside the earth. The earth and the body must be left

---

[16]Plato (42), 23.

[17]For the major writings of intertestamental apocalyptic, see R. H. Charles, *The Pseudepigrapha of the Old Testament* (Oxford: Clarendon Press, 1913).

[18]For the major gnostic literature, see James M. Robinson, ed., *The Nag Hammadi Library* (San Francisco: Harper and Row, 1977).

[19]Cyril Richardson, ed., *Adv. Haer*, by Irenaeus, vol. 1 of *Early Christian Fathers* (Philadelphia: Westminster, 1953) 387-98.

behind in order to ascend to another, heavenly world of disembodied life. Even though the Hebrew idea of resurrection of the body was retained, increasingly this notion was envisioned as a vehicle of immortal light for the soul, not the material body in all its distasteful physical processes, which they saw as the very essence of sin as mortal corruptibility.[20]

The view of women in this ascetic Christian system was profoundly ambivalent. A part of ascetic Christianity imagined women becoming freed from subordination, freed both for equality in salvation and to act as agents of Christian preaching and teaching. But this freedom was based on woman rejecting her sexuality and reproductive role and becoming symbolically male. The classic Christian "good news" to woman as equal to man in Christ was rooted in a misogynist view of female sexuality and reproduction as the essence of the sinful and mortal, corruptible life.[21]

But, for most male ascetic Christians, even the ascetic woman who had rejected her sexuality and reproductive role was too dangerously sexual. Ascetic women were increasingly deprived of their minor roles in public ministry such as deaconesses, and locked away in convents where obedience to God was to be expressed in total obedience to male ecclesiastical authority. Sexually active woman, drawing male seminal power into herself, her womb swelling with new life, became the very essence of sin, corruptibility and death, from which the male ascetic fled. Eternal life was disembodied male soul, freed from all material underpinnings in the mortal bodily life, represented by woman and nature.

Medieval Latin Christianity was also deeply ambivalent about its view of nature. One side of medieval thought retained something of Irenaeus' sacramental cosmos, which becomes the icon of God through feeding on the redemptive power of Christ in the sacraments of bread and wine. The redeemed cosmos as resurrected body, united with God, is possible only by freeing the body of its sexuality and mortality. Mary, the virgin Mother of Christ, assumed into heaven to reign by the side of her son, was the representative of this redeemed body of the cosmos, the resurrected body of the Church.[22]

But the dark side of medieval thought saw nature as possessed by demonic powers that draw us down to sin and death through sexual temptation. Women, particularly old crones with sagging breasts and bellies,

---

[20]Origen, *On First Principles*, ed. G. W. Butterworth (New York: Harper and Row, 1966) 2:83-94. Also Gregory Nyssa, *On the Soul and the Resurrection, Nicene and Post-Nicene Fathers*, 2nd ed., (New York: Parker, 1893) 5:464-65.

[21]See Kari Vogt, "Becoming Male: A Gnostic and Early Christian Metaphor," *Image of God and Gender Models in Judaeo-Christian Tradition*, ed., Kari Borresen (Oslo: Solum Forlag, 1990).

[22]See Otto Semmelroth, *Mary: Archetype of the Church* (New York: Sheed and Ward, 1963) 166-68.

still perversely retaining their sexual appetites, are the vehicles of the demonic power of nature. They are the witches who sell their souls to the Devil in a satanic parody of the Christian sacraments.[23]

The Reformation and the Scientific Revolution

The Calvinist Reformation and the Scientific Revolution in England in the late 16th and 17th Centuries represent key turning points in the Western concept of nature. In these two movements the medieval struggle between the sacramental and the demonic views of nature was recast. Calvinism dismembered the medieval sacramental sense of nature. For Calvinism nature was totally depraved. There was no residue of divine presence in it that could sustain a natural knowledge or relation to God. Saving knowledge of God descends from on high, beyond nature, in the revealed Word available only in scripture, as preached by the reformers.

The Calvinist reformers were notable in their iconoclastic hostility toward visual art. Stained glass, statues and carvings were smashed, and the churches stripped of all visible imagery. Only the disembodied words, descending from the preacher to the ear of the listener, together with music, could be bearers of divine presence. Nothing one could see, touch, taste or smell was trustworthy as bearer of the divine. Even the bread and wine was no longer the physical embodiment of Christ, but intellectual reminders of the message about Christ's salvific act enacted in the past.

Calvinism dismantled the sacramental world of medieval Christianity, but it maintained and reenforced its demonic universe. The fallen world, including both physical nature and human groups outside of the control of the Calvinist church, lay in the grip of the Devil. All that was labeled pagan, whether Catholics or Indians and Africans, were the playground of demonic powers. But even within the Calvinist church women were the gateway of the devil. If women were completely obedient to their fathers, husbands, ministers and magistrates, they might be redeemed as good wives. But in any independence of women lurked heresy and witchcraft. Among Protestants, Calvinists were the primary witchhunters.[24]

The Scientific Revolution at first moved in a different direction, exorcising the demonic powers from nature in order to reclaim it as an icon of divine reason manifest in natural law.[25] But in the 17th and 18th centuries the more animist natural science that unified material and spiritual lost out to a strict dualism of transcendent intellect and dead matter. Nature was secularized. It

---

[23]Montague Summers, ed., *Malleus Maleficarum* (London: J. Rodker, 1928).

[24]William Perkins, *Christian Oeconomie*. London, 1590; also his *Discourse on the Damned Art of Witchcraft*. London, 1596. See also Carol F. Carlsen, *The Devil in the Shape of a Woman: The Witch in 17th Century New England* (Ph.D. Diss: Yale University, 1980).

[25]Brian Easlea, *Witchhunting, Magic and the New Philosophy* (Highlands, NJ: Humanities P, 1980).

was no longer the scene of a struggle between Christ and the Devil. Both divine and demonic spirits were driven out of it. In Cartesian dualism and Newtonian physics it becomes matter in motion, dead stuff moving obediently according to mathematical laws knowable to a new male elite of scientists. With no life or soul of its own, nature could be safely expropriated by this male elite and infinitely reconstructed to augment their wealth and power.

In Western society the application of science to technological control over nature marched side by side with colonialism. From the 16th to the 20th centuries, Western Europeans would appropriate the lands of the Americas, Asia and Africa, and reduce its human populations to servitude. The wealth accrued by this vast expropriation of land and labor would fuel new levels of technological revolution, transforming material resources into new forms of energy and mechanical work, control of disease, increasing speed of communication and travel. Western elites grew increasingly optimistic, imagining that this technological way of life would gradually conquer all problems of material scarcity and even push back the limits of human mortality. The Christian dream of immortal blessedness, freed from finite limits, was translated into scientific technological terms.[26]

The Ecological Crisis

However, in a short three-quarters of a century this dream of infinite progress has been turned into a nightmare. The medical conquest of disease, decreased infant mortality and the doubling of the life span of the affluent, insufficiently matched by birth limitation especially among the poor, has created a population explosion that is rapidly outrunning the food supply. Every year ten million children die of malnutrition.[27] The gap between rich and poor, between the wealthy elites of the industrialized sector and the impoverished masses, especially in the colonialized continents of Latin America, Asia, and Africa,[28] grows ever wider.

This Western scientific, industrial revolution has been built on injustice. It has been based on the takeover of the land, its agricultural, metallic and mineral wealth, appropriated through the exploitation of the labor of the indigenous people. This wealth has flowed back to enrich the West, with some for local elites, while the laboring people of these lands grew poorer. This system of global affluence, based on exploitation of the land and labor of the many for the benefit of the few, with its high consumption of energy and waste, cannot be expanded to include the poor without destroying the basis

---

[26]Antoine-Nicholas de Condorcet, *Sketch for a Historical Picture of the Progress of the Human Mind,* 1794.

[27]Dr. Nafis Sadik. Talk. London, 29 May 1989; see David Broder, Report, *Chicago Tribune* 31 May 1989, 1:17.

[28]Francis Wilson and Mamphela Ramphele, *Uprooting Poverty: The South African Challenge* (Capetown: David Philip, 1989).

of life of the planet itself. We are literally destroying the air, water and soil upon which human life and planetary life depends.

In order to preserve the unjust monopoly on material resources from the growing protests of the poor, the world becomes more and more militarized. Most nations are using the lion's share of their state budgets for weapons, both to guard against each other and to control their own poor. Weapons also become one of the major exports of wealthy nations to poor nations. Poor nations grow increasingly indebted to wealthy nations while buying weapons to repress their own impoverished masses. Population explosion, exhaustion of natural resources, pollution and state violence are the four horsemen of the new global apocalypse.

The critical question of both justice and survival is how to pull back from this disastrous course and remake our relations with each other and with the earth.

Toward an Ecofeminist Ethic and Culture

There are many elements that need to go into an ecofeminist ethic and culture for a just and sustainable planet. One element is to reshape our dualistic concept of reality as split between soulless matter and transcendent male consciousness. We need to discover our actual reality as latecomers to the planet. The world of nature, plants and animals existed billions of years before we came on the scene. Nature does not need us to rule over it, but runs itself very well and better without humans. We are the parasites on the food chain of life, consuming more and more, and putting too little back to restore and maintain the life system that supports us.

We need to recognize our utter dependence on the great life-producing matrix of the planet in order to learn to reintegrate our human systems of production, consumption and waste into the ecological patterns by which nature sustains life. This might begin by revisualizing the relation of mind or human intelligence to nature. Mind or consciousness is not something that originates in some transcendent world outside of nature, but is the place where nature itself becomes conscious. We need to think of human consciousness, not as separating us as a higher species from the rest of nature, but rather as a gift to enable us to learn how to harmonize our needs with the natural system around us, of which we are a dependent part.

Such a reintegration of human consciousness and nature must reshape the concept of God, instead of modeling God after alienated male consciousness, outside of and ruling over nature. God in ecofeminist spirituality is the immanent source of life that sustains the whole planetary community. God is neither male nor anthropomorphic. God is the font, from which the variety of plants and animals well up in each new generation, the matrix that sustains their life-giving interdependency with each other.[29]

In ecofeminist culture and ethics, mutual interdependency replaces the hierarchies of domination as the model of relationship between men and women, between human groups and between humans and other beings. All racist, sexist, classist and anthropocentric assumptions of the superiority of whites over blacks, males over females, managers over workers, humans over animals and plants must be culturally discarded. In a real sense the so-called superior pole in each relation is actually the more dependent side of the relationship.

But it is not enough simply to humbly acknowledge dependency. The pattern of male-female, racial and class interdependency itself has to be reconstructed socially, creating more equitable sharing in the work and the fruits of work, rather than making one side of the relation the subjugated and impoverished base for the power and wealth of the other.

In terms of male-female relations this means not simply allowing women more access to public culture, but converting males to an equal share in the tasks of child-nurture and household maintenance. A revolution in female roles into the male work world, without a corresponding revolution in male roles, leaves the basic pattern of patriarchal exploitation of women untouched. Women are simply overworked in a new way, expected to do both a male work day, at low pay, and also the unpaid work of women that sustains family life.

There must be a conversion of men to the work of women, along with the conversion of male consciousness to the earth. Such conversions will reshape the symbolic vision of salvation. Instead of salvation sought either in the disembodied soul or the immortalized body, in a flight to heaven or to the end of history, salvation should be seen as continual conversion to the center, to the concrete basis by which we sustain our relation to nature, and to one another. In every day and every new generation we need to remake our relation with each other, finding anew the true nexus of relationality that sustains rather than exploits and destroys life.[30]

Finally ecofeminist culture must reshape our basic sense of self in relation to the life cycle. The sustaining of an organic community of plant and animal life is a continual cycle of growth and disintegration. The Western flight from mortality is a flight from the disintegration side of the life cycle, from accepting ourselves as part of that process. By pretending that we can immortalize ourselves, souls and bodies, we are immortalizing our garbage and polluting the earth. In order to learn to recycle our garbage as fertilizer for new life, as matter for new artifacts, we need to accept our selfhood as

---

[29]Sallie McFague, *Models of God: Theology for an Ecological Nuclear Age* (Philadelphia: Fortress, 1987) 69-77.

[30]Rosemary Reuther, "Envisioning our Hope: Some Models of the Future," *Women Spirit Bonding* (New York: Pilgrim Press, 1984) 325-35.

participating in the same process. Humans also are finite organisms, centers of experience in a life cycle that must disintegrate back into the nexus of life and arise again in new forms.

These conversions from alienated, hierarchical dualism to life-sustaining mutuality will radically change the patterns of patriarchal culture. Basic concepts, such as God, soul/body and salvation, will be reconceived in ways that may bring us much closer to the ethical values of love, justice and care for the earth. These values have been proclaimed by patriarchal religion, yet contradicted by patriarchal symbolic and social patterns of relationship.

But these tentative explorations of symbolic changes must be matched by a new social practice which can incarnate these conversions in new social and technological ways of organizing human life in relation to one other and to nature. This will require a new sense of urgency about the untenability of present patterns of life and compassionate solidarity with those who are its victims.

FOUR QUESTIONS IN RESPONSE TO
ROSEMARY RADFORD RUETHER

Jay B. McDaniel

Rosemary Ruether is a prime mover behind what has come to be called "the ecofeminist movement." The movement proposes, as Dr. Ruether puts it in her essay, that there are "historical, social, economic and cultural" connections between the oppression of women and the oppression of nature. Recognizing that there is much work to be done in tracing these connections on all fronts, Dr. Ruether applies her considerable talents in this paper to tracing "some symbolic connections of the domination of women and domination of nature in Mediterranean and Western Europe."

Toward the end of her paper, she briefly explores "the alternative ethic and culture" which might be envisioned if these patterns of domination and destructive violence to women and to the natural world are overcome. Because I am persuaded by most of her historical analysis, I will focus on the alternative she proposes at the end. I have four questions concerning the alternative to be developed under the auspices of ecofeminism.

First Question

The first question stems from my own interest in the animal rights movement. How compassionate towards *animals* is the ecological vision of ecofeminism? Let me rephrase the question in order to make my point clearer.

Granted that ecofeminism is sensitive to the ecological matrices in which we live and move and have our being, is it also sensitive to the unnecessary suffering and loss of life that we inflict upon individual animals? Granted that it is cognizant of the need to recognize our embeddedness in the web of life, does it also enable us to recognize the intrinsic value of each node in the web? Granted that it encourages a respect for natural systems, does it also encourage a respect for those animals--both wild and domestic--whom those systems support?

I ask this question for two reasons. First, I am led to do so by Dr. Ruether's own paper. Her paper introduced the problem of the enslavement of animals in its discussion of the pre-Hebraic roots of Western attitudes toward nature, but does not speak to contemporary forms of enslavement. She notes that, with the development of plow agriculture, animals were placed in a "new relation to humans." They were "yoked and put to the plow, driven under the whip . . . enslaved and coerced for their labor." Her words suggest that a new form of oppression entered into human history, that animals were the first slaves.

When it comes to articulating the parameters of an alternative ethic for our time, however, she does not mention the current fate of these "slaves." She speaks of care for the earth, which suggests a concern for habitats and species; but she does not speak of care for the billions of animals that are reared, transported, and slaughtered for food under atrocious conditions; the billions who are subjected to cruel tests for cosmetics and household products, the billions more who are subjected to cruel experiments and wasteful loss of life in science, the billions more who are subjected to deplorable forms of recreation. From an ecofeminist perspective, does "justice" include justice for these animals; does "love" include love for them; does "care for the Earth" include compassion for these, our closest biological kin? Does ecofeminism have anything to say about the nodes in the web?

Second, I ask this question out of my own dissatisfaction with (a) the "dichotomy" between environmentalism and animal rights that has emerged in secular environmental philosophy and (b) the tendency of environmentalists to lapse into what Tom Regan calls "ecological fascism" or "reductionist ecology," the view that individual living beings are "nothing more" than cogs in the ecosystem. My hope is that ecofeminism might bridge this gap. My view is that Rosemary Ruether can bridge it.

Indeed, I am convinced that when feminist theologians such as Dr. Ruether lend their voices to the contemporary ecofeminist movement, they are in a unique position to bridge the gap between environmentalists and animal rights activists, because they know all too well the dangers of approaching individual human "centers of experience" merely as helpmates in a larger system. Ecofeminist theologians such as Rosemary Ruether are in a position to say that the same danger applies to nonhuman "centers of experience" as well. A deep ecology that neglects what we are doing to individual animals is not deep enough. A truly deep ecology will be as interested in the individual trees as in the forest, in the nodes as the web. It will move beyond the current dichotomy of patriarchal environmental thinking.

Second Question

How multicultural, and open to insights from non-Western perspectives, is the ecological vision of ecofeminism? Granted that ecofeminism invites us to experience a respect for the "web of life," and that it learns about this web from the science of ecology; does it also recognize--with so many African Christians, for example--that the "web of life" can include departed ancestors, terrestrial and celestial spirits, heavens and hells, the living Jesus? Can these less tangible lives--lives accessible only to the realm of shamanic imagination--

be among the inhabitants of a living ecology? Or must a living ecology be limited to "the organic community of plant and animal life" as understood by the science of ecology, with spirits therefore understood as "mere projections" constructed in the context of a "flight from mortality." Granted that we must find our salvation in "the concrete basis by which we sustain our relation to nature and one another," what are we to make of those non-Western peoples whose concrete bases, whose living ecologies, are broader and more imaginative, less scientistic, than our own?

Why ask these questions? Again, I have two reasons. First, I am uncertain concerning Dr. Ruether's own position. On one hand, (a) her own writings are quite sensitive to the multicultural context of contemporary feminist thinking. And (b) they are at least open to certain ways of considering "life after personal death." Implicit in that openness is a recognition that there may be more to reality, and indeed to the web of life, than is contained in the visible world. And yet, on the other hand, (c) she persistently warns us against flights from mortality, and in this regard her writings can suggest a rejection of even the possibility of transterrestrial existence. It can sound, at least from this paper, as if "the organic community of plant and animal life" on Earth is what there is and all there is. That ecology is limited to Earthology.

Second, I ask this question because I am dissatisfied with a kind of reductionism of secular environmental thinking, a reductionism that does indeed reduce Ecology to Earthology. This reductionism can take one of two forms: *geocentrism* or *scientism*. By geocentrism I mean the view that the Earth is itself a larger, more mysterious story: that of cosmic evolution. Much secular environmental thinking is, I believe, geocentric at the expense of being cosmically aware. If not geocentric, however, much secular environmental thinking can be scientistic. By scientism I mean the view that the visible world as disclosed through the techniques of the natural sciences is what there is and all there is. Symptomatic of such scientism is an easy dismissal of the worldviews of indigenous peoples as mere superstition.

I am of the conviction that feminist theologians, particularly in their sensitivity to multicultural forms of feminist thought, are in a position at least to be open to wider, more imaginatively rich notions of "ecology." Here as well, Rosemary Ruether can lead the way.

Third Question

How open is the ecological vision of ecofeminism to the ambiguity of natural processes, and indeed to the "fallenness" of creation? Granted that the language of a "fallen creation" has often functioned in the West to legitimate dominating control over nature and women, and granted that ecofeminists want to reject such control; does Ecofeminism nevertheless recognize a tragic dimension in nature itself? Consider the fox chasing the rabbit. From an outside perspective, of course, this predator-prey relation is part of a larger harmony. But how about from the rabbit's perspective? Is the rabbit's will-to-live not frustrated, is the rabbit's eros for life not cut off? Is there not something violent, cruel, perhaps even tragic about life as we know it?

Dr. Ruether has herself appropriated the symbol of "fallen" nature in her book *Sexism and God Talk*, writing that "nature can be seen as fallen, not that it is evil in itself, but that it has been marred and distorted by human misdevelopment." But is there any sense in which nature is fallen apart from human misdevelopment? And if so, does this not lead us to have a concern for the eschatological redemption of the Earth and other animals? How might Dr. Ruether's own feminist understanding of eschatological redemption for humans be extended to include an eschatological redemption of the Earth and other forms of life?

Fourth Question

What is the role of God in ecofeminism? Is ecofeminism truly in need of a "God," or can it do quite well without reference to the divine? What does reference to the divine add to ecofeminism that is not already present in its secularized versions? Conversely, in what ways might ecofeminism add to our understanding of God?

Let me offer a suggestion in the latter regard: In Dr. Ruether's paper she speaks of God as the "font, from which the variety of plants and animals well up in each new generation, the matrix that sustains their life-giving interdependency." The emphasis is on the generative and sustaining power of the divine Matrix. Yet ecological studies show mutual dependence between all things. They suggest, I believe, that God, however understood, will in some way be dependent on the Cosmos, the Earth, plant and animal life, on us. The seeds for such a dependence are already in some of Dr. Ruether's writings. In her essay "Eschatology and Feminism" she speak of the divine as a "fabric of Being" in which "our personal achievements and failures are gathered up and assimilated into the fabric of Being, to be preserved in eternal memory." Would not the false starts and dead ends of evolution, the sufferings and pleasures of animals, the quiet harmonies and illnesses of plants, also be "gathered up and assimilated into the fabric of Being, to be preserved in eternal memory"? And could not the Memory itself--the very Fabric of Being-- be enriched by the harmonies and impoverished by the tragedies? Would not a truly ecological understanding of the Divine suggest a dependence of the Divine on the cosmos, the earth, on other animals, on us? And would not this kind of dependence, too, be an antidote to that patriarchal consciousness which sees God as generative but not receptive, powerful but not vulnerable, affecting but not affected? At least so I suggest.

CREATION MYSTICISM AND THE
RETURN OF A TRINITARIAN CHRISTIANITY

Matthew Fox

First, I should confess where I get the dual title for my presentation. In January of 1990 I was doing a series of conferences and lectures in New Zealand and Australia and at my last stop, that of the University of Western Australia in Perth, there was a particularly energetic experience with an overflow crowd of eager learners who had heard the renowned British physicist Paul Davies speak on the New Cosmology the previous evening.[1] My talk on "Creation Theology and Western Religion" was followed by a discussion in which one person, in the midst of exciting dialog on environment and creation spirituality, asked the somewhat familiar question: "But are you a Christian? Do you believe Jesus is the Son of God?" I paused for a moment and replied: "I do not deny the divinity of Jesus, but I am a Trinitarian Christian. To focus on Jesus alone is heretical."

I repeat this story because it pertains profoundly to the theme of ecology. As long as we western Christians[2] succumb to this fundamentalist "Jesusolatry" that appears in so many religious guises we shall continue to commit gross sins of omission, ones that result in sins of oppression towards the earth and therefore towards the peoples of the earth and towards our children, those who are destined to inherit our debts of degradation and sickliness. As poet/farmer Wendell Berry put it recently in an interview: "Rural America is a bona-fide part of the Third World. It's a colony."[3]

We cannot create an ecological theology on the basis of "Jesusolatry. A Trinitarian Christianity--one that honors cosmology and thereby the Creator and the co-creative process of the universe; one that honors Jesus as prophet and Liberator as well as a unique bearer of the Cosmic Christ or Sophia

---

[1]See Paul Davies, "Cosmogenesis," *Creation* (May/June, 1990), 10-13.

[2]Eastern Christians are less tempted to do this since they reject Augustine's introspective conscience in favor of a more cosmic Trinitarian spirituality. See Krister Stendahl, "the Apostle Paul and the Introspective Conscience of the West," in Krister Stendahl, *Paul Among Jews and Gentiles* (Philadelphia: Fortress Press, 1976), 78-96.

[3]Carol Polsgrove and Scott Sanders, "An Interview with Wendell Berry," *The Progressive* (May, 1990): 35.

tradition,[4] and one that honors the on-going Spirit who makes "all things new" and is found "pervading and permeating all things" (Wis. 7.24): it is a Trinitarian theology of this sort that is necessary for an ecological theology.

The second part of my title is "Theology in Ecological Perspective." I have chosen to reverse the words in the title of this Conference because it is the universe which gives birth to theology and theologians, and not the other way around. Theology and theologians have been invented by the universe and the earth over about eighteen billion years of history, and not the other way around. Earth begets theology and theologians; theologians do not beget earth. "Every creature is a word of God and a book about God," Eckhart declared six centuries ago.[5] Every creature was already a revelation about God, billions of years before Holy Scripture came to be in books. Scripture does not make holy the creation God made billions of years before books.

There are many challenges that the ecological peril and an ecological mindset or consciousness puts to theology in praxis and theory today. It might be summarized as the challenge to let go of anthropocentrism. I think that there is a hidden anthropocentrism in the theme of ecology in theological perspective that needs to be corrected. Ecology is judging theology, not the other way around.

In this presentation I hope to offer some reflections on how the ecological issues challenge theology itself to renewal. I detect at least nine ways in which theologians are being asked to undergo what theologian Leonardo Boff calls a "different way of doing theology and being a theologian"[6] for the ecological crisis of our time. It is people like college theology teachers who will provide the leadership for altering theology according to the demands of ecology, for these are more on the frontlines with the young and with the lay persons who always hold the future for church renewal in a time of cultural upheaval and potential renaissance, as Pere Chenu pointed out.[7] Clearly, the future for theological exploration lies other than in theological seminary establishments.

1. Cosmology as the basis for theology instead of anthropology or psychology or any other expression of anthropocentrism.

"Eco" in the word "ecology" means "home." Economics is about managing our home and ecology is about studying our home. What is our home? It is

---

[4]See Susan Cady, Marian Ronan, Hal Taussig, *Sophia: The Future of Feminist Spirituality* (San Francisco: Harper & Row, 1986) and Kathleen M. O'Connor, *The Wisdom Literature* (Wilmington: Michael Glazier, 1988). Cosmic wisdom is also the Cosmic Christ tradition. See Matthew Fox, *The Coming of the Cosmic Christ* (San Francisco: Harper & Row, 1988).

[5]See Matthew Fox, *Meditations with Meister Eckhart* (Santa Fe: Bear & Co., 1982) 14.

[6]Leonardo Boff, Clodovis Boff, *Introducing Liberation Theology* (Maryknoll, New York: Orbis, 1988) 22.

[7]M. D. Chenu, *Nature, Man, and Society in the Twelfth Century* (Chicago: University of Chicago Press, 1968) 219-20.

not just western culture, not just educational apparatuses, most of which were invented during the Cartesian era when Descartes declared, "We shall be masters and owners of nature."[8] Our home is the universe itself, which in turn, has given us this amazing planet which we call Earth with its stunning four and a half billion year history. This is the context for grasping both ecology and theology.

Adelard of Bath in the twelfth century warned us of the danger in neglecting to study this home: "Were we to neglect coming to know the admirable rational beauty of the universe in which we live, we would deserve to be cast out from it like guests incapable of appreciating a home in which hospitality is offered to them."[9]

In the same century--the last one in which the West truly woke up to a cosmology and thereby birthed a renaissance--Hildegard of Bingen also warned of what happens when humans neglect their home: "If humanity breaks the web of justice that is creation, then "God's justice permits creation to punish humanity."[10] As humans scurry about looking for places to dump nuclear waste and other trash, Hildegard's prophetic insight seems to be coming ever closer to home. Thomas Berry alerts us to the price we now pay for neglecting our home when he warns that we are involved in a "supreme pathology" as we go about "closing down the major life systems of the planet."

> We are upsetting the entire earth system that has, over some billions of years and through an endless sequence of experiments, produced a magnificent array of living forms, forms capable of seasonal self-renewal over an indefinite period of time.[11]

And anthropologist Loren Eisley comments on current attitudes:

> We have reentered nature, not like a Greek shepherd on a hillside hearing joyfully the returning pipes of Pan, but rather as an evil and precocious animal who slinks home in the night with a few stolen powers. The serenity of the gods is not disturbed. They know on whose head the final lightening will fall.[12]

All ecological theology must begin with cosmology: the story of how the universe got here, what it is doing today, and where "here" is. The story of time *and* space and how together they have birthed and been birthed in a universe of at least a hundred billion galaxies, each glowing with its many billions of stars.[13]

---

[8]Rene Descartes, *Discours de la Methode* 6.

[9]Chenu 13.

[10]Matthew Fox, *Illuminations of Hildegard of Bingen* (Santa Fe: Bear & co., 1985) 45.

[11]Thomas Berry, *The Dream of the Earth* (San Francisco: Sierra Club Books, 1988) 206.

[12]Berry 204.

[13]For summaries see: Brian Swimme, *The Universe is a Green Dragon* (Sante Fe: Bear & Co., 1985) and Thomas Berry and Brian Swimme, *The Universe Story* (Unpub. MS, 1989). For a beautiful commentary from the perspective of a Central American spiritual writer see Ernesto

2. Mysticism as Awe and Awe as Blessing.

An awakened cosmology results in an awakened mysticism. Thomas Aquinas, who devoted his life to integrating cosmology and theology, offers a one-word exegesis of the Psalmist's prayer: "They shall be drunk with the plenty of thy house," when he writes, "*i.e., the universe.*" (Ps. 35.8.)[14] The universe and the ecosystems are not just our home--they are sources of delight, and of awe, of wonder and intoxication. Therefore they are the matrix for a renewed mysticism, for to *enter these mysteries* as cosmologists are now naming them is a mystical experience. There is awe to be experienced in all of our relationships with creation. Instead of the sacred as "wholly Other"--a designation that can easily reinforce theistic relationships to divinity and subject/object relationships with nature--we need to recover the sense of the sacred as the sense of the <u>awesome</u>. Heschel indicates that there are three ways we can respond to creation: "We may exploit it, we may enjoy it, we may accept it with awe."[15] Awe for Heschel is the beginning of wisdom, the basis of biblical mysticism and of our "radical amazement." Awe is a categorical imperative." Without it everything becomes a subject for consumerism. "Forfeit your sense of awe, let your conceit diminish your ability to revere, and the universe becomes a marketplace for you," Heschel tells us.[16] He also points out--in what may be an understatement for graduates of an anthropocentric educational and ecclesial system--"We are shocked by the inadequacy of our awe, at the weakness of our shock."[17] Awe is about an increased sense of the sacred in things--and beyond them. Thanks to the new cosmic story we are learning how sacred our home is.

There are those who feel that an ecological theology can be addressed from the perspective of the concept of "stewardship." I disagree. Stewardship still denotes a dualistic relationship between humans and creation (as if we humans are not totally interdependent with all other created things). Because this concept is not consistent with the cosmic law of interdependence,[18] it flies in the face of any true cosmology--it remains anthropocentric and subtle sado-masochistic. It is still one species taking upon itself the right to manage another. The word "steward" means "a person who manages another's property, or who administers anything as the agent of another." Joseph

Cardenal, *Cantico Cosmico* (Managua, Nicaragua: Editorial Nueva Nicaragua, 1989).

[14]Thomas Aquinas, *II Contra gentes* 2. Translated by Thomas Gilby, *St. Thomas Aquinas: Philosophic Texts* (Durham, North Carolina: The Labyrinth Pres, 1982) 128.

[15]Cited in John c. Merkle, ed., *Abraham Joshua Heschel: Exploring His Life and Thought* (New York: Macmillan, 1985) 126.

[16]Cited in John C. Merkle, *The Genesis of Faith: The Depth Theology of Abraham Joshua Heschel* (New York: Macmillan, 1985) 169.

[17]Merkle 115.

[18] See Erich Jantsch, *The Self-Organizing Universe* (New York: Pergamon Press, 1980) and Rupert Sheldrake, *The Presence of the Past* (New York: Timesbooks, 1988).

Meeker observes that "stewardship of the earth" is a "vision of benevolent, non-violent management, enlightened by science, and intended to create a garden-like Earth where all creatures will thrive in peace." Are we here to be benevolent managers of the entire planet? Meeker comments on the fallacy of stewardship theology--a theology that was present in the Jewish, Christian and Islamic texts of the Assisi Declaration derived from the conference of world religions held at Assisi in 1986.

> However green and compassionate may be the language of these three religions, their concepts of stewardship emphasize the power and dominance of humanity. These stewards are kings, managers, pilots, and executive officers who serve as benevolent bosses of the natural world for its absentee landlord. All specific references to nature in their statements are to domesticated plants and animals and to habitats used for human benefit. Wilderness has no place in their thinking, and there is no intrinsic value in the nature they speak of.[19]

Stewardship theology offers a *moral* model but it lacks *mysticism*, for it is not about relationships among equals. It reinforces images of God as distant from nature--God is viewed as an absentee landlord, and we are God's serfs or managers. It will not serve us as an ecological theology.

Meeker finds a true ecological spirituality in the two eastern religions represented at Assisi. The Vedas of Hinduism "celebrate 'all objects of the universe, living or non-living, as being pervaded by the same spiritual power.'" The Buddhist section of the Assisi Declaration states that "Spirit is everywhere, 'in the rivers, mountains, lakes, and trees,' and it must be revered as fully as human spirit."[20]

Yet the West boasts an alternative to the Stewardship model as well. The Wisdom tradition and the Cosmic Christ are deeply mystical. In the Book of Wisdom we learn that wisdom "permeates all things" and Hildegard of Bingen says "no creature lacks a spiritual life."[21] Eckhart taught the "isness is God" and that there exists an "equality of being" among all creatures.[22] A reawakening to a theology of the spirit is essential for a truly ecological theology. The struggle for ecological justice cannot be waged without mysticism because ecology is about our relationship to things and to the divine, the Spirit, permeating all things. Indeed, it is an awakening to what scientists today are calling the "mind" in all things--an idea very close indeed to that of the Biblical Sophia.[23] Ecology is not one more item for our political agendas; it is a non-negotiable reality--Creation cannot be destroyed without the

---

[19]Joseph W. Meeker, "The Assisi Connection," *Wilderness* (Spring, 1988): 62.

[20]Meeker 62.

[21]Fox, *Illuminations* 53.

[22]Matthew Fox, *Breakthrough: Meister Eckhart's Creation Spirituality in New Translation* (Garden City, New York: Doubleday, 1980) 91-101.

[23]Jantsch 308-10.

destruction of the Spirit itself.

Only an awakened mysticism can usher in an era of deep ecology. The dominance implied in a stewardship model--however benign it is--needs to give way to the *participation* that is implicit in all mystical experience. To make this paradigm shift we have to heed the warning of Biblical scholar Claus Westermann to reimmerse ourselves in a theology of blessing, for to concentrate solely on salvation as deliverance constitutes a "serious distortion of the biblical data."

> From the beginning to the end of the biblical story, God's two ways of dealing with mankind[sic]--deliverance and blessing--are found together . . . Here lies the error that led Western theology to a number of further misinterpretations of and deviations from the message of the Bible. . . . In the primeval history (Gen. 1-11) blessing is found in the context of creation and extends to all living creatures.[24]

In other words, blessing is cosmological. Blessing and awe go together, for awe can be said to be our response *of* blessing *for* blessing.

3.   Images of God.

It is not just our manner of imaging our *relationship* with divinity that is challenged by ecology. Rather, the very images of the Divinity to whom we relate also undergo change. Today, under the impetus of the paradigm shift from an anthropocentric and patriarchal theological model to a more curved and maternal one, there is occurring simultaneously a veritable explosion of images of God. New names for the divine one--that are often deeply ancient ones--are emerging from many places. For example: Godhead; Goddess; Isness; the Beloved; God as Mother; God as Caring Father, not Theistic Father; Great Spirit; Holy Spirit; Sophia; Cosmic Christ; Cosmic Wisdom; the Sacred; the Face behind the Face; Compassion; the "I am" in every creature; Beauty; Justice; Underground River; Life--all these invite us to rediscover the Divine all about us and within us.

We encounter God's face whenever we encounter being itself--if we are prepared for it. Altering our images of God or, if you will, allowing new ones to bubble up from our collective memories and traditions, is a significant move on the part of believers. Eckhart gives us a clue to the reason for this when he says that "all the names which the soul gives God, it receives from the knowledge of itself."[25] To change our images of God is to allow ourselves to undergo change as well. It is little wonder, then, that a time of paradigm shift would be a time of rich re-naming of divinity, a time for *letting God be God in all new--and ancient forms*. It is a time for doing what Eckhart dared

---

[24]Claus Westermann, *Blessing in the Bible and the Life of the Church* (Philadelphia: Fortress Press, 1978) 4.

[25]Fox, *Breakthrough* 175.

to do: "I pray God to rid me of God," he declared.[26] That is, we need to give ourselves permission to let go of clinging to images of God that are not serving us or the earth or divinity as well as they should in order to allow new images to emerge.

4. Images of our relationship to God.

"Awe awakens," poet Bill Everson observes. Part of the awakening that occurs in a creation mysticism is the developing of new images of our relationship to divinity. The environmental imperative challenges us to reconsider the ways we image our relationship to divinity. In particular it challenges us to move from theism to panentheism with all the implications of this move. It is telling that the word "environment" derives from the French word, *environ*, meaning "around." We seek a more rounded, a more encompassing, imagery for our relationship to divinity. Creation mystics offer us such a rounded, circular imagery, which derive from panentheism the awareness of God in us and us in God, when the "us" does not refer to humans alone but to all of creation and all created things. Here are some examples:

> The reign of God is among you. (Lk 17.21)
> Make your home in me, as I make mine in you. . . . Whoever remains in me, with me in him or her, bears fruit in plenty. (Jn 15.4,5)
> God is the one in whom we live, move and have our being. (Acts 17.28)
> God hugs you. You are encircled by the arms of the mystery of God (Hildegard of Bingen)
> God is a wheel, a space, a circle. (Hildegard of Bingen)[27]
> The day of my spiritual awakening was the day I saw and knew I saw all things in God and God in all things. (Mechtild of Magdeburg)
> God speaks: When your Easter comes I shall be all around you, I shall be through and through you. (Mechtild of Magdeburg)[28]
> God is round-about us completely enveloping us. (Meister Eckhart)
> God created all things in such a way that they are not outside himself [sic], as ignorant people falsely imagine. (Eckhart)[29]
> We have all been enclosed with God. (Julian of Norwich)
> We are in God and God, whom we do not see, is in us. (Julian)
> God is our clothing that wraps, clasps and encloses us so as never to leave us. (Julian)
> The deep Wisdom of the Trinity is our Mother. In her we are all enclosed. (Julian)[30]

---

[26]Fox, *Breakthrough* 221.

[27]Fox, *Illuminations* 24.

[28]Sue Woodruff, *Meditations with Mechtild of Magdeburg* (SantaFe:Bear & Co.,1982) 42, 95.

[29]Fox, *Breakthrough* 73.

[30]Brendan Doyle, *Meditations with Julian of Norwich* (Santa Fe: Bear & Co., 1983) 27, 89, 24, 90.

Panentheism is basic to a true environmental spirituality because it celebrates the sacred presence of the divine--the Cosmic Christ or the goddess--in all things.

Is it surprising that so many of the citations I offer come from feminists? Not really. Theism gives us the imagery of Jacob's Ladder; panentheism, on the other hand, is better imaged as "Sara's Circle."[31] Theism supports a flight upwards away from earth, matter and the mother principle; panentheism keeps us grounded in eye-to-eye contact with the divine one in us all.

5. Renewal of Worship.

It is rare to find persons today--Protestant or Catholic--who feel nourished by the forms of worship being offered them, and yet there is a renewed passion for rituals that heal, that tell the new creation story, that allow us to tell *our* stories of interaction with the Spirit in non-verbal ways, that bind young and old, that teach letting go, that involve the body, that cause us to breathe deeply again (hence "ruah" or spirit), that delight. This should not surprise us, for a time of cosmology is a time of renewed worship, a time when we discard forms that are not effective and integrate other forms--often more ancient ones--into our traditions. We live in such a time. As Joseph Campbell puts it:

> The first function of mythology--myths and mystical rituals, sacred songs and ceremonial dances--is to waken in the individual a sense of awe, wonder, and participation in the inscrutable mystery of being.[32]

The ecological imperative requires rituals that get the new cosmological story into our bodies and imaginations, whence they will give birth to a renewal of politics, economics, and education. Ritual with curves, play, unself-consciousness, body, circle dancing that mirror the sense of our curved universe--all this is required by the new ecological era. Artists are needed to tell the story in drama, dance, song, poetry and ritual and to elicit it from the people--thus liturgy as "the work of the people." Aboriginal peoples with their ancient ways of sweat lodges and circle dance, of animal totems and drumming,[33] will bear of wisdom in this.

Thomas Kuhn points out that at a time of paradigm shift "education becomes all-important."[34] A dimension of worship we often neglect is that

---

[31]See Matthew Fox, *A Spirituality Named Compassion* (San Francisco: Harper & Row, 1990 ed.,) chapter two.

[32]See John M. Maher and Dennie Briggs, eds., *An Open Life: Joseph Campbell in Conversation with Michael Toms* (Burdett, New York: Larson Publications, 1988) 17.

[33]For a discussion on bringing the drum back to Western worship see Jim Roberts, "Creating Ritual," in *Creation* (May/June, 1990) 39.

[34]Thomas Kuhn, *The Structure of Scientific Revolutions* (Chicago: University of Chicago Press, 1970).

of education. Education in the cosmological/ecological worldview is sorely lacking when we rely on prayer as reading from books instead of prayer as the opening up of the heart.[35] Worship is the most basic of all art forms--when we renew it we are renewing our relationships to the Earth and to all creatures, including ourselves, and to God. "All our relations," the Lakota people pray in their prayer ceremonies. Ritual is too important to leave to committees and bureaucracies. New forms are emerging, and will continue to emerge, at the level of grass-roots praxis. Scientist Rupert Sheldrake points out that in the previous paradigm of a mechanistic universe "there was no freedom or spontaneity anywhere in nature. Everything had already been perfectly designed."[36] Often our ritual-life imitates such a paradigm today. We need to develop rituals that mirror the facts of our universe; including the reality of its deep, deep creativity.

6. An awakened eros, earthiness and passion.

Compassion simply means "passion with," to be in a solidarity of feeling with the joy and pain of another. An awakened passion can lead to a renewal of compassion, a fuller, deeper living out of our interdependence with all creation. As Hildegard put it, "O human, why do you live without a heart and without blood?"[37] Erotic justice flows from moral indignation, from the passion of moral outrage. Yet, as Heschel observes, "We are a generation that has lost the capacity for outrage."[38] If this was true in the seventies, how much more true it is after the sleepy eighties. Our country is engaged in a war against the poor--a war being carried on in Central America for ten years and being carried on in our own country as well. And through it all the middle class--who are in fact also becoming poorer--are asleep. Our passion has been muted.

Consider the following statistics about the income distribution of recent years in our country.

-- Between 1980 and 1984 the richest 20% of American families gained $25 billion in income and the poorest 20% lost $6 billion.

-- In 1968 the poorest 20% of American families had an estimated 91% of the income needed for basic requirements; by 1983 they had only 60%.

-- In 1985 the top 20% of American families took in 43% of all family income, a postwar high. The bottom 20% got only 4.7%--their lowest share in 25 years. And those in the middle dropped from 46% to 39%.

-- Since 1977 the pre-tax income of the lower 60% of American taxpayers, adjusted for inflation, has declined 14%. Yet taxes on this group have

---

[35]For an analysis of how cosmology can and needs to alter worship, see Fox, *Cosmic Christ* 211-27.
[36]Sheldrake 51. (See footnote 18.)
[37]Fox, *Illuminations* 83.
[38]Merkle 136.

increased by $19 billion. In the same period, the pre-tax income of the top 1% of all Americans, with inflation adjustments, has soared 86% to an average of $549,000.

-- Since 1977, tax changes for the poorest 90% of Americans has resulted in $25.6 billion less. For the richest 10%, a savings of $93.1 billion.

-- The richest 1% of Americans are paying an average of $82,000 less in taxes today than they would have under the tax system before changes in 1978. The lower 90% are all paying higher taxes.

Thus Barbara Ehrenrich comments that "a massive upward redistribution of wealth occurred during the Reagan years" and our society "has succeeded in reducing large numbers of the American poor to the condition of their third-world counterparts--beggars, vagrants, and dwellers in makeshift shelters."[39]

When people learn of the ways in which our society is abusing the earth--its waters, forests, land, air--we can also ignite passion. Joanna Macy reports, from doing workshops recently in Eastern Europe, that it was the ecological disasters that motivated people to demand their democratic rights in the streets. They decided they would "rather die of bullets than of choking."

7.   New Images of Justice and Compassion.

Hildegard of Bingen says that when people are asleep they are asleep to injustice. As we learn to deanthropocentrize justice and place it within a larger, more cosmological setting, we experience new images. Cosmic laws of interdependence and celebration, of interdependence and justice, are being laid out today in the new cosmic story. Justice is not just a moral category for humans--it is a cosmic law, a cosmic "habit" as scientist Rupert Sheldrake would say,[40] into which humans also can fit. The quest for balance and equilibrium is built into our bodies, into our minds (dreams come to bring balance back when we are out of balance) and into the earth body. Scientists call this cosmic habit "homeostasis." Erotic justice occurs when passion over injustice unites with a sense of cosmic awe. Cosmos, after all, is the opposite of chaos. Injustice unravels the ropes of order in the universe and justice brings them together again.[41]

Ecological facts lay bare issues of justice and responsibility between "first" and "third" world peoples, or rather, "1/3" and "2/3" world. One North American does twenty to one hundred times more damage to the planet than one person in the "third" world. One rich American causes 1,000 times more destruction due to our gas-guzzling luxury cars, air-conditioning and what scientist Paul Ehrlich calls our "high-intensity-the-hell-with-tomorrow agriculture." The people of Sweden on the other hand, while still maintaining

---

[39]Barbara Ehrenreich, *Fear of Falling: The Inner Life of the Middle Class* (New York: Pantheon Books, 1989) 202, 190.

[40]Sheldrake, 36-38. (See footnote 18.)

[41]See Hildegard's paintings of this phenomenon in Fox, *Illuminations* 22-25, 86-89.

a quality lifestyle, have learned to use 60 percent less energy than the average American.[42]

8. People of Color and People of the Land.

These people, including aboriginal peoples and family farmers, will increasingly emerge as sources of non-elitist wisdom. Wisdom in the bible, after all, "walks in the streets" and offers an everyday encounter. She is not elitist. James Cowan, in his excellent book on the spirituality of the Aboriginal people of Australia--the oldest tribe of humans in the world--summarizes his study in the following manner: "As long as there is no wish to recognize the divinity in all things, then Aboriginal belief will always be regarded as a suspect philosophy grounded in superstition and strange ritual practices."[43]

If our religions and theologies lack a deep awareness of the *Cosmic Christ*--which is our tradition of "the divinity of all things," then our racism continues. African-American theologian Howard Thurman, who studied Meister Eckhart with Quaker Rufus Jones as a young man in college and knew Eckhart's creation mysticism well, also tells us about his cosmic mysticism as a black person in America.

> As a child, the boundaries of my life spilled over into the mystery of the ocean and the wonder of the dark nights and the wooing of the wind until the breath of nature and my own breath seemed to be one--it was resonant to the tonality of God. This was a part of my cosmic religious experience as I grew up.[44]

Elaborating on this "cosmic religious experience," he says: "There is magic all around us--in the rock, the trees and the minds of men. [sic] . . . There can be no thing that does not have within it the signature of God."[45] Thurman's theology was a significant influence on that of Dr. Martin Luther King. Another example of the deep cosmological spirituality of African-Americans would be that of Alice Walker. A cosmological mysticism opens doors to deep ecumenism and new relations between the peoples of the earth. It honors the wisdom of people of color.[46]

9. Youth and a Renewed Education.

Youth the world over are in despair and with good reason. They sense the peril of the planet--the future home for their children and grandchildren--the

---

[42]Cited in Tara Bradley-Steck, "Americans Destroying the Planet," *Oakland Tribune* (April 6, 1990) A-5.

[43]James Cowan, *Mysteries of the Dreaming: The Spiritual Life of Australian Aborigines* (Dorset, Great Britain: Prism Press, 1989) 125.

[44]Howard Thurman, *With Head and Heart* (New York: Harcourt, Brace, Jovanovich, 1979), 177.

[45]Thurman 268.

[46]For more on "Deep Ecumenism," see Fox, *Cosmic Christ* 228-44.

diminished beauty and health of the earth that they will inherit along with massive debts, unemployment, useless but dangerous weaponry, nuclear wastes, garbage, and overpopulation from the adult world. Adultism reigns from church to school to government to workplace, and the young are the victims of this sin. But an awakened cosmological/ecological mysticism can assist the young in several significant ways. First, by calling for the mystic in every adult--the divine *child* or *puer/puella* in each adult--a mystical awakening gets to the heart of the oppression of the young which is the repression of the mystic or child in the adult. When this child is allowed to "play in the universe" again, there is less need to oppress the young out of a kind of violent envy and projection.

In addition, by regrounding education in cosmology the young are empowered, for they learn that they are desired by the universe over an 18 billion year history and that their lives count for something significant. Hildegard of Bingen says that when humans do good work they make "the cosmic wheel go around." Now there lies a challenge for the young! By re-defining work beyond the narrow, man-made definitions of the industrial revolution, to include the arts, with their power to evoke healing, the art of gardening, the art of creating rituals and teaching adults to play again and be mystical again, a cosmic mysticism can create *good work* for the masses of unemployed youth in the world. Many youth today, acknowledging that they simply are not wanted in an adultist, capitalist economic system, are being called by history to *create their own culture* with its own work, its own economic system based on bartering, its own entertainment, ritual, and lifestyles. A cosmology assists this important project--a project not unlike that of Benedict sixteen centuries ago or of the Celtic monasteries that were also places of lay leadership and youthful imagination.

By insisting that education train body *and* mind, heart *and* head, intuition *and* intellect, a creation-centered spiritual education *honors* the youth by emphasizing process and self-discovery in the context of cosmological discovery. Education and spirituality can be renewed simultaneously. A team of scientists, artists and mystics as teachers in search of a common cosmology will not bore the young but will challenge them to self-discipline. Art as meditation will prove to be a powerful tool for both self-discipline and learning to relate to the universe. We must remember, when we speak of education and the young, the vast and increasing numbers of incarcerated persons in our society who are young. They too deserve to be reached with these new models of education and with the Good News of their empowerment by way of cosmological education and art as meditation.

These nine points indicate some directions that theology might take when we move from an excessive emphasis on Jesus alone to a Trinitarian Christianity, and from an excessive emphasis on a single article of faith (Redemption) to all three articles, thus including *Creation* and *Sanctification* or, in the Eastern tradition, divinization. All this can happen when we understand faith in the context of the glimmering light of a cosmological/ecological awakening--an awakening that requires, but also effects, a "Greening" of the Trinity and each of its Persons. Hildegard celebrated this "viriditas" or "greening power" as the "vitality to bear fruit" and she credits Christ who is "the green figure itself" with bringing "lush greenness" to "shriveled and wilted" peoples and their institutions.[47] Perhaps theology and education themselves might be rendered green and lush by the ecological imperative in our time and thus contribute to a much-needed renaissance in our species.

---

[47]Fox, *Illuminations* 30, 32.

THE UNICORN AND THE RHINOCEROS:
A RESPONSE TO MATTHEW FOX

J. Patout Burns

Father Fox has certainly addressed the theme of ecology by placing theological science within the context of contemporary understanding of the effects of human industry, consumption and warfare on the nonhuman world. Our ability and apparent tendency to disrupt and even destroy the very processes which support all earth's life forms present a truly new challenge to religious traditions. Although he criticizes contemporary Christian theology for its contribution to the ecological crisis, Father Fox moves beyond criticism to develop or recover a Christian spirituality which might inspire a more effective response to the situation. For this he is certainly to be commended.

I should like to begin with a sort of summary of what I take to be Father Fox's principle points, set within the context of his other writings. In so doing, I will be engaged in a transposition of his message into another form of discourse, the more formal language of the academy, in which his proposal can be more effectively discussed, at least by the likes of us.

Father Fox proposes a move away from major tendencies in contemporary Christian theology and practice, particularly its traditional theism and its more recently emphasized anthropocentrism. By the word "theism" Fox wants to point to that objectification of the divine which not only distinguishes but separates God from humanity and the cosmos. When the analogy of being fails to function, and knowing is identified with taking a look at the already-out-there-now-real, God is imagined as an object set over against the human knower. In this way of knowing, humans regard the cosmos as one set of objects and the divine as a distinct, and even dissimilar, object. God, however, is imagined as spatially separated or intellectually over against both humanity and the cosmos.

Within a theistic context, humanity's relationships to the divine and to the cosmos may be governed by morality or mysticism. Humanity's moral relationship to the divine within theism is defined by what Father Fox calls a fall-redemption spirituality, dominated by the notions of promise and command, obedience and reward, guilt and punishment, satisfaction, forgiveness and restoration. The cosmos, in contrast, neither has rights nor imposes obligations. Rather God establishes humans as stewards of the universe, holding them responsible for prudent development and consumption of the resources placed at their disposal.

Christian theocentrism supports a personal mysticism, adapted from the Platonic tradition, in which humans seek union with the divine by separating from and going beyond the cosmos. This spirituality begins with a contemplation of the universal order which reveals the vestiges of the Creator who is wholly other than the creation. A mystical encounter or union with the transcendent divine being can occur only after asceticism has freed a person not only from sensible forms and bodily appetites but from all intelligible concepts drawn from the created world. We should note, however, that during the second millennium of Christianity, the humanity of Jesus Christ was identified as an alternative mystical way, offering a union with the transcendent divine through sensible and emotional attachment to the human Christ. The cosmos, though it may provide analogies, figures and allegories for the divine, has not itself been perceived as the medium or locus for encountering the divine.

The anthropocentrism which relies on anthropology, psychology and the social sciences to develop contemporary Christian theology and spirituality has also, Father Fox contends, resulted in the isolation of humanity from the cosmos. As the Enlightenment strengthened the hold of theism on theology, so eighteenth century idealism focused attention on the human subject, which serves as the starting point for reflection. These idealistic theories tend to emphasize the striving of the human subject; they may even understand the very notion of the cosmos as a construct of the human drive for order. By way of contrast, the divine is often identified primarily as the most fundamental presupposition and the ultimate horizon of all human activity.

In place of this anthropocentric theism, Father Fox has undertaken to develop or, as he would prefer to say, to recover a mystical spirituality centered on a divine person living in the cosmos itself, a creation-centered spirituality. Using the notion of panentheism (God in all things and all things in God), he asserts that the divine spirit or wisdom indwells and animates the entire creation, both human and cosmic. Thus he proposes that humanity can be joined to the divine only by recognizing and recovering its rightful place within the cosmos. In stark contrast to the Enlightenment view of nature as matter in motion, Father Fox views the cosmos as organic and even personal, animated by the Cosmic Christ. Thus he calls for an end to the Platonic mysticism of ascetic and intellectual withdrawal from the body and asserts that the true Christian mystic encounters the divine within the living cosmos. From his recent remarks, I gather that he would also oppose a mysticism focused on the human Jesus.

In a creation-centered spirituality, asceticism trains the senses not to turn away from the world but to discern the divine within the cosmos. It guides the person to awe and delight in the world and in the God who is its life. Worship and contemplation celebrate the mysteries of cosmic process, the blessing bestowed upon all creatures.[1]

By an awakened sense of the divine within the cosmos, by standing in awe of and becoming attuned to the life of the cosmos, humans are called to enter into a totally new relationship with God, the world and one another. As a result, we are promised, the justice of the cosmos itself, the harmony and balance of its operations, will transform human social relationships. Reverence for the divine within the cosmos will replace the moral category of stewardship with the mystical sense of interdependence and thereby inspire an ecologically sound economy and life-style. These and many other benefits will follow if only we would recognize the error of Platonic theism, cast off the chains of an anthropocentric fall-redemption theology, and embrace this creation centered spirituality.

A Brief Critique

This theory of a living cosmos might be, and I am sure has been, examined from many different angles. I propose to inquire into the question raised in the title and introduction to the paper we have just heard: is it Christian? Father Fox posed this question as one of heresy and orthodoxy; he attempted to reverse the charge of heterodoxy onto his questioner. I propose instead a noetic or epistemological question: on what basis might we affirm the truth of this theory? Does Christian faith, grounded in scripture and tradition, offer an intelligible and reasonable basis for affirming a Cosmic Christ?

Father Fox offers two different kinds of warrants for the Christian truth of this creation centered spirituality: its grounding in the normative documents and traditions of Christianity, and its self-authentication in the experience of Christian practitioners. Thus he cites scriptural evidence and theological traditions. In addition, he both quotes the writings of Christian mystics, such as Hildegard and Eckhart, and he refers to the witness of many who have heard and now follow this way.

I propose that we begin with a consideration of the scriptural evidence which has been advanced to support the thesis that the divine wisdom animates the entire cosmos. Should the scriptural texts cited and the method of interpreting them prove convincing, we would be encouraged to undertake the more elaborate evaluation of the subsequent mystical traditions.

---

[1]The difference between the traditional theistic and this creation centered mysticism might be clarified by reference to the Song of Songs. An ancient and well established school of both Jewish and Christian interpretation has prayed this song as a figure or allegory of the soul's love and union with the Word of God or, especially in medieval piety, as an image of the Christian's bridal love for the human Christ. Creation centered spirituality, in contrast, focuses instead on the human lovers' enjoyment and union with one another, locating their union with God in the very midst of that human encounter.

Father Fox anchors the notion of the Cosmic Christ in the references to Divine Wisdom in the Hebrew Scriptures and in the applications of this title to Christ in the New Testament. The primary text is of course the hymn of Proverbs 8:22-36, in which a personified Divine Wisdom describes its role in the creation and governance of the world. In the Deuterocanonical books this notion was elaborated in the Wisdom of Solomon, chs. 7 and 8, but was most fully developed in Sirach, ch. 24.

The text of Proverbs probably reflects an ancient Mediterranean tradition of a distinct divine being who assisted in the formation of the world. As the hymn was appropriated in the sixth or fifth century, it was of course modified to conform to the strict monotheism of Israelite religion. Modern commentators agree that the personification of the divine attribute of wisdom was turned into a literary device to illustrate the richness of the divine life; the biblical editors avoided an ontological assertion of a second divine or semi-divine being.[2] We note, moreover, that although the text speaks of Wisdom working as a craftsman in the process of creation and of Wisdom's joy in the beauty of the cosmos, it does not present Wisdom as animating the creation. In fact, the initial portion of the hymn associates Wisdom with the divine transcendence and superiority to the cosmos.

The two deuterocanonical texts, Wisdom of Solomon and Sirach, belong to a much later period, the second century B.C.E., and are associated with the Jewish community in Alexandria. Both reflect Judaism's attempt to come to terms with Hellenistic civilization prior to the Maccabean revolt.

The text of the Wisdom of Solomon, which seems to have been composed in Greek rather than Hebrew, takes over the vocabulary of Hellenistic speculation. Though the text highlights the cosmological functions of wisdom, it focuses on wisdom as a guide in human affairs and wisdom's sharing of the divine transcendence is never abandoned.[3] Sirach, which was composed in Jerusalem, counters the Hellenistic orientation echoed in the Wisdom of Solomon by locating the indwelling of wisdom not in the creation as a whole but only in Israel, and specifically in Torah.[4] Both these texts do reflect the Hellenistic tendency to hypostatize, to grant distinct personal existence to, mental attributes and operations, a tendency which most of us encounter in gnostic texts. They are, indeed, much more restrained than other texts of the genre.

---

[2] Thus Roland Murphy and Terrence Forestall in *Jerome Biblical Commentary*, (Englewood Cliffs, N.J.: Prentice Hall, 1968), 494-505; R.B.Y Scott in *Proverbs and Ecclesiastes, Anchor Bible*, vol. 18, (Garden City: Doubleday, 1965), 66-73.

[3] David Winston, *The Wisdom of Solomon, Anchor Bible*, vol. 43 (Garden City: Doubleday, 1979), 162-99.

[4] Patrick W. Skehan, *The Wisdom of Ben Sira, Anchor Bible*, vol. 39, (New York: Doubleday, 1987), 327-38. Skehan allows the personification of wisdom but insists that the text presents this hypostasis as a creature rather than identifying it with the divine.

I submit that these three texts from Proverbs, the Wisdom of Solomon and Sirach provide little, if any, foundation for the hypothesis of a hypostatic divine wisdom which serves as the animating principle of a living cosmos. The theory of the Cosmic Christ would require a more elaborate foundation in order to meet contemporary theological standards.

As we all know, however, these scriptural texts were given a very different interpretation by Christians in their attempt to identify the person of Jesus and to locate him within the religious history of Israel and the culture of the Greco-Roman world. In the Prologue of John's Gospel and Colossians 1:15-20, Christians identified Jesus as the incarnation of a divine principle distinct from the Father God who had operated in the creation and governance of the cosmos. I believe that it can be demonstrated that the Christian doctrine of the Trinity developed from this judgment, which is very clearly articulated in John's Gospel, that Jesus Christ was personally identical with the divine wisdom. The "I am" statements in that gospel, as well as its elaboration of the miracles stories, are intended to correct the synoptic presentation of Jesus as the bearer of a divine energy or power.[5] Jesus, the Johannine tradition insists, is not a man raised up to divine status but a god come down to human status.

This Johannine experience of Jesus as a divine person, as identical with the divine wisdom, provides the epistemological basis for turning the literary personification of wisdom in Proverbs, Wisdom of Solomon and Sirach, into an ontological assertion of a second divine being. In the absence of the Johannine portrait of Jesus as a divine person, speaking to the Father and about the Spirit as near equals, Christians would have no basis in revelation for a Trinitarian doctrine. In other words, the worship of Jesus as divine person, not just a bearer of the divine spirit or wisdom, is not some deviation or heresy but the very foundation for Trinitarian Christianity. It is, moreover, the necessary scriptural foundation for asserting that the divine power which governs the universe is personal, living and purposeful.

In his objection to what he calls "Jesusolatry," Father Fox has identified a proper Trinitarian Christianity as "one that honors Jesus as prophet and Liberator as well as a unique bearer of the Cosmic Christ or Sophia tradition." As I follow his exposition in this paper and his discussion in *The Coming of the Cosmic Christ*, I find him avoiding a Johannine understanding of Jesus as the incarnation or enfleshment of the divine wisdom and preferring instead a Markan interpretation of Jesus as a human person who was uniquely inspired or indwelt by the divine wisdom. I believe that such a view of Jesus undercuts the scriptural foundation for the claims that Father Fox makes for the Cosmic Christ.

Even the acceptance of a Johannine Christology, however, would not put an end to the difficulties in reconciling the theory of the Cosmic Christ with

---

[5]I take this to be the thesis of Raymond Brown's ground-breaking study in *The Community of the Beloved Disciple* (New York: Paulist Press, 1979).

the conciliar interpretation of the scriptural revelation. Let me review the subsequent development of this Johannine Christology into the orthodox Christian doctrine of the Trinity.

Christian theologians of the second century, such as Justin, Irenaeus and Tertullian, used the interpretation of Jesus proposed in John's Gospel and the Colossians hymn to construct a synthesis of the Israelite and Hellenistic religious cultures. They presented Jesus as the incarnation of a secondary divine being, subordinate to the Father, who served as his agent in creating the world and governing human history. None of them, however, spoke of this divine wisdom as indwelling the creation or as its life-force. Like the scriptural texts, they maintained a clear distinction between the divine wisdom and the cosmos. Moreover, each of them recognized the historical as well as the cosmological functions of the divine Word.

During the third and fourth centuries, some Christian theologians did attempt to adapt the Platonic notion of the world soul. The Arian controversy, however, closed off that avenue of interpretation. By the end of the century, orthodox Christianity confessed that in their cosmological functions, the Son as divine word and the Spirit as divine wisdom enjoy that transcendence which had always been attributed to the first principle of all reality by Christians, Jews and Hellenes alike. Distinctions between the divine persons were made only for their historical or anthropocentric functions.

In the fifth century, the standard for Christian orthodoxy became the decree of the Council of Chalcedon which reaffirmed the personal identity of Jesus and the divine Word as a single subsistent or individual. The subsequent monophysite and iconoclast controversies never challenged this identification. In fact, the doctrine of divine transcendence was so firmly established that, even in the Hesychast controversy, no attempt was made to personify the divine light or energy which divinizes the mystic.[6]

Father Fox has attempted to draw upon the Christian scripture and doctrinal tradition to provide the foundation for a cosmo-centered theology, a spirituality in which both divine and human are located and united within the cosmos. I suggest that the tradition will not support the theory he is

---

[6]Even as we recognize that Father Fox's theory of the Cosmic Christ cannot be grounded in the Christian dogmatic tradition, we have identified its pedigree. The theory draws on the resources of Hellenistic religious thought which attempted to bridge the distance between an increasingly transcendent divine being and the cosmos by positing a number of intermediary beings. In fact, the theory of the Cosmic Christ closely resembles the Hellenistic doctrine of the World Soul, at once one and many, which animates the entire cosmos and every individual within it. But the fundamental orientation of this Hellenistic speculation is contrary to the intention and spirit of the theory of the Cosmic Christ, which avoids the assertion of the divine transcendence and even tends to identify the divine with the cosmos. Platonic mystics have a distinct preference for the divine in its pure, supersensible and superintelligible form. Moreover, they do not understand the divine as a personal reality which can be encountered and addressed.

proposing. The divine wisdom he has described cannot, I believe, be identified with Jesus Christ. Nor, I submit, does this tradition allow him to abandon the historical or anthropocentric functions of the divine wisdom which are epistemologically prior and foundational to recognition of cosmic functions. He must find some other grounds for affirming that this theory is true.

Two Further Issues

With your indulgence, I would like to address two related issues: panentheism and anthropocentrism.

In proposing this mystical vision of the relation between the divine and the cosmos, Father Fox intends to assert that God is living and working in all things. I believe that in choosing this theory, he intends to avoid pantheism, that God is all things and all things are God. In his attempt to block a spirituality of withdrawal from the cosmos, however, he denies or at least neglects the divine transcendence, the ways in which God is other, indeed wholly other, than the cosmos. The creation-centered spirituality affirms that the mystic encounters the divine in the midst of cosmic process and internalizes this experience of the living cosmos. Asceticism and worship sharpen the senses and activate the right brain for perceiving, appreciating and celebrating the wonder of the divine within the world. Moreover, he rejects those forms of Christian spirituality which cultivate the God who is wholly other than the cosmos.

We note that in his presentation, Father Fox regularly personifies the cosmos and attributes Christian theology reserves to the divine: "Earth begets theology and theologians;" "the universe has given us this amazing planet which we call Earth;" and, "they [the young] learn that they are desired by the universe. . . ." This language, which is foundational to *The Coming of the Cosmic Christ*, identifies the divine as the life principle of the cosmos. In rejecting theism and the otherness of God, Father Fox has unwittingly reduced the divine to the cosmos and embraced pantheism.

As a consequence of this neglect or refusal of divine transcendence, the proposed panentheism collapses into a functional pantheism: the cosmos must be reverenced as divine and the divine is accessible only in the cosmos. Obviously, such a theory is not based on Christian teaching and practice.

I detect a parallel reduction of the human to the cosmic in the proposed shift from anthropocentrism to cosmocentrism. In developing his assertion that the cosmos is a living being, he establishes the standards and norms for human performance in the laws which seem to govern the evolution and operation of the universe itself. For example: the indeterminism which current scientific theory attributes to the cosmos is proposed as a grounding instance of human freedom and creativity; the justice which regulates interpersonal and social interaction is proposed as a special instance of the scientific postulates of cosmic principles of harmony, coherence and balance. I understand this theory as an attempt to integrate humanity into the cosmos and block recourse to a fall-redemption theology.

Actually, however, Father Fox overlooks not only the capacities of individual human beings for deliberation, choice and purposeful action but, even more importantly, the structures of human culture which shape the individual actions into social movements. Yet these capacities and structures are foundational to Israelite religion, to Christian belief, and indeed to any responsible ecological theory. As I mentioned earlier, the Christian appropriation of the biblical and Hellenistic traditions of divine wisdom focuses on the historical interventions of the Word and places its cosmic functions in a supporting role.

Thus I have argued that Father Fox should not claim a foundation in Christian revelation for his theory of the Cosmic Christ. By neglecting both the divine transcendence and the distinctiveness of the human, his theory tends to reduce both the divine and the human to the cosmos.

In closing, I would like to present an image which has accompanied my study of Father Fox's work. It is not the musical, mystical bear, but the unicorn. This animal gently and gracefully symbolizes the power of sexuality and warfare. Of course, such a beast neither is nor could be. The skeleton and muscular structure of a horse will not support such a wondrous horn; the animal would itself be the first casualty of an attempt to use its horn.

So, I believe, is the theory of the Cosmic Christ. Wonderful as it seems and powerful as it is promised to be, I have found no basis for believing that such a reality exists. Moreover, Dr. Santmire convinced me that the theory is impotent in the face of contemporary social and ecological problems.

Yet all is not lost. God did indeed make a unicorn, a great and powerful beast, though not so beautiful and graceful as its mythic cousin. The rhinoceros strikes me as an apt symbol for the Christian belief of God living and working in human history and society. I refer of course to the mysticism of the church as the Body of Christ and the living Temple of the Holy Spirit.

I suggest that a renewed mysticism of the church and indeed of human culture or society as a sacrament of God's presence and faithful power might provide a more necessary and resource. More importantly, we have some evidence for believing that it might be true.

Part Three

MOMENTS IN THE CHRISTIAN TRADITION

FOR ECOLOGICAL AWARENESS

THE RICH FOOL AND THE SPEECH ON MARS HILL: FROM THE COMIC TO THE COSMIC IN LUKE'S CREATOR-CENTERED THEOLOGY

Dennis Hamm, S.J.

Luke, universalist though he was, did not possess a planetary consciousness; nor *could* he. He had no way of knowing that he lived on Planet Number Three. The atmosphere was relatively unpolluted. Beyond his horizon, rain forests breathed freely, their species unthreatened. And though the agricultural system of the Eastern Mediterranean was in many ways unjust, it was at least sustainable. Obviously, we cannot expect Luke to provide answers to our contemporary planetary crises. All the same, it is the thesis of this paper that there is a cosmic and moral vision embedded in Luke-Acts that sits at the root of Christian ethical thinking and can inform and energize our struggles to rescue and heal our fragile and endangered biosystem.

I shall defend this thesis by making two soundings in the text of Luke-Acts: Paul's speech on Mars Hill (Acts 17:22-31) and the parable of The Rich Fool (Luke 12:16-21). I choose the Areopagus speech because it provides one of the most explicit treatments of the relationships between creator, cosmos, and humanity. I pick the Rich Fool parable because it provides a vivid, almost cartoon-like, illustration of the Christian explication of Jesus' teaching regarding those relationships of God, cosmos, and humanity. We will look at the speech first and the parable second because the speech is relatively abstract and the parable stunningly concrete.

The Areopagus Speech

I approach this episode in Acts with these presuppositions, which generally reflect the consensus of Lukan commentators: (1) Using a convention current among Hellenistic historians, Luke has composed the speeches of his second volume as vehicles for presenting his interpretation of the history he narrates. (2) Using traditions current in Christian preaching, Luke rather freely composes cameo discourses that, while they are roughly plausible within his story line, speak more to the reader than to the audience in the world of the narrative. (3) Consequently, the theology of the speeches in Acts is that of the author and it is coherent with the dominant theological interpretation conveyed by Luke-Acts as a literary whole. Thus, as part of the speech material (where the author's hand and mind are especially evident), elements in the speech of Acts 17 illuminate and are illuminated by elements in the other speeches of Acts; and we should expect that theology to be consistent with the vision expressed in the same author's first volume, Luke's Gospel.

Rather than rehearse all the issues of this controverted passage, I will simply engage those aspects that bear on our focus, the relationships of God, cosmos, and human behavior.

The audience. Luke's highlighting of the Stoics and Epicureans in verse 18 (both named only here in the whole of the NT) is significant. Their mention evokes philosophical positions regarding humanity, nature, and the gods--a stereotyped complex that would have been accessible to Luke's readership.[1] The Stoics perceived reality as a unified, organic cosmos in which the divinity inhered pantheistically as a kind of "law." Humanity was part of that cosmos and found happiness by harmonizing with that essentially benevolent law of the cosmos. Epicureans, on the other hand, had a more mechanistic notion of the world, in which the divine was conceived in a "deistic" way at best (the divinity causing but remaining uninvolved). Human destiny meant dissolution after death. Meanwhile, Epicureans sought happiness by prudently doing what was most sensibly pleasant.

In makes sense, then, for Luke to describe the crowd reactions as divided between those who heckled Paul, calling him a "seed-picker," and those who, though they were initially confused (thinking Paul to be speaking of new gods *Iesous* and *Anastasis* ["resurrection," mis-heard as the name of the divine consort of *Iesous?*]), nevertheless remained open to the preacher and wanted to hear more. This portrayal fits the expected reactions of the Epicureans, who would have found Paul's teaching radically incompatible with their own, and the Stoics, who would have found some tantalizing convergences with their worldview and lifestyle and would have been drawn to further inquiry.[2]

Now a quick reading of the speech. First, verses 22-25:

22b You Athenians, I see that in every respect you are very religious. 23 For as I walked around looking carefully at your shrines, I even discovered an altar inscribed, 'To an Unknown God.' What there you unknowingly worship, I proclaim to you. 24 The God who made the world [*kosmon*] and all that is in it, the Lord [*hyparchon kyrios*] of heaven and earth, does not dwell in sanctuaries made by human hands, 25 nor is he served by human hands because he needs anything. Rather it is he who gives to everyone life [*didous pasi zoen*] and breath and everything.[3]

---

[1]The following references to the worldviews of the Epicureans and the Stoics depend heavily on the fine survey of their philosophies by F. E. Peters, *The Harvest of Hellenism: A History of the Near East from Alexander the Great to the Triumph of Christianity* (New York: Simon and Schuster, 1970), esp. pp. 119-50.

[2]For an excellent discussion of the Areopagus speech as a presentation of Christian theodicy against the Epicurean denial of theodicy, see Jerome H. Neyrey, S.J., "Epicureans and the Areopagus Speech: Stereotypes and Theodicy," in a *Festschrift* honoring Abraham Malherbe.

[3]Unless otherwise indicated, the English translation used here is the NAB 1986 revised version of the NT.

The notion that the deity is not captured in sanctuaries and does not need human worship would have been congenial to Stoics and Epicureans alike. But against Stoic pantheism, Luke's Paul asserts the biblical notion of a transcendent creator who *made* everything and, moreover, sustains everything. Haenchen rightly notes that Luke creates v 24a and v 25b by adapting LXX Isaiah 42:5, which reads,

> Thus says the Lord God, who made the heaven, and established it; who settled the earth, and the things in it, and gives breath to the people on it, and spirit to them that tread on it.

Luke's key changes: (1) he introduces the word *kosmos*, a word faithful to the biblical vision and also congenial Greek thought. (2) He uses the formula *hyparchon kyrios*, which emphasizes *continuing* lordship of God. (3) In describing God as the source of all good things, he substitutes *zoen* for Isaiah's *pneuma* (since for Christians God gives *pneuma* only to believers), he drops *to lao* (which in the LXX usually means the chosen people) and adds the fully inclusive "all, (*pasi*)" and he adds "and everything" (*ta panta*) to emphasize that God is the giver of all that there is.[4] Adapting and clarifying the biblical language for his readership, Luke has affirmed the essential vision of Isaiah: God is the initiator and sustainer of all that is. And the appropriate response to this creator is not in the first place man-made temples and temple liturgy.

The speech continues:

> 26 He made from one the whole human race to dwell on the entire surface of the earth, and he fixed the ordered seasons [*horisas prostetagmenous kairous*] and the boundaries of their regions [*kai tas horothesias tes katoikias auton*], 27 so that people might seek God, even perhaps grope for him and find him, though indeed he is not far from any one of us.

Verse 26 has been an interpretive *crux*. One problem has been whether to translate *pan ethnos anthropon* as "every nation of [humans]" (RSV) or "the whole human race" (NAB '86). Another question has been how to translate words for time and space. *Kairoi* can mean either historical epochs or natural seasons. *Horothesiai* can mean either national borders or natural boundaries (shorelines, for example). These choices are illustrated by comparing the NAB translation just given with the following rendering by the RSV:

> And he made from one every nation of men to live on all the face of the earth, having determined allotted periods and the boundaries of their habitation. . . .

---

[4]See E. Haenchen, *The Acts of the Apostles: A Commentary* (Philadelphia: Westminster, 1971), 522, n. 7.

The issue here is a crucial one for our purposes, for it is a question of whether Luke's emphasis is in picturing God as governing the history of diverse nations *or* as providing the gift of the earth and its seasons for the one human family. For us, who are reading the text within an ecological horizon, these differences, obviously, are crucial. Rather than rehearse here the pros and cons of the commentaries, I marshal the arguments for the latter interpretation:

(1) The context of creation naturally recalls Genesis 1, where in the LXX *kairoi* refers to natural periods, most likely seasons (1:14). More immediately, in the parallel speech to the Lycaonians, *kairous karpophorous* (14:17) clearly refers to harvest seasons.[5] Equally pertinent is LXX Jer 5:24:

> And they have not said in their heart, Let us fear now the Lord our God, who gives us the early and the later rain, according to the season of fulfillment of the ordinance of harvest [*kata kairon pleroseos prostagmatos therismou*], where *kairoi* refers to ordained seasons as a work of the Creator that should evoke conversion.

(2) Regarding *horothesias tes katoikias* (national borders? or natural boundaries?), again, creation provides the context and suggests natural boundaries in the sense of the imagery of Genesis 1, where God is pictured as separating water and from dry land to provide fit habitation for animals, plants, and people. Haenchen notes that LXX Ps 73 (74):17 stands behind our passage: *sy epoiesas panta horia tes ges theros kai ear sy epoiesas* ["You have made all the boundaries of the earth; summer and winter you have made"].[6] This verse of the Psalm follows a creation passage (about establishing the sea and preparing the sun and the moon) and connects boundaries and seasons (see vv 11-17 of the Psalm). Thus the NAB's "seasons" works better than the RSV's "periods."

Katoikia means essentially "dwelling-[place], habitation"[7]--not a geographical region. Luke has already twice used the verbal form of that word, *katoikeo*, in the speech, in v 24 referring to divine dwelling (not in man-made temples) and in v 26 referring to human dwelling (possibly picking up on the irony of 2 Sam 7 [You will make me a house? I will make you a house]). Here the RSV's "habitation" works better than the NAB's "regions."

(3) Regarding *pan ethnos anthropon* (RSV's "every nation of [people]"? or NAB's "the whole human race?), either rendering is possible, but "the whole human race" best parallels the holistic meaning of the use of *pan* in the phrase that follows, "the whole face of the earth," and best carries through the

---

[5]Thus, Haenchen, *Acts*, 523. See also H. Conzelmann, *Acts of the Apostles* (Philadelphia: Fortress, 1983), 143.

[6]Haenchen.

[7]Walter Bauer, *A Greek-English Lexicon of the New Testament and Other Early Christian Literature*. Adapted and transl., William F. Arndt and F. Wilbur Gingrich. Chicago: University of Chicago Press, 1957, 424. Hereafter: *BAGD* (Bauer-Arndt-Gingrich Dictionary).

note of unity struck with the notion of *ex henos* ("from one").[8]

In short, I hold that v 26 should be translated this way, modifying slightly the NAB '86: "He made from one the whole human race to dwell on the entire surface of the earth, having fixed the ordered seasons and the boundaries of their habitation."[9]

The upshot is that Luke's emphasis in this picture of the creator is *not* that of God providentially guiding human history in its ethnic and geographical diversity. It is rather a picture of the creator providing and sustaining the gift of creation as the habitat for a single humanity.

Four verses complete the speech:

> 28 For 'In him we live and move and have our being,' as even some of your poets have said, 'For we too are his offspring.' 29 Since therefore we are the offspring of God, we ought not to think that the divinity is like an image fashioned from gold, silver, or stone by human art and imagination. 30 God has overlooked the times of ignorance, but now he demands that all people everywhere repent [*metanoein*] 31 because he has established a day on which he will 'judge the world with justice' through a man he has appointed, and he has provided confirmation for all by raising him from the dead.

In v 28 Luke appropriates Hellenistic language to assert against the Stoic pantheism what we might call a biblical pan*en*theism. Against the Stoic notion of endless cycles of cosmic rebirth and death, he announces the biblical doomsday. Against the coldness of Epicurean "deism" he asserts the biblical notion of God's intimate involvement with creatures. If Luke has said in v 24 that human handicraft cannot *house* God, here in v 29 he argues that human skill and wit cannot *image* the divinity. The unarticulated element of the argument is the biblical idea that the only adequate image of the living God is living human beings, who are images of the King of the universe insofar as they are stewards of the earth.[10]

From cosmos to christology? The wind-up of the speech seems to be a leap from cosmology to christology, totally unprepared for by the earlier part of the speech. But this "leap" from creation to redemption was indeed prepared for in the very Isaiah passage that provided the language of vv 24-25, the first Servant Song and its extension, Isa 42:1-7. Let us hear it in its entirety (in a translation of the Septuagint version, Luke's preferred source):

> Jacob is my servant, I will help him: Israel is my chosen, my soul has accepted him; I have put my Spirit upon him; he shall bring forth judgment [*krisin*] to the gentiles. He

---

[8]Thus, Haenchen 523.

[9]C. K. Barrett ("Paul's Speech on the Areopagus," in M. E. Glasswell (ed.) *New Testament Christianity for Africa and the World* [London: SPCK, 1974] 72) supports this interpretation when he lists among the familiar points of contact between the speech and well-known Stoic doctrines "the unity of mankind (v. 26)" and "the divine appointment of seasons and natural boundaries (26)."

[10]Conzelmann 145.

shall not cry, nor lift up his voice, nor shall his voice be heard without. A bruised reed he shall not break and smoking flax he shall not quench; but he shall bring forth judgment to truth. He shall shine out [*analampsei*] and shall not be discouraged, until he has set judgment [*krisin*] on the earth and in his name shall the gentiles trust [*elpiousin*].

Thus says the Lord God who made the heaven and established it; who settled the earth and the things in it, and gives breath to the people on it and spirit to them that tread on it. I the Lord God have called you in righteousness [*en dikaiosyne*], and will hold your hand and will strengthen you. And I have given you for the covenant of a race [*genous*], for a light of the gentiles [*eis phos ethnon*] to open the eyes of the blind to bring the bound and those that sit in darkness out of bounds and the prison-house.

In the servant imagery of II Isaiah we touch the biblical home base of much of the vision of Luke-Acts. Jesus, in his earthly ministry and as risen Lord working through his church, fulfills the role of the prophet and leader sketched in Isaiah. Jesus becomes a "light to the nations" mainly as risen Lord working through the likes of Paul and Barnabas (see Acts 13:43; 26:18-23). What has not been adverted to before is that the link between God's creation and redemption through the Servant has been prepared for in Luke's source, Isaiah 42:1-7.

Conversion to What? What is the content of the call to *metanoia* issued at the climax of the speech in v 30? Using the same imagery of Second Isaiah, Luke elaborates on this "turning" of conversion in the speech of Paul before Agrippa II (esp. Acts 26:17-28). The first words are those of the risen Lord's commission to Paul in this third account of the Apostle's experience on the road to Damascus:

17 "I shall deliver you from this people and from the Gentiles to whom I send you, 18 to open their eyes that they may turn from darkness to light and from the power of Satan to God. . . ."

And Paul finishes the speech with these words:

22 "But I have enjoyed God's help to this very day, and so I stand here testifying to small and great alike, saying nothing different from what the prophets and Moses foretold, 23 that the Messiah must suffer and that, as the first to rise from the dead, he would proclaim [*katangellein*][11] light both to our people and to the Gentiles."

That would seem to describe what Paul is about in the Areopagus scene, bringing light to the gentiles, or, in the language of the episode itself, moving them from ignorance to knowledge. What, then, is the knowledge here? Is it simply the *fact* of the resurrection and Jesus' future role as mediator of God's judgment? But that would ignore the talk of cosmic creation that preceded the final announcement. It would seem that the *metanoia* in question would mean

---

[11]The word used by Paul to describe his preaching in our speech, Acts 17:23, katangello; see v 17.

a turning to God precisely as described in this speech. It would mean an acceptance of God as transcendent creator and sustainer of the cosmos, fashioned as the human habitat and nurtured by the seasons. Here the reader presumably has in memory the early version of this approach to the pagans at Lystra (Acts 14), where the auditors are challenged to turn from idols to the living God who made the heaven and the earth and the sea and all that is in them, the God who "satisfied your hearts with food and gladness" (14:17, RSV). Conversion, then, would also include *behaving* according to that interpretation of reality, that is, stewarding the goods of the earth to meet human needs, not for self-aggrandizement.

Why Jesus as Judge? If that idea seems to make a big leap to the language of post-biblical reflection on the common good, back up a moment and ask another question: why does the announcement of the appointment of Jesus as God's future judge of all cap the speech? Is it simply a way of asserting that there will be a general reckoning? Or is the naming of *Jesus* as judge a reminder that the person and teaching of Jesus provides the very *criteria* upon which judgment will be made? The synoptic tradition abounds in cues that this is the case. But even more to the point, the teaching of Jesus as presented in Luke-Acts is especially attentive to the relationships of God, cosmos, and humanity as sketched in the Areopagus speech. This is the point that Halvor Moxnes makes when he argues that the teaching of Jesus, especially as presented by Luke, advocates "generalized reciprocity and redistribution," according to a model of human interaction that acknowledges God as the ultimate patron and benefactor and human beings as equal clients.[12]

One could demonstrate this from a variety of Lukan texts, Luke 14:25-33, the treatment of wealth in Luke 16, and special sayings like Luke 11:40 ("Fools! Did not he who made the outside make the inside too?"). But one passage may, more than any other in the Third Gospel, illustrate the relationship between Creator, world, and humanity--the parable of The Rich Fool, to which we now turn.

The Rich Fool

It is striking that the Lukan setting of Jesus' telling of The Rich Fool is told in language that anticipates the issues of the Areopagus speech.

12:13 One of the multitude said to him, "Teacher, bid my brother divide the inheritance with me."

---

[12]Halvor Moxnes, *The Economy of the Kingdom: Social Conflict and Economic Relations in Luke's Gospel* (Philadelphia: Fortress, 1988).

Since inheritance in a peasant society is mainly a matter of land,[13] Luke, by way of this introductory conversation, establishes the topic of the possession of that basic gift of creation after human life:

12:14 But he said to him, "Man, who made me a judge or a divider over you?"

One need look no further than the UBS marginal notes to recognize that Exod 2:14 is being alluded to here--the words that were spoken by Moses' kinsman when he tried to break up their fight. That this incident is important to Luke becomes clear when we read in the speech of Stephen in Acts, where Luke twice alludes to that Mosaic episode: at 7:27 where he quotes the LXX of Exod 2:14 exactly ("Who made you prince or judge [archonta kai dikasten] over us?") and at 7:35, where the speech reflects back on that incident with irony, "This Moses, whom they had rejected with the words, 'Who appointed you ruler and judge?' God sent as both ruler and deliverer, through the angel who appeared to him in the bush." The point in the speech, of course, is that this is another example, like the patriarch Joseph, of the rejected one becoming the savior, a pattern which climaxes in the person of Jesus.

Surely this is what Luke would want the reader/auditor to have in mind as the ironic background against which to hear Jesus' retort to these quarrelling brothers. The Christian reader, looking through Easter glasses, knows very well the answer to that question: the Creator has appointed Jesus judge (and, apparently to bring it closer to the language of acts, Luke here substitutes krites for the LXX's dikastes; see Acts 10:42). 12:15 And he said to them, "take heed and beware of all covetousness; for not even when it abounds to one does a person's life consist in one's possessions [hyparchonta]." [My own very literal translation]

As in the Areopagus speech, the focus is on the gift of life [zoe]. Hyparcho means "to be" but the participial form, hyparchonta means "substance, possessions," which gives rise to some wordplay on the subtle distinction between being and having. The Areopagus speech uses the word three times in ways that seem to play on this dimension. Verse 24 in describing God, "being Lord [hyparchon kyrios] of heaven and earth." V 27 describes the God for whom people seek as "not being far from any of us" [kai ge ou makran apo henos hekastou hemon hyparchonta]. And v 29 describes human beings as "being [hyparchontes] offspring of God." Since in Luke's Greek the word used here for "being" sounds much like the word for possession it is possible to hear the subliminal message that the best "possession" is the kind of "being" which is relationship with God--precisely the point of the beatitudes. Whether

---

[13]This observation from Kenneth Bailey, Through Peasant Eyes: More Lucan Parables (Grand Rapids, MI: Eerdmans, 1980) 59; much of my understanding of the nuances of this parable is indebted to Bailey's discussion, 57-71, esp. on the implied communitarian context and the wordplay on eu-phraino/a-phron.

such a wordplay is intended here, the point is clear: life is not to be equated with possessions.

12:16 And he told them a parable, saying, "The land of a rich man brought forth plentifully." 17 And he thought to himself, "What shall I do, for I have nowhere to store my crops?'

It is crucial to the meaning of this parable to notice that the subject of the opening sentence is "the land." It is mainly the earth itself--that primary gift of God's creation--that has brought forth this abundance. It is indeed the possession of the rich man but, whatever part human work played, it is the land itself that has brought forth this abundant crop. The response of the rich man is not gratitude or an impulse to share. Rather he sees himself in a crisis of accumulation ("Where shall I store it all?").

18 And he said, 'I will do this: I will pull down my barns and build larger ones; and there I will store all my grain and my goods. 19 and I will say to my soul, Soul, you have ample goods laid up for many years; take your ease, eat, drink, be merry.'

Here is a person rich enough to purchase a vacuum as his dwelling place. In a highly communitarian society, we have a picture of a person whose sole conversation partner is himself. Luke's diction highlights the oddly asocial quality of this monologue: *dielogizeto en heauto* ("he thought to himself" v 17); the repeated use of the first-person possessive pronoun "my crops," "my barns," "my grain and goods," (*mou . . . mou . . . mou*), climaxing with the statement, "I will say to my soul, `Soul. . .' This RSV rendering *ero te psyche mou, Psyche* . . . catches this parody of radical selfishness fairly well. Even better is the inspired paraphrase of Clarence Jordan: "And I will say to myself, 'Self, you've got enough stuff stashed away to do you a long time. Recline, dine, wine, and shine!'"[14] That catches in American English the humorous parody of selfishness audible in the Greek. The reader/listener is now ready for the punch-line:

20 But God said to him, 'Fool! This night your soul is required of you; and the things you have prepared, whose will they be?'

The landowner is surprised to learn that what he had thought was an interior monologue had in fact at least one other partner, God. He hears an unexpected message from his (forgotten) sponsor, and the words are full of irony. The last word hanging in the air from the landowner's soliloquy was *euphrainou* ("be merry", etymological, "have a good belly" *eu-phren, phren* meaning both belly and mind). The first word from the *bat qol* of God is

---

[14]*The Cotton Patch Version of Luke and Acts: Jesus' Doings and the Happenings* (New York: Association Press, 1969) 53.

Aphron (etymological, *a-phren*, i.e., no-mind, and no-belly), which could have been heard as a wordplay *euphrainou* ("You speak of having yourself a good tummy. Dummy, you are not going to have any belly at all after tonight").[15] The news of the fool's approaching death might be more accurately translated, "This night they are foreclosing on your soul [*ten psychen sou apaitousin apo sou*]." For *apaiteo* is a legal term meaning to "ask for or demand something back, e.g., a loan or stolen property."[16] Thus, even this *psyche* that he was addressing so possessively is something that comes from another source (implicitly, God). The final verse drives home the obvious lesson:

> 21 Thus will it be for the one who stores up treasure for himself [*thesaurizon heauto*] and is not gathering riches toward God [*eis theon plouton*].

The issue is laid bare. The orientation of the rich fool is such that he has violated all of the primary relationships possible to a human being. (1) He has neglected his relationship with the very *land*, thinking of it first as a possession, rather than a gift to be implemented in stewardship for the common good. (2) He has withdrawn from *community* relationships, as evidenced by his impulse to grab all for himself and to "dialogue" about this in almost solipsistic isolation. (3) He has even lost a proper relationship with his very *self*, forgetting that his *psyche* is not simply a possession but a gift

---

[15]This word for "fool" turns up in important contexts in the LXX. Ps 13 (14):1 ("The fool has said in his heart, There is no God"); a few verses later this psalm describes the fool as one who has not "sought after God," an important motif from Acts 17. The same words appear in Ps 52(53), the doublet of Ps 13(14). Ps 38(39):8 uses the word in the context or the psalmist speaking to God precisely as creator and meditating on the human proclivity to substitute wealth for relationship with God: "he lays up treasures [*thesaurizei*] and knows not for whom he shall gather them," exactly the situation of our landowner. Ps 48(49) is a meditation on the folly of trusting in wealth rather than in God and uses the word "fool" in a verse that resonates with our parable: " . . . the fool and the senseless one shall perish together; and they shall leave their wealth to strangers" (v 10). The double use of *aphron* in Ps 73(74) is particularly striking: immediately after an eight-verse passage celebrating God as cosmic creator, including the verse we found reflected in v 26 of the Areopagus speech (about borders and seasons), Ps 73(74):17, v 18 goes, "Remember this thy creation ; an enemy has reproached the Lord and a foolish people [*laos aphron*] has provoked thy name" and v 22, "Arise, O God, plead your cause; remember your reproaches that come from the foolish one [*aphronos*] all the day." Thus the psalm associates the epithet "fool" with refusal to recognize God precisely as creator. Ps 91(92):6 calls the person who does not magnify the works of God *aner aphron* ("a foolish man"). Again, Ps 93(94):8-9 makes the same connection between foolishness and failure to acknowledge one's Maker: "Understand now you simple [*aphrones*] among the people and you fools [*moroi*], at length be wise. He that planted the ear, does he not hear? Or he that formed the eye, does not he perceive?" Thus in all eight instances of the epithet *aphron* in the LXX Psalms, it is applied to those who do not recognize God as Creator. In this light, the other instance of *aphron* in Luke is clearly seen to be cut from the same cloth: "Fools [*aphrones*]! Did not he who made the outside make the inside too?" (Luke 11:41).

[16]BAGD 80.

from God. And, (4) in all of this, he has of course lost his sense of connection with *God*. And so the final verse of the parable can sum up his life as treasuring up for himself instead of becoming "rich" in his relationship with God, by being grateful for the gift of his own life and living that out by sharing the gifts of the earth with his fellow creatures.

In short, the comic parable illustrates, by way of reverse example, what Luke spells out in the abstract cosmic vision of the Areopagus speech.

Conclusions

Obviously, we cannot expect Luke to address the ecological crises of our day. Yet we find in the text of Luke-Acts, as illustrated in our two soundings, the parable of The Rich Fool and the Areopagus speech, a biblical vision of the relationships of God, cosmos, and humanity which provides a sound basis for grounding an ethic capable of addressing these crises.

To both the exponents of Deep Ecology, who would center their ethics on a paradigm of "*bio*centric equality," and to the mainline conservation movement, which is essentially *anthropo*centric, Luke reminds us that the Judeo-Christian understanding of our ecological context is radically *theo*centric.[17] Just when some Christians may be drawn to a romanticizing of nature, Luke reminds us that ours is a Creator-centered theology. Yet he does this in a way that affirms human dignity ("offspring of God" . . . in whom we "live and move and have our being"). To those who think that Jesus and christology have nothing to offer in our struggle to be more friendly "users" of the gift of Planet Number Three, Luke reminds us that the Creator has affirmed Jesus as judge of our stewarding of this habitat because the relationship of God, earth, and people is at the heart of his teaching about the Reign of God.[18] Although the Third Evangelist does not offer solutions to our ecological problems, his two-volume work, ranging from the cosmic to the comic, helps us see that the context of our life of faith is nothing less than that of the whole human family sharing the single gift of the heavens, the earth, and all that they contain. Both the parable of The Rich Fool and the speech on Mars Hill remind us that individualism and idolatry have been, and still are, primary impediments to living lives of fully conscious creaturehood.

---

[17]For a helpful review of some current approaches to ethics and ecology, see Drew Christiansen, S.J., "Ecology, Justice and Development," *TS* 51 (1990) 64-81.

[18]For a suggestive review of the state of the question in creation spirituality, see Thomas E. Clarke, S.J., "Creational Spirituality," *The Way* 29.1 (1989) 68-79.

MARTYRS, MONKS, INSECTS AND ANIMALS

Maureen A. Tilley

Even people who agree that we should care for all of creation still argue among themselves about just how we ought to value the various components of the created world. Animals are a case in point. Some attribute intrinsic importance to animals, declaring all parts of creation to be of equal value. Others are more anthropocentric, insisting that humans, the rational animals, are of greater importance and value, precisely because of rationality. Other animals are valuable because they serve human beings. The earliest Christians had their own disagreements on this issue. They did not form environmental groups or put forth formal statements on ecology. But the stories they told about animals reveal how they might have addressed this twentieth-century problem.

My investigation of the early Christian attitude toward the natural world began when I was reading texts from fourth-century North Africa, the hagiography of the Donatist Christians.

The old bishop Marculus refused to recant his faith. As we enter the story he is about to be martyred by being thrown off a cliff onto the jagged rocks below. The author of the text was an expert at suspense. As the good bishop falls to his doom, we read line after line about his descent--how his hair is caressed by the breezes, how his garments billow out, how his body cuts through the liquid air. On and on it goes as we wait for the climactic splat. We are further delayed as we read of the difficulty with which the soldiers and the friends of the bishop descend from the precipice to the place of death. When we all finally arrive at the base of the cliff, we look for the grisly evidence of a faith which is true even to death. We examine the jagged rocks and--mirabile dictu--there's no body there. Confused the soldiers and supporters of the bishop look back up the side of the cliff. The bishop was not caught on any craggy outcropping. But as they gaze upward, they notice his profile in the clouds of the sky. Moments later they do find his body, in the posture of sweet repose, laid out on the rocks of a nearby canyon. In witness and deference to the holiness of this martyr the rocks themselves had refused to harm the body of the martyr.[1]

---

[1] *Passio benedicti martyris Marculi* (Migne PL 8.766).

The next day I read another story of Carthaginian martyrs. This time the Romans are frustrated by their own policy of persecution. The more people they martyr, the more relics the Christians have to venerate, and the stronger their faith grows. So they decide on an ingenious policy, one which will execute Christians and annihilate their bodies. They load Christians and other convicts, the living and the dead, onto a ship and row out into the Mediterranean several miles where they dump them all into the sea. Even if the tide eventually washes the bodies back to shore, the remains of the martyrs will be so disfigured by several days in the sea and so intermingled with the bodies of common criminals that the Christians will be unable to tell the difference. They will refrain from venerating any of the bodies for fear of honoring murderers and robbers.

This case is no less wondrous. Immediately dolphins came to the aid of the Christians and bring back only the bodies of their revered saints before the sea can take its toll.[2]

Reading stories from fifth-century Syria, I came across another case of animals assisting martyrs. A woman named Anahid was being tortured by the Persians for her adherence to Christianity. Her interrogators tried many ingenious forms of torture but were unable to break her resolve. At last she was condemned to death and such a grisly death it was to be: she was chained by her wrists and ankles to a cliff. Her body was smeared with honey and she was left as prey for hungry animals and stinging insects. But the creatures never harmed her. For a swarm of wasps descended on the hillside. It formed a wall five arms thick to protect her. The wasps could not liberate her but they did protect her from danger and ridicule. When the Christians came to take her body for burial, the swarm parted like a curtain.[3]

Good stories, but not simply tales of another time. There I was in the grocery store waiting in line and I glanced at the tabloids. It was the usual: "Wild West Town Found on Venus," "Faith Healer Fixes Cars by Touch," "Elvis Sighted in Mississippi Drugstore." But Holy Ecology, Batman: "Drowning child snatched from death by heroic seal."[4] Not too much later it was "Pet rooster pulls drowning child from icy pond,"[5] and "Hero dog pulls crippled kid from swimming pool,"[6] and the story of ants which fed a toddler trapped in the jungle.[7] And there were more and more which paralleled stories of the early martyrs and ascetics.

---

[2]*Passio Maximiani et Isaac Donatistarum auctore Macrobio,* Migne PL 8.772-73.

[3]*Holy Women of the Syrian Orient,* introduced and translated by Sebastian P. Brock and Susan Ashbrook Harvey (Berkeley: University of California Press, 1987) 98.

[4]*Weekly World News* (Oct. 11, 1988): 1 and 5.

[5]*Weekly World News* (April 11, 1989): 1 and 11.

[6]*Weekly World News* (July 18, 1989): 1 and 3; cf. "Heroic dog saves toddler from drowning," *Sun* (October 18, 1988): 5.

[7]"Lost Tot Found Alive Inside Giant Anthill, *Sun* (October 18, 1988): 1 and 35.

What can I say? I was hooked. I was not interested in the historical accuracy of the stories, either the martyr stories or the tabloids. What I did find interesting were the various similarities between the stories in content. Each of the stories involved a single victim in peril and a single animal (except in the case of the ants where it was a single anthill, analogous to Anahid and the wasps). Each told of a daring rescue not otherwise expected.

The similarities in content led me to contemplate similarities in audience and purpose. Neither these stories of martyrs nor the tabloid tales were written for the literati of their societies. The martyr stories were written to be recited aloud at the annual commemoration of these heroes and heroines of faith. The stories of the ascetics were written to encourage others who had chosen the path of self-denial. These are popular forms of literature which invite participation in the story, giving importance to one's own life. So too the tabloids. People read them for amusement, for titillation, to relieve the boredom of a humdrum life. Both are written to delight the reader and to confirm already held beliefs, whether those are beliefs about the nature of holiness and its manifestation in the martyrs or the nature of Elvis and the afterlife. Both stress the ripe balance between the bizarre and the ordinary. Both involve their readers in scenarios which might well, under the right circumstances, happen to them.

How do the animals function here? In the tabloids they always seem to be rescuing young or crippled children, the innocents, the helpless. Where the person is an adult there is generally some prior contact with the animal. A dog rescues an adult woman, but the woman had been the veterinarian who had cared for the animal on another occasion.[8] In general between children and beneficent adults, animals have positive relationships only with good or innocent people. On the flip side, animals in the tabloids attack evil people or people who have invaded their territory.[9] The lesson seems to be that animals have some sixth sense about the identity of humans and put it to good use.

But what of the stories of the saints of antiquity? It used to be a commonplace that the ascetics and the animals of Late Antiquity got on so well because the ascetics were trying to recreate Eden in this life and the animals were joining their effort. However, before jumping to any conclusions I want to look at a variety of animal stories. In this paper I will survey stories of animals from Greco-Roman sources, including Jewish and Christian sources. Each time I will look at folklore and theology. By examining how animals functioned in the earlier stories available to patristic writers, one should be able to detect what, if anything, is distinctive about patristic attitude toward animals and what opinions about animals they challenged or accepted

---

[8]"Hero hound rescues nurse who saved HIM 2 months earlier," *Weekly World News* (April 25, 1989): 46.

[9]E.g. "Incredible Photo of a Killer Crock Attack," *Weekly World News* (May 22, 1990): 4-5.

obiter dicta. I hope these stories will bring to the surface issues which relate to our contemporary relationships with animals and the earth itself.

Greco-Roman Stories

In Greco-Roman stories animals exemplified justice, gratitude, and love. Those stories which represented justice or fair play preserved a sense of order within a world in which good seemed in danger of losing out to evil. Animals, especially elephants, protected the innocent, and avenged graft, adultery and murder by their caretakers.[10]

A variant on the theme of justice appeared in stories about the gratitude shown by animals for the favors done them. A stork fledgling had its broken wing mended by a kind woman. Later the bird repaid her with a gem it found.[11] A snake spared by a hunter rescued the innocent man from an ambush.[12] An eagle saved its benefactor from poisoning.[13] A dolphin played with the son of the elderly couple who had cared for it.[14] And of course there is the story of Androcles and the lion who refused to eat him in the arena, since Androcles has previously removed a thorn from the animal's paw.[15]

There are also stories of love and devotion. Contrary to modern expectations, dogs do not figure prominently here.[16] Snakes were more widely known for combining prescience and fidelity in their care for children.[17] Again one finds eagle stories, including one in which a bird was so devoted to its young master and life-long companion that when the boy died the bird threw itself on his funeral pyre.[18]

Sea mammals were the most highly praised of animals in this respect. They performed the accustomed task of saving their benefactors.[19] They went

---

[10]Protection of the innocent: Aelian, 3.46 and 12.21 in Claudius Aelianus, *Aelian. On the Characteristics of Animals*, with an English translation by A. F. Schoelfield, 3 vols., Loeb Classical Library (Cambridge: Harvard University Press; and London: William Heinemann, 1958), 1.206-09 and 3.38-41). Graft: Plutarch, *De sollertia animalium (Whether land or sea animals are better)* 12, 968D-E in *Plutarch's Moralia*, with an English translation by Harold Cherniss and William C. Helmbold, 12 vols., Loeb Classical Library (Cambridge: Harvard University Press; and London: William Heinemann, 1957), 12.374/75. Adultery: Aelian 8.20 (Loeb 2.206-207). Murder: Aelian 8.17 (Loeb 2.202/203).

[11]Aelian 8.22 (Loeb 2.208-11).

[12]Aelian 10.48 (Loeb 2.344-49).

[13]Aelian 17.37 (Loeb 3.368-71).

[14]Aelian 2.6 (Loeb 1.192-95).

[15]Aelian 7.48 (Loeb 2.166-71).

[16]An exception is the story from Gelon of Syracuse of a dog who wakes its owner from his nightmares in Aelian 6.62 (Loeb 2.84-87).

[17]Aelian 4.54, 6.17 and 6.63 (Loeb 1.276-79, 2.30-33 and 2.86-89).

[18]Aelian 6.29 (Loeb 2.46-49).

[19]Aelian 8.3 (Loeb 2.180/81).

beyond justice to inter-species love as several authors attested.[20] Plutarch said that they were the only creatures which love human beings for their own sake and not for any recompense for any kind human actions.[21] Aelian provided the love story of the dolphin who beached himself in grief over the death of his human lover, and of the seal who surpassed all other creatures by loving an ugly person who seems to have had no other friend.[22]

Is it mere coincidence that the animals are agents in the restoration of earthly equilibrium, that they seem to have gratitude, that they love human beings? Are the authors of these stories not simply anthropomorphizing animal behavior? Or do these creatures of the gods have the equivalent of human intelligence? While folklore is single-minded in its recognition of the wisdom of the animals, the philosopher-theologians were divided.

The Stoics considered animals to have a place in the natural world not unlike trees and rocks but definitely distinct from that of human beings.[23] Animals were there to be used by human beings, though not to be harmed. Even the bed bugs were there for human beings. The bugs kept people from sleeping too much.[24] But they were not rational.[25] They did not know how to obey laws.[26] Morality itself was alien to them for the gods allowed them to eat one another.[27] They did not even have language, nor did they participate in politics, friendship and philosophy, the *sine qua non* of the rational being (at least according to the philosophers).[28]

On the other side of the question were the Neo-Platonists. Their emanationist view of the universe would not allow them to draw a sharp distinction between humans and animals even on the subject of reason.[29] Plato himself had considered animals to be the reincarnation of evil human beings. So there was a continuum running both ways between animals and humans.[30]

---

[20]Cf. "Don Juan Dolphin Tries to Mate with Lady Trainer," *Weekly World News* (May 22, 1990): 37.

[21]Plutarch, *De soll.* 3.6, 984C (Loeb, p. 470/71).

[22]Aelian 61.5 and 4.56 (Loeb 2.26-29 and 1.278/79).

[23]Porphyry, *On Abstinence* 3.1 in *Select Works of Porphyry containing his four books on abstinence from animal food* ... Translated by Thomas Taylor (London: Thomas Rood, 1823) 94-95.

[24]Chrysippus in *SVF* 2.1152.

[25]See Howard Cherniss and William C. Helmbold in *Plutarch*, 313.

[26]Cicero, *De finibus* in *SVF* #371, (p. 3.90).

[27]Hesiod, *Works and Days*, 11. 277-79, cited in Plutarch, *De soll.* 964B (Loeb 348/49).

[28]See Philo, *De animalibus adv. Alexandrum* 45 and 84, in *Philonis Alexandrini de Animalibus*, Armenian text with an introduction, translation and commentary by Abraham Terian (Chico, CA: Scholars Press, 1981) 87 and 103.

[29]Porphyry 3.6 (Taylor, pp. 100-01).

[30]Plato, *Timaeus* 42C and 91D-92C translated by H. D. P. Lee (Baltimore: Penguin, 1965) 58 and 121.

At the beginning of the first century C.E., Plutarch deflected much of the Stoic disdain for the abilities of animals by attributing their critiques to simple lack of knowledge. In his estimation, animals did not only rely on instinct as the Stoics claimed. The variety of abilities within even a single species was proof that they were rational and capable of learning.[31]

Two hundred years later the debate was still going on. Porphyry looked at the acute sense perception of the animals, their prudence and what he interpreted as their ability to learn and concluded that the difference between the rationality of humans and animals was one not of essence but of degree, like that between the gods and humanity.[32] Where the Stoics had claimed that animals' lack of language was evidence of their irrationality, Porphyry answered that animals did indeed have languages but human beings had not yet learned them, as they had not yet learned the languages of all other humans.[33] He asserted that they were part of the realm of morality for they practiced virtues and vices. The theriomorphic form of the gods of Egypt even provided them with congenial objects of worship.[34] The general attitude of the Neo-platonists was that humans and animals were part of a single web of creation.

Finally, there was the mediating point. Aelian, a third-century Greek philosopher, tended toward Stoicism in most matters, but in the animal stories he collected he found a divine providence regarding these creatures: "The gods have taken thought for them, neither looking down on them nor reckoning them of small account. For although destitute of reasoning power, at any rate they possess *understanding proportionate to their needs*."[35]

Which of these positions would Christians take? Any answer would be premature before taking a look at the other major influence on the early Christians, i.e., Judaism.

Judaism

Stories of animals interacting with people are fairly rare in Judaism. Biblical stories and intertestamental literature view them as instruments of divine aid or justice. Ravens feed Elijah (1 Kings 17.6); the dogs lick up the blood of Ahab and Jezebel (1 Kings 21.19); bears killed the children who twitted Elisha as "Old Baldy" (2 Kings 2.23); and lions refused to eat Daniel but gobbled up his tormentors (Daniel 6). The Psalms of Solomon affirm that animals attack the wicked but not the just.[36] Rabbinic sources have one great

---

[31]Plutarch 14, 970E (Locb 12.386/87).

[32]Porphyry 3.7 (Taylor, 101).

[33]Porphyry 3.3 (Taylor, 95).

[34]Porphyry 3.8-10 and 3.16 (Taylor, 102-06 and 110).

[35]Aelian, 11.31 (Loeb 2.396/397).

[36]*Ps. Sol.* 13.1-4 in *The Old Testament Pseudepigrapha*, edited by James H. Charlesworth, 2 vols., (Garden City, New York: Doubleday, 1983 and 1985) 2.662.

animal story. When Moses and Aaron were in Egypt, servants of Pharaoh let loose lions to attack them. But when Moses raised his staff the ferocious lions traded their accustomed demeanor for that of playful puppies.[37] The animals reacted properly while their captors did not. In all these cases the animals acted better than many of the people. These irrational creatures were still wiser than the supposedly rational humans.

Generally, Judaic writers presented a positive view of animals, a view arising no doubt from the belief in the direct creation of the animals by God.[38] The Jewish philosopher Philo even departed from his Neo-Platonic tendencies to affirm the primal goodness of animals and their ensoulment by their creator.[39] But that positive view was tempered by two details. First, animals may have souls, i.e., a life-bearing element within them. They may also have sense perception and therefore, a mind. But this mind is not a rational one, for animals do not have the higher reasoning powers like human beings.[40]

But even though they were not like humanity in this respect, the animals like humans were affected by the Fall. Tame before the Original Sin, they now reflected the sin of Adam and Eve. Other Jewish traditions held that there were no carnivores before the Fall and that as a result of the disorder brought by sin, the animals now fail to obey human beings.[41] But when the Messiah would come they would revert to their original state.[42] However, even in their fallen state, some animals were better than others. The animals that Noah took onto the ark were less tainted that those which remained outside.[43]

Even in this state of imperfection, animals were valuable for three reasons, sometimes of an intrinsic value, sometimes as useful for some divine or human purpose.   First, animals recognized good in people and responded appropriately. In the *Testament of Job* they wept over Job's wife because of

---

[37]Louis Ginzberg, *The Legends of the Jews*, 7 vols., (Philadelphia: Jewish Publication Society of America, 1937, 1966, 1982, 1983), 2.332; cf. 5.425 and 435.

[38]Gen. 1.20-25.

[39]Philo, *On the Creation* (*De mundi opificio*) 20,62-21,64 in *Philo*, with an English translation by F. H. Colson and G. H. Whittaker, 10 vols and 2 suppl. vols., Loeb Classical Library (Cambridge: Harvard University Press; and London: William Heinemann, 1956), 1.46-49.

[40]Philo, *On the Creation* 24,73 (Loeb 1.56-59).   For the distinction between mind and reasoning as they exist in human beings and in animals, see *De animalibus adv. Alex.* 12-16 and comments in Terian, pp. 71-73.

[41]Theophilus, *Theophilus to Autolycus* 2.18 in *The Ante-Nicene Fathers*, edited by Alexander Roberts and James Donaldson, 10 vols. (repr. Grand Rapids, Mich.: Eerdmans, 1983) 2.101; Novatian, *On the Jewish Meats* 2 (*ANF* 5.646); the *Life of Adam and Eve* 24.4 (Charlesworth 2.283).

[42]Is. 11.6-9. See the list of rabbinic references in Ginzberg, 5.102.

[43]Sanh. 108a, 108b, cited in Ginzberg 1.160.

her piety.[44] In the *Testament of the Twelve Patriarchs* wild animals recognized good people and did them no harm.[45]

Second, the animals acted as witnesses to the good or evil that people do. In *2 Enoch*, God preserves the souls of animals until the day of judgment so that the animals can give evidence regarding the ethical treatment of animals by their caretakers.[46] They are not preserved for any value of their own but solely to act as witnesses.[47]

Third, animals have an overtly symbolic function. In their conduct they exemplify the virtues and vices which human beings ought to have.[48]

It is just this sort of symbolism that one will find in earliest Christianity alongside the idea that animals recognize good and respond accordingly.

The New Testament and Apocryphal Literature

The New Testament contains very little about animals. The birds of the air, the foxes with their dens all act as place markers for recommended or discommended conduct.[49] So too in the Gospel of Thomas. The significant exception to this is a passage by Paul, Rom. 8.18-23, which speaks of all creation in bondage waiting for redemption. The sentiment is not singular: first, it is perfectly congruent with the Jewish belief that animals suffer the results of the sin of Eve and Adam; and second, it presages the cooperation of inanimate nature with the saints.

Outside the New Testament, in apocryphal material, we reenter the world of the folk tale. Material from the second century shows the recognition of goodness by the world of nature. The *Acts of Peter* contains a story in which a dog obtained a human voice in order to bear witness against Simon Magus.[50] In the *Proto-Evangelium of James* not only animals but inanimate nature recognizes and responds to holiness. As the child John the Baptist and his mother Elizabeth fled the soldiers of King Herod, Elizabeth appealed to the mountains for help. They opened to hide her and her son.[51] Meanwhile the Baptist's father had been slaughtered in the Temple by the soldiers and "the panelwork of the ceiling of the temple wailed" at his death.[52]

---

[44]*Testament of Job* 40.13 (Charlesworth 1.860).

[45]*Testament of Napthali* 8.4 and *Testament of Benjamin* 3.4-5 (Charlesworth 1.813-14 and 824-25).

[46]*2 Enoch* 58.4-6 (Charlesworth 1.184-85).

[47]*Questions of Ezra* 5 (Charlesworth 1.596 and 599).

[48]*Letter of Aristeas* 153-54 (Charlesworth 2.23); Ginzberg 1.43-46.

[49]See, e.g., Mt. 8.20.

[50]*Acts of Peter* 4.9-5.12 in Edgar Hennecke, *New Testament Apocrypha*, edited by Wilhelm Schneemelcher, English translation by R. McL. Wilson, 2 vols. (Philadelphia: Westminster, 1962) 2.291-92.

[51]*Protoevangelium of James* 22.3 (Hennecke 2.387).

[52]*Protoevangelium of James* 24.3 (Hennecke 2.388).

The third century *Acts of Thomas* and the *Acts of Paul* contain the same sort of stories we have seen in the pagan literature. In the Thomas story dogs preserved the balance of justice in an incident similar to the biblical story of the death of Jezebel. Just as the apostle predicted, the animals attacked and killed a man who had insolently slapped him.[53]

Stories of the Martyrs

The stories of the martyrs contain many incidents of animals interacting with human beings. In two separate incidents in the *Acts of Paul* lions recognized the goodness of Paul and Thecla and refused to harm them just as the lion had refused to attack Androcles.[54] Animals were also on the side of the martyrs in the story of Perpetua and Felicitas. A bear brought in to torture the martyrs refused to come out of its cage, and a boar refused to attack the martyrs, turning against the Romans instead.[55] When animals could not prevent martyrdom, they could at least reverence the bodies of the holy ones as they did in the case of Anahid and the wasps, and that of the Carthaginian martyrs whose bodies the dolphins brought back to land for proper burial and veneration.

In these stories animals give up their bestial nature at the same time the persecutors of the saints are being described with feral epithets. This is no return to Eden for the animals but a role reversal with evil human beings.[56]

Inanimate nature too respected the martyrs. Many stories tell of bonfires prepared for martyrs. The rains soak the pyres and the martyrs are temporarily saved.[57] Divine justice is served here as it was in the story of the bishop Marculus whose body the rocks would not tear.

In general, the animals and the world of nature recognize the holiness of the martyrs and refuse to harm them.

Stories of the Ascetics

Not every story of saints and animals involved martyrdom. Many more were devoted to the relationship between the saints of the desert, the ascetics. In these stories animals took on many roles in a mutually beneficial relationship.

---

[53]*Acts of Thomas* 5 and 8 (Hennecke 2.445 and 447).

[54]*Acts of Paul* 7 and 26 (Hennecke 2.372 and 360).

[55]*Passio Perpetuae* 19.5 in *The Acts of the Christian Martyrs*, introduction, texts and translations by Herbert Musurillo (Oxford: Clarendon Press, 1972) 126-27.

[56]For a catalogue of such stories and a structuralist analysis, see Alison Goddard Eliot, *Roads to Paradise: Reading the Lives of the Early Saints* (Hanover, N. H., and London: University Press of New England for Brown University, 1987) 149-50.

[57]E.g., *Passio Sanctorum Montani et Lucii* 3.3 in Musurillo, 216-17.

The animals called on the monks for help. A hyena prevailed on the monk Macarius to heal one of her cubs which had been born blind. She recognized his spiritual power and realized it could benefit her brood. In return for his care she brought him an ram's skin to use as a bed covering.[58]

In their turn, the animals may come to the aid of the monks of the wilderness. The animals provide an atmosphere in which the monks can learn to repent for their sins.[59] On a more mundane level, the animals help the monks with smaller tasks. The Abba Amoun called on snakes to guard his cell.[60] The Abba Helle was ferried across the river by a crocodile. However, once he had returned from the other side, he turned to the animal which had previously terrorized the neighborhood and said: "It is better for you to die and make restitution for all the lives you have taken." The animal immediately went belly up and died.[61]

This should be no surprise for the animals were generally responsive to the preaching of the champions of asceticism. The Abba Bes in Egypt preached to both hippos and crocodiles. Inspired by his words they ceased their ravaging of the countryside.[62]

Often the beasts simply responded to the presence of the goodness of the holy ones. Animals delighted in the presence of the holy monk Antony. As the demons recognized his holiness and fled, the beasts approached.[63] The animals reacted more sanely than the demons.

But when the holiness of the monk departed so also did the good relationship with the animals. The best example is the story of the monk Sabas. This holy man had a servant named Flavius. Flavius was a real Sancho to the monk's Don Quixote. The servant tended a lion which guarded the monk's donkey from other beasts of prey. One day the servant fell into sin. On that day the lion ate the donkey.[64]

---

[58]*The Lives of the Desert Fathers: The Historia Monachorum in Aegypto*, section 21.15-16, translated by Norman Russell, introduction by Benedicta Ward (London and Oxford: Mowbray ; and Kalamazoo: Cistercian, 1981) 110.

[59]*Ephraemi Syri, Rabulae, Balaei aliorum opera selecta*, edited by J. J. Overbeck (Oxford, 1895), p. 117, cited in Arthur V bus, *History of Asceticism in the Syrian Orient: A Contribution to the History of Culture in the Near East*. Vol. 2: *Early Monasticism in Mesopotamia and Syria* (Louvain: Secretariat du Corpus SCO, 1960), 2.27

[60]*The Lives of the Desert Fathers* 9.7, (Russell, 81).

[61]*The Lives of the Desert Fathers* 12.7-9 (Russell, p. 91). A similar story is found in Palladius, *Historia Lausiaca* 59 (Migne PL 73.1167).

[62]*Lives of the Desert Fathers* 10 (Russell, 66).

[63]Athanasius, *The Life of Antony* 53, in *Athanasius, The Life of Antony and the Letter to Marcellinus*, translation and introduction by Robert C. Gregg, Classics of Western Spirituality (New York: Paulist, 1980) 70.

[64]Eliot, p. 156, citing Cyril of Sytholopolis, *Life of Saint Sabas* 3.2, from A. J. Festugi re, *Les Moines d'orient: Introduction au monachisme oriental* (Paris: Cerf, 1961) 65.

Thus in the stories of the ascetics the animals assist the monks, but only so long as they remain holy. As in the stories from the Greco-Roman traditions, animals recognize innocence and act with proper awe and gratitude. But the monks also find peace and repentance in the company of the animals, and in their turn are able to inspire repentance in the animals. These folk tales all witness to some rationality or mind in the animals.

The Theologians' Responses

We now leave the realm of folk tale to contemplate the response of Christian theologians to popular beliefs about animals. Many treated the animals as their pagan predecessors had. The behavior of the animals was anthropomorphized to provide object lessons for Christians in acquiring virtues and avoiding vice. The Christians took up the preaching of Jesus on the lilies of the field and the birds of the air who provided models of trust for the disciples.[65] In their attempt at utilizing the entire Bible without taking it literally, they treated discussions of animals allegorically. In the division between clean and unclean animals they saw the categorization of people of virtue and of vice. At the beginning of the second century, the *Epistle of Barnabas* used this technique which was adapted from Jews like Philo. By the end of the century Clement of Alexandria saw the clean ruminating animals as people with the proper attitude toward scripture, mulling it over in their minds.[66] Lactantius saw the command to abstain from pork as an order to avoid sin. Christians must avoid being enslaved to their appetites as swine were.[67] John Chrysostom saw the animals as visual aids in the pursuit of Christian virtues. Wise as serpents, harmless as doves, industrious as ants and spiders: each animal had something to offer.[68]

The allegorical interpretations of behavior ignored whether animals were rational or not. The question which had so strongly vexed Greco-Roman philosophers was no longer an issue for many.

But not all Christians sidestepped the issue. Among those who did treat the question we find echoes of the old Stoic/Neo-platonic split.54 Christian folklore came down squarely on the Neo-platonic side with a sense that the animals knew what they were doing and with whom they were dealing. Thus they acted appropriately around the saints, martyrs, and ascetics.

---

[65]Mt. 6.28-33, Lk. 12,24-31.

[66]Clement of Alexandria, *Stromata* 7.18 (*ANF* 2.555-56).

[67]Lactantius, *The Divine Institutes* 4.1 (*ANF* 7.119).

[68]*Homilies on the Statues* 12.5-6 in *A Select Library of the Nicene and Post-Nicene Fathers of the Christian Church*. Vol. 9: *Saint Chrysostom: The Priesthood; Ascetic Treatises; Select Homilies and Letters; Homilies on the Statues* (New York: The Christian Literature Co., 1894), 419-20.

The theologians, on the other hand, had a strong commitment to a Stoic universe in which humans were qualitatively different from animals. The apologist Origen appeared to take the Stoic side in his dispute with Celsus. Reason, said Origen, was common to human and heavenly beings, perhaps even to God, but not to animals.[69] If animals appeared to have organizational, governmental, or military skills, these were appearances only. They did not act from reason. They could not have reason because their souls were shaped differently.[70] Yet this did not make them totally different from human beings. Origen's Neo-Platonism, however, would not allow him to divorce humanity from the animal world entirely, for both participate in the divine. Since both emanated from the divine, all participated in some degree in God.[71] So Origen held in tension the Stoic and Neo-Platonic attitudes toward animals.

A century and a half later that tension was still being maintained. We see it most acutely in John Chrysostom. He commented on the passage from the book of Jonah in which the animals of Nineveh, like the people, put on sackcloth and fasted (Jonah 3.10). The animals, like the people, needed to know the message of the prophet. But while the humans were rational and could perceive the message in a rational manner, the animals being irrational could not. So the animals in their fasting *felt* the message of God. Thus all could understand.[72]

The patristic tradition was thus heir to three traditions. There was the Stoic which saw all of nature, both sensate and non-sensate, as part of the landscape, for the use of human beings. On the other hand, there was the Neo-platonic which saw all creation, non-sensate, sensate and rational as emanating from the same divine principle. Christianity held these two in tension but was constantly drawn by its Jewish heritage to a consideration of animals as fellow creatures.

The results of this tension were most succinctly put by one of the desert fathers. The abbot Alonius was once asked, "What is contempt?" He replied "To be below the creatures that have no reason and to know they are not condemned."[73] The human sinner is higher than the animal in rationality. When that person sins, however, s/he has to look up to the creature with no mind, no ability to think, no ability to observe the law, or to participate in politics, all those things that are human.

---

[69]Origen, *Contra Celsum* 4.85, in *Origen: Contra Celsum*, translated and edited by Henry Chadwick (Cambridge: Cambridge University, 1980) 251; cf. *De principiis* 3.1.3 in *ANF* 4.303.

[70]Origen, *Contra Celsum* 4.81-83 (Chadwick, 249-50).

[71]Origen, *De principiis* 1.3.6 (*ANF* 4.253).

[72]John Chrysostom, *On the Statues* 9 (*NPNF* 9.358).

[73]*The Desert Fathers*, edited by Helen Waddell (Ann Arbor: University of Michigan, 1957) xxxvi.

Perhaps what made the Christian attitude toward animals unique was the knowledge that rationality, that which separates humanity from animality was not the grand mark of *haute culture* before God. Virtue counted much more than mental abilities.

So we return to the tabloids: "Scientific experiments reveal your pet can read your mind . . . and even detect [your] serious illnesses."[74] They can predict an owner's epileptic seizures, helping to guarantee safety for the owner and her pet. The animals have understanding proportionate to their needs living in a web of relationships with the human animal. Can the rational human say the same? The early Christians offer a variety of attitudes from which to choose.

---

[74]*National Examiner* (March 20, 1990) 29.

A ROOTED FLOWER, A RADIANT STONE:
ECKHART ON NATURE

Jonas Barciauskas

Carolyn Merchant, an environmental historian, has written persuasively of "the death of nature as a living being and the accelerating exploitation of both human and natural resources in the name of culture and process."[1] She claims that the Scientific Revolution caused a shift from the organism to the machine "as the dominant metaphor binding together the cosmos, society, and the self."[2] Christianity has also been described as a major historical factor behind the modern ecological crisis. Some have argued that the Christian tradition has neglected nature because of its overwhelmingly anthropocentric perspective.[3] I would prefer to say along with Paul Santmire "that kind of historical verdict has been too hastily and too simplistically rendered."[4] Taking seriously his call for "a much more adequate account of . . . [Christian] thought about nature,[5] I will examine the writings of Meister Eckhart who, I believe, has some provocative things to say about the interaction of the human realm and the natural world.

A close reading of Eckhart's works, especially those with his doctrine of detachment, reveals the Dominican mystic's profound vision of the relationship between God, human person, and the universe. It is a vision which describes how a Christian believer may experience a oneness between the divine, human and natural realms which is not monistic but dialectical. According to Eckhart, God transcends his creation by virtue of his very immanence.

Nothing created can be so immanent to a being or so fundamental to its existence as its Creator; therefore God absolutely transcends the created

---

[1]Carolyn Merchant, *The Death of Nature: Women, Ecology, and the Scientific Revolution* (San Francisco: Harper & Row, 1989), xxii.

[2]Merchant xxii.

[3]H. Paul Santmire, *The Travail of Nature: The Ambiguous Ecological Promise of Christian Theology* (Philadelphia: Fortress Press, 1985), 1-7.

[4]Santmire 7.

[5]Santmire 7.

realm. Moreover, for Eckhart the highest reality of a thing resides in the process of its being created in the eternal Now by the immanent transcendent God. But in order to be able to experience the unmediated divine creative activity, we must transcend the creaturely realm through detachment in order to see things in their highest reality, their divine ideas in the Logos.

The significance of Eckhart's thought for its current struggle with ecological issues has been suggested by others. Those familiar with the writings of Matthew Fox know his description of Eckhart's mysticism as creation-centered.[6] Moreover, Zen Buddhist philosophers of the Kyoto school well-trained in the Western philosophical tradition, like Masao Abe and Keiji Nishitani, have found Eckhart's ideas to resonate with Zen doctrines,[7] and no religious tradition is more intimately tied to nature than Japanese Zen.[8]

The first two sections of the paper will include examinations of relevant themes in Eckhart's works.[9] In the first section, I will examine some of the fundamental metaphysical themes behind Eckhart's understanding of God's creative activity. In the second section, I will explore the ways in which his spirituality weaves together human, natural, and divine realms. In the third section, I will attempt to relate his metaphysical and spiritual ideas to visual images in an effort to render them more experientially real to a modern reader unfamiliar with the Meister's Neoplatonic terminology. In the final section, I will raise some issues concerning Eckhart's contribution to a Christian ecological theology and spirituality.

---

[6]See, for example, Matthew Fox, "Creation-Centered Spirituality from Hildegard of Bingen to Julian of Norwich: 300 Years of an Ecological Spirituality in the West," in *Cry of the Environment*, pp. 85-106, and Fox's introduction to *Breakthrough: Meister Eckhart's Creation Spirituality in New Translation* (Garden City, N.Y.: Image Books, 1980).

[7]Masao Abe, *Zen and Western Thought*, ed. William R. LaFleur (Honolulu: University of Hawaii Press, 1985), 133; Keiji Nishitani, *Religion and Nothingness* (Berkeley: University of California Press, 1982) 61-68.

[8]One need only consider haiku poetry and Zen monastery gardens, both of which are meant to intensify a person's awareness of the natural world. See Daisetz T. Suzuki, *Zen and Japanese Culture* (Princeton: Princeton University Press, 1970), 215-67, 329-95.

[9]The texts consulted include the critical edition of Eckhart's Latin and Middle High German works as well as modern English translations. They include: Meister Eckhart, *Die lateinischen Werke*, 5 vols., ed. Josef Koch et al. (Stuttgart: Kohlhammer, 1936), hereafter abbreviated LW; *Meister Eckhart: The Essential Sermons, Commentaries, Treatises, and Defenses*, trans. Edmund Colledge and Bernard McGinn (New York: Paulist Press, 1981), hereafter abbreviated as CM; *Meister Eckhart: An Introduction to the Study of His Works with an Anthology of His Sermons*, trans. James M. Clark (London: Nelson, 1957), hereafter abbreviated as Cl; *Breakthrough: Meister Eckhart's Creation Spirituality in New Translation*, trans. Matthew Fox, et al. (Garden City, N.Y.: Image Books, 1980), hereafter abbreviated as F. Eight sermons are translated in Reiner Schurmann, *Meister Eckhart: Mystic and Philosopher* (Bloomington: Indiana University Press, 1978); when Eckhart quotations are taken from this translation, this work will be abbreviated as S.

Once God Has Spoken, Twice I Have Heard This

Eckhart's metaphysics of God's creative activity is spelled out in his Latin commentaries on the first chapters of Genesis and John.[10] The fundamental themes are as follows:

1. God creates "in the beginning"--which translates the Latin *in principio*. The *principium* is God, and to create principially means God does not create outside of himself. "God created" means he who is One is his creativity.[11]

2. The *principium* is the *ratio idealis* of all created things, which--within the Christian Neoplatonic tradition--is identified with the second Person of the Trinity. The Son is the *imago et ratio idealis omnium*.[12]

3. God is most essentially intellect.[13] In one Latin treatise he goes so far as to say that God is more intellect than being.[14] This means, for Eckhart, that God acts freely in creating the world and not out of necessity.[15]

4. God creates in a timeless present. For a beginning to be truly a beginning, it must be outside time, because time implies duration with a before and an after, and there cannot any temporal period antecedent to the beginning of time. Thus creation, taking place in an eternal now, is a *creatio continuo*.[16]

5. Created beings are grounded in God's Being. They are continuously being created by their Creator. But somehow they appear to us to have been created in time and to have a separate existence. In their deepest relationship to God, however, they have no separate being. Eckhart quotes a scriptural verse to characterize the difference between human and divine perspectives of the created cosmos: "Once God has spoken, twice I have heard this" (Ps 62:11 RSV).[17] God speaks once and thus generates the Logos and the divine ideas; we seem to hear him speaking twice: once inwardly in generating the Word and once outwardly in creation.

In order to explain how God may be understood to be both deeply present in and yet not identified with his creation, Eckhart at times refers to the light in the air as an example. Although the sun shines through the air, the air can never be described as possessing the light. In Eckhart's words:

---

[10]The Latin texts we will examine can be found in LW I: 185-206 for Genesis 1:1 and LW III: 3-114 for John 1.

[11]CM 97.

[12]CM 84, 123-24.

[13]CM 84.

[14]*Meister Eckhart, Parisian Questions and Prologues*, trans. Armand Maurer (Toronto: Pontifical Institute of Mediaeval Studies, 1974), 45 f. For a German text on this theme, see Cl 207-08; DW I: 150.

[15]CM 84.

[16]CM 84-85, 124-25.

[17]CM 85; passages in Eckhart containing the verse: LW I; 191; LW III: 61; DW II: 98, 536.

> Anyone who sees the truth knows that God, the heavenly Father, gives everything that is good to the Son and to the Holy Spirit; but to his creatures he gives nothing good; he lets them have it as a loan [ze borge]. The sun gives heat to the air, but makes a loan of light; and that is why as soon as the sun goes down, the air loses the light, but the heat remains there, because the heat is given to the air to possess as its own.[18]

This notion of a loan to the creature is in keeping with Eckhart's ontology. By itself, the creature is nothing; all its being is on loan from God and indeed it is only God who is truly *esse*. But to leave it at that would be to imply that for Eckhart, God is ultimately transcendent, perhaps monistic: God is all, creaturely existence merely an illusion. This, however, would be to overlook the extremely dialectical nature of his thought, which leads me to my last theme: the dialectic of infinite Being and finite beings which plays between the poles of univocal identity and equivocal difference.

6. Vladimir Lossky and Bernard McGinn have offered extended examinations of the Meister's dialectic.[19] The most significant texts in Eckhart's Latin writings include his commentaries on Wisdom 7:27 and Exodus 20:4b.[20] In Eckhart's commentary on Wisdom, he says that God is distinct from creatures because of his very indistinction or absolute oneness: no created being is as indistinct or without limitation. Stated dialectically, the more God is indistinct, the more he is distinct. The German works are also filled with dialectical expressions, for example: "God is in all things. The more he is in all things, the more he is outside of things."[21] God's immanence and transcendence cannot be defined as separate attributes but must be seen as mutually interdependent: God is so transcendent because he is so immanent.

Having identified what I believe are six basic themes in Eckhart's doctrine of creation, I would like to consider some passages from his Middle High German works, for it is in these works that the Meister brings together his various metaphysical notions in order to formulate his characteristic doctrines of spirituality.

A Fly, a Flower, a Piece of Wood

Tom Berry was once asked to define nature; the discussion had been a philosophical one but he didn't respond in the expected manner with a metaphysical definition. Instead, he replied that nature was trees, stones, rivers, and birds.[22] In Eckhart's more mystical, less scholastic writings, we

---

[18]CM 224; DW V: 36.

[19]Bernard McGinn, "Meister Eckhart on God as Absolute Unity," in *Neoplatonism and Christian Thought*, ed. Dominic O'Meara (Albany: SUNY Press, 1981) 132 ff.; Vladimir Lossky, *Theologie negative et connaissance de Dieu chez Maitre Eckhart* (Paris, Vrin, 1960), 261-75.

[20]LW II: 110-17, 438-91.

[21]F 65.

[22]Related by Fr. Berry during a class at Fordham University during the fall of 1979.

begin to get closer to what the Dominican Meister hoped his readers would realize experientially: an intimate awareness of the natural world in its most essential being. In Eckhart's spiritual teachings, his metaphysics and particularly his dialectic become incorporated into a dynamic vision of inner transformation.

Much has been written about Eckhart's modes of expression. Reiner Schurmann argues that he is less interested in presenting a rational explanation of God's presence in the world and more concerned about describing the stages of the spiritual journey to God.[23] This may help explain certain dramatic differences between the Meister and his Dominican brother Thomas, whom he quotes often and with great respect. Schurmann has distinguished between an indicative mode which is characteristic of the Angelic Doctor and the imperative mode which typifies Eckhart's writings, especially his German sermons and treatises.[24] Thus, much of what Eckhart says must be understood as his way of urging his listeners or readers onto the mystical path.

A critical term in the Meister's spiritual teachings is detachment or *abegescheidenheit*. Its dynamic successfully weaves together the various metaphysical themes within the whole of Eckhart's mystical thought. Given its central significance, it can suggest Eckhart's fuller sense of nature.

Scheiden in modern as well as Middle High German means to separate or divide. *Ab* (Middle High German variant--*abe*) as a prefix to *scheiden* means "from." A strict translation of *abegescheidenheit*, then would be "a state of being separated from."[25] According to Eckhart, "detachment is freedom from all created things."[26] Formulated this way, detachment seems like a form of withdrawal, an ascetic rejection of the realm of nature. But this interpretation of *abegescheidenheit* is incomplete. The essential elements of detachment are as follows:

1. God in his oneness contains no distinctions. The human person who was made in God's image enjoyed oneness with the Absolute, a state of identity which is described in the German treatise *On Detachment* as existing "before ever God made created things."[27] More accurately speaking, however, this state refers less to time before time began than to the timelessness of eternity which is without the distinction of "before" or "after."

2. But God viewed purely as Creator is often distinguished from his creatures. This is a common viewpoint for an untransformed believer to accept: the world of beings is a realm of distinct objects, but unfortunately God as Creator is then considered as just another member of this realm,

[23]Schurmann 29-30.
[24]Schurmann 29-30.
[25]Schurmann 84
[26]CM 285; DW V: 401.
[27]CM 285; DW V: 401.

albeit as the Absolute Being who has caused all contingent beings. It is precisely this pitfall of Christian theistic thinking and spirituality that the Meister wishes to avoid with his doctrine of detachment. The imperative character of his writings on *abegescheidenheit* urges the reader to enter into a dynamic experience of the place of the universe of beings in God.

If the believer is dependent on a vision of a static cosmos of individual substances, there is no possibility for transformation. Within the indicative mode of a Christian natural theology of Creator and creation, detachment could be viewed as a harsh breaking away from concrete reality. But within the imperative mode of a spiritual theology, it is the beginning step of a transformative process.

3. Detachment is not a simple act of a human individual but an act of grace, i.e., God's own gift. Although it often sounds as if the believer must cut him/herself off from the world, it is God who "draws" us away through his own divine action.

> It [detachment] then draws a person into purity and from purity into simplicity, and from simplicity into unchangeability, and these things produce an equality between God and the person; and the equality must come about in grace, for it is grace that draws a person from all temporal things, and makes him pure of all transient things.[28]

4. Does this mean that the transformed state, even if effected by grace, is one of spiritual removal from the world? According to Eckhart, God's oneness, his absolute all-inclusiveness, the indistinction of his being which distinguishes him from all beings, means that he ultimately grounds all beings: "insofar as he [God] remains within he is an end of the Godhead *and of all created things*."[29] Therefore, the believer who cuts him/herself off from the realm of created things finds them again in the One who is the end of all his creation.

From the perspective of the untransformed human individual, the cosmos is populated by separate substances. The believer who is awakening to his/her spiritual dimension may see that all creatures long for their source. Ultimately, as transformed believer, he or she sees the universe of beings in their origin: the unindividuated unity of God. This God is no longer a Creator who because of our incomplete vision is considered as distinct from his creation. In the following passage from *Sermon 52*, Eckhart gives a powerful expression to the equality of beings which exists in God who in his absolute oneness surpasses the Creator-creature distinction. God as a distinct Creator is here noted in quotation marks:

> Now I say that God, so far as he is "God," is not the perfect end of created beings. The least of these beings possesses a great abundance in God. If it could be that a fly had

---

[28]CM 288; DW V: 412-3.
[29]CM 192 (emphasis added); DW I: 252.

reason and could with its reason seek out the eternal depths of the divine being from which it issued, I say that God, with all that he has inasmuch as he is "God," could not fulfill or satisfy the fly. So therefore let us pray to God that we may apprehend and rejoice in that everlasting truth in which the highest angel and the fly and the soul are equal.[30]

The least of all beings, exemplified by a fly, possesses a great richness in God and enjoys total equality with the human soul because in God's indistinct unity, there is no subject-object division, no possibility of anything outside of any other thing. McGinn indicates the Neoplatonic roots of Eckhart's thought where created beings are seen by the detached believer in the realm of divine ideas, i.e., pure reason, at times characterized by the Meister as a realm of light.[31] In Eckhart's words: "If someone saw a piece of wood in that light, it would become an angel and a rational being, and not merely rational; it would become pure reason in primal purity."[32] This, of course, is related to the Plotinian notion of the mutual coinherence of the ideas in the realm of *Nous*, a notion that also refers to light as a characteristic of this realm.[33]

5. Does this mean that Eckhart is more Neoplatonic than Christian in his interpretation of the blessed state? It would be more correct to say that his purpose is to elevate creation, to raise a single act of creation to the realm of on-going creative activity. He does this by explaining that creation of the world and generation of the Word, or the two beginnings of Genesis and John, are one process: "God did not create heaven and earth in the temporal fashion in which we describe it--'Let there be!'--because all created things were spoken in the everlasting Word."[34] This theme appears throughout his writings. According to Eckhart, if God's creation and generation are perceived as two processes, that is because of our incomplete understanding. We have already referred to one of the Meister's favorite scriptural verses--"Once God has spoken, twice I have heard this" (Ps 62:11 RSV) in order to emphasize that our blurred vision sees double what is in reality a unity.

From the viewpoint of traditional theology, this fusion of beginnings, *In principio erat Verbum* and *In principio creavit Deus caelum et terra*, was a dangerous step in the direction of the unacceptable notion of the eternity of the universe. But as Ueda has argued, much of Eckhart's theological and philosophical thought must be read as an *Ausgangspunkt*, a point of departure for his spiritual message.[35] One must keep in mind Eckhart's ultimate goal--a spiritual healing, a reintegration of the inward self. Within the dynamic of his mysticism, the doctrine of creation is not rejected as such but is used within

---

[30]CM 200; DW II: 493.
[31]McGinn, "Summary," 41.
[32]CM 194; DW I: 383.
[33]Plotinus, *Enneads* 5, 8, 4, 6, 7, 12.
[34]CM 290; DW V: 418.
[35]Ueda 49.

a spirituality leading one back to God. In Lossky's words, "In making the creation operation an interior act of God, Meister Eckhart wants to liberate it from all that is duality, imperfection, *recessus ab Uno*."[36] And from all that may lead to division and brokenness in the human being and his or her relationship with the natural world, we might add.

The purpose of detachment, then, is to achieve the freedom of God in his freely-willed relationship with the created world of beings. Moreover, *abegescheidenheit* preserves the playful presence of God to beings which, like the fly or the piece of wood or the detached soul, enjoy equality with him in the light of reason or intellect.

> God gives equally to all things; and as they flow from God they are equal. . . . If they are thus equal in time, they are much more equal in God in eternity. . . . God is so joyful in this equality that in it he completely pours out his nature and his being through himself. . . . In the same way, if one were to let a horse run about in a green meadow, which was flat and level, it would be the horse's nature to pour forth its whole strength in leaping about in the meadow.[37]

One could say that the world of beings is both eternal and temporal, but the larger, more joyous reality is that it is eternal--and this truth is realized through detachment. We see then that in Eckhart, detachment is a separation from the created world of things in order to realize a new relationship with the universe of beings as they are continually being created in God's Word.

We could say a great deal more at this point--especially since we are on the verge of introducing what many consider to be Eckhart's greatest theme, the birth of the Son in the soul.[38] The believer, in the ground of the soul where God's ground is the soul's ground,[39] is both one with the Father in generating the Son and one with the Son in the realm of the divine ideas where created beings are realized in their greatest reality.[40] But we shall close this section of the discussion with a final example of Eckhart's vision of the equality of all beings in a community of radiant being:

> If we were to know the smallest object as it is in God--say, if we were to know only a flower that has being in God--this object would be more noble than the whole world. To know that smallest object in God--to the extent that it is being--is better than it would be for someone to know an angel.[41]

---

[36]Lossky 59 (translation mine).

[37]C1 225-6; Q 215.

[38]John Caputo, "Fundamental Themes in Meister Eckhart's Thought," *Thomist* 42 (1978), 198; see also Josef Quint, "Einleitung," in Q, 21-2.

[39]CM 192; DW I: 252-3.

[40]See in particular S 4-5; DW I: 27-31.

[41]F 85; DW I: 132.

Seeing the Flower

Perhaps the greatest challenge for a modern reader of Eckhart is to ask: how do we interpret the Meister's doctrines in terms of contemporary or personal experience? This issue is complicated by the fact that Eckhart's spiritual teaching, because of its medieval Neoplatonic vocabulary, may for some readers seem archaic or obscure.

Most simply, we can say that Eckhart's spiritual vision is inviting us to see things as they really are. In the Meister's Neoplatonic framework, this is to see them in their divine ideas which means to experience them beyond all images, thoughts, or any other forms of mediation. But what does this mean? Can we translate this into a more modern idiom? In the following passage, Jacob Needleman offers a description of seeing things as ideas that sounds somewhat like Eckhart:

> I know now that when I learned about the structure of a leaf or the means of spore propagation in the mushroom, *I was taking in a real idea.* . . . What were called ideas were the theories of the scientists--such as the theory of evolution, the theory of the gene, etc. The theories interested me very much, but not as much as I pretended to myself. What I really loved was the description and the observation of natural phenomena. But these descriptions were given the names of *data, facts* by my teachers and peers. Only now do I see that in these descriptions I was coming into contact with *ideas* of a very different order than the theories of the scientists which purported to explain the data. Here we all were surrounded by the living reality of incarnate ideas, while being told to direct our minds to mere thoughts, ingenious though they may have been.[42]

Of course, he is not having a mystical experience, nor seeing into the realm of the Logos or divine ideas, but the sense of a freshness of seeing the physical world is one that Needleman seems to share with Eckhart.

How, then, do we incorporate the notion of divine origin in our understanding of what Eckhart is trying to say? Rather than a purely conceptual exercise in exegesis, it might be a helpful strategy to attempt to interpret the Meister in a more experiential manner. In an attempt to do so, I will offer a reflection in the form of a visit to three sacred spaces, Chartres Cathedral, Daitoku-ji, which is a Zen temple in Kyoto, Japan, and Thorncrown Chapel in Eureka Springs, Arkansas. Our goal will be to achieve a more intuitive sense of Eckhart's spirituality of nature; we will try to realize our goal by a simple, concrete objective--trying to see a flower, not in order to name it a rose or any other name, a la Umberto Eco's semiotic medieval mystery, but simply to see it in its truest being, in its divine idea.

Sacred space is where the believer of a particular religious tradition encounters the holy, or experiences more intensely the higher realms of being,

---

[42]Jacob Needleman, *A Sense of the Cosmos: The Encounter of Modern Science and Ancient Truth* (Garden City, NY: Doubleday, 1975) 74.

or--in theistic language--comes closer to God. The significance of Chartres to sacred architecture of the Middle Ages in the West is well-known.[43] It is interesting I believe, that in comparison to the next two architectural examples, the natural realm is invisible from within the building.

For an observer within Chartres, two overwhelming impressions are the height of the vaulted ceilings and the intense colored light from the stained glass windows. Theologically and spiritually, we can say that these two features illustrate Christian Neoplatonic themes. In order to approach God, the believer begins a spiritual ascent from the mundane world to realms of higher reality. According to Bonaventure in *The Soul's Journey into God*, the natural world contains vestiges of God. The earth is a mirror reflecting the Trinity; in Bonaventure's words: "The Creator's supreme power, wisdom and benevolence shine forth in created things."[44] In another text, the Seraphic Doctor compares creatures to stained glass windows where "the divine ray shines forth in each and every creature in different ways and in different properties."[45] However, the subject matter of the Chartres windows is drawn predominantly from scripture and history. Within Chartres, there is no immediate contact with the natural world. It is as if the natural world is already transcended as one enters this magnificent architectural expression of medieval Neoplatonism.

Daitoku-ji is composed of several temples. In most of their interiors, space appears to be structured more horizontally than vertically. Ceiling beams establish long lines paralleling floorboards and tatami mats. Here, spiritual practice is not to ascend but to sit in cross-legged posture on the floor and practice zazen meditation. Some of the temples contain brush paintings of natural subjects including flowers.[46] But the greatest contrast to Chartres is the openness of many temple interiors to the outside world. The Bosen tearoom and the Daisen-in's Main Hall, for example, afford views of gardens with trees and large stones.[47]

An intimate awareness of the natural world, therefore, is an important aspect of Zen practice. It is not shut out of Zen's most sacred spaces, but can easily become the object of one's meditative gaze while one sits inside the temple. D. T. Suzuki discusses the poem by Basho where that great haiku master appreciates a particular flower as an integral part of nature, of

---

[43]"The erection of Chartres Cathedral is perhaps the single most important event in the history of Gothic architecture." From George Henderson, *Chartres* (Harmondsworth, England: Penguin Books, 1968) 111.

[44]Bonaventure, *The Soul's Journey into God. The Tree of Life. The Life of St. Francis*, trans. Ewert Cousins (New York: Paulist Press, 1987) 63.

[45]*Hexaem.* 17 (V, 332). Quoted in Bonaventure, *The Soul's Journey*, 26.

[46]See plates 34 and 48 in Jon Covell and Yamada Sobin, *Zen at Daitoku-ji* (Tokyo, New York: Kodansha, 1974).

[47]*Zen*, plates 15 and 23.

existence as such.[48] Basho did not need to pull it from the ground; rather he enjoyed it in its simplicity, rooted in the ground, perfect as it was. The Zen garden presents the meditator with a microcosm of the earth community and invites a deep appreciation of our oneness with its inhabitants of stones, trees and flowers.

Thorncrown Chapel, designed by Fay Jones and completed in 1980,[49] has aspects of both Chartres and Daitoku-ji. In its interior, one is reminded of Gothic verticality by the height of its ceiling and the upward thrust of its peaked roof. But in place of stone walls and stained glass windows are walls of perfectly transparent glass held in place by a fragile grid of wooden beams. Thus, like in Chartres, the soul is invited to a spiritual ascent, but also like Daitoku-ji, the inward journey includes an intimate relationship with the exterior natural world, in this case a forest setting in northwestern Arkansas.

I believe that, of the three sacred spaces, Thorncrown is the most architectural expression of Eckhart's spirituality in all its dialectical richness and complexity. God's utter transcendence, embodied in the high peaked ceiling, and his indistinct pervasiveness, almost palpable in the quiet landscape outside the chapel's nearly invisible walls, may indeed lead the believer to undergo spiritual rebirth, perhaps the birth of the Son in the soul which is in the Meister's most powerful theme of divine fruitfulness.

In choosing Fay Jones' forest chapel over Chartres, I believe that Eckhart's relationship with the created world is more immediate than Bonaventure's doctrine of exemplarity would allow. For the Franciscan theologian, created beings are like colored bits of glass transmitting God's radiant being. For the Dominican mystic, things considered as exemplars are still outside of God and removed from their truest reality, the realm of the Logos and the divine ideas. For Bonaventure, contemplation of exemplars in nature is a prelude to contemplation of God's image in the soul and ultimately of God. For Eckhart, to behold things in their ideas is not a prelude to deeper experiences but an experience of the divine essence itself. Not stained glass but clear windows are necessary for the believer who, while worshipping God within the chapel, may wish to meditate upon a flower in its natural environment, to see a thing in its true being.

The other possibility, Daitoku-ji, does permit direct experience with nature. But the space lacks a sense of the divine transcendence which is articulated by Thorncrown's graceful Gothic arches. The openness of Daitoku-ji to the concrete beauty of the natural world can be a revelation for western Christians as a stimulus for rethinking the boundaries of the sacred. However, Christian spirituality requires a dialectic between God and creation as well as between self and world, and I think Thorncrown provides more of a sense of

---

[48]Suzuki 262-5.

[49]See Charles K. Gandee, "A Wayfarer's Chapel by Fay Jones," *Architectural Record* 169 (March 1981): 88-93.

a presence of the divine origin of the earth and humankind than does the Zen temple. Therefore, from within this forest chapel we may be able to see things as they are, not only simply as they are, as a Zen monk might say, not as ideas, as Needleman said above, but in their divine ideas in the Logos, i.e., with all the Christian associations of God, divine personhood, and creativity that are embedded in that expression. The possibility of such seeing, Eckhart would insist, is dependent on God's graceful activity in our souls.

Seeing and Doing

I would like to close with a few remarks concerning Eckhart's potential role in the contemporary ecological movement. It has been the burden of this paper to indicate how Eckhart can provide a particular form of a Christian spirituality of nature. Despite the medieval character of Eckhart's Neoplatonic vocabulary, his works can be regarded as a rich resource for a contemplative experience of creation. To see things in their purest form is to recognize their ground in God. Eckhart's teachings can show Christians a way of healing the subject-object division that characterizes much of Western attitudes toward nature. We and the community of created beings around us share the same divine ground, and Eckhart's mystical theology can offer another contribution toward achieving a more holistic contemporary worldview.

But we must also ask: does Eckhart's teaching provide more than a contemplative path? On the whole, his terminology is intellectualistic, and his focus is inward. In one of his more remarkable sermons, he clearly praises the active life over the contemplative.[50] But as mentioned above, for Eckhart creatures apart from God are nothing. This particular notion is revealing, because it clearly indicates that for Eckhart, created beings possess little or no ontological reality of their own but receive it directly from God. The path of access to that reality lies inwardly, within the believer's soul, through the discipline of detachment.

This contrasts strongly, I believe, with Teilhard de Chardin's view of the cosmos as an enveloping universe of physical bodies, each with a spiritual center, a "within," of its own which is deeply related with an equally evolving human consciousness.[51] A Teilhardian spirituality, then, can include a "science of human energetics" which aims to enable the human community along with the universe of beings to approach their fullness of being in the divine Omega.[52] We may ask: can Eckhart's strong emphasis on primary causality over secondary causality (to borrow from scholastic vocabulary) as the source of a creature's being support the kind of scientific involvement that contemporary ecology requires?

---

[50]F 478-86; DW III: 481-92.
[51]Teilhard de Chardin, *The Phenomenon of Man* (New York: Harper, 1959) 53-66.
[52]Chardin 283.

No doubt, Eckhart presents us with a magnificent vision of a community of beings in the divine essence. But we have found it necessary not only to see things as they are but to alter the environment and draw on its resources. Such an interactive relationship with the natural world has been historically necessary for our survival; it still is, but we now recognize the need to assure the survival of the environment as well. The necessary communality of the human and natural realms has become painfully obvious, and Eckhart's teachings can provide a deeply spiritual basis for that sense of interdependence.

But it is not clear yet how Eckhart's teachings can contribute toward a serious reorientation of modern science and technology from a position of dominating to cooperating with the natural processes of the earth. Secular ecological thought is deeply involved with this project of reorientation. Much of the Christian world is still struggling to articulate helpful spiritual doctrines which would guide believers both inwardly and outwardly in their ecological activities. In short, for the modern Christian, the ability of spiritual seeing must somehow be complemented by a capacity for spiritual doing. Intuitively, I think Eckhart can offer a great deal in formulating a contemporary Christian ecological spirituality, but the specifics of his contribution need to be explored further on both spiritual and scholarly levels.

Part Four

SPIRITUALITY

AND ECOLOGICAL AWARENESS

PSYCHOSPIRITUALITY: THE ECOLOGICAL MATRIX

Eugene Bianchi

> "'One only understands the things that one tames,' said the fox."
> Men have no more time to understand anything. They buy
> things already made at the shops. But there is no shop
> anywhere where one can buy friendship, and so men have no
> friends anymore. If you want a friend, tame me."[1]

I want to explore some relationships between ecological awareness and human development, both spiritual and psychological. In a recent article, I criticized psychotherapy for not being ecological enough.[2] Therapeutic work over the last century has focused on the intrapsychic, the interpersonal and the socio-psychological. Of course, these are crucial dimensions for dealing with conflictual situations and stimulating personal growth. But was there nothing therapeutically important about Henry Thoreau going to Walden pond to learn to "live deliberately?" He certainly thought so, if we can judge by his intended goal: to avoid dying without ever having lived.[3] He saw solitude and contemplation with nature as vital to deeper living. Had he lived at the turn of the century, he might have told Freud that to love and to work better required wilderness experience. A similar critique can be laid at the door of pastoral psychology, which has taken its cue from various clinical psychology movements. Although religious retreats are frequently held in bucolic surroundings, the serious work about sin and grace is usually anthropocentric. Nature becomes mere backdrop. Was there nothing spiritually therapeutic for Francis Assisi who talked with birds and plants as his siblings?

---

[1]Antoine de Saint Exupery, *The Little Prince* (New York: Reynal & Hitchcock, 1943).

[2]Eugene C. Bianchi, "Psychotherapy as Religion: Pros and Cons," *Pastoral Psychology* 38.2 (1989): 67-82.

[3]Henry David Thoreau, *The Illustrated Walden* (Princeton: Princeton University Press, 1973) 90.

Before we address these question, I wish to explain a few terms in my title. I take liberty of linking psychotherapy and spirituality in the only moderately felicitous word "psychospirituality." Elsewhere I argue that spiritual and psychological development are closely intermeshed.[4] Without trying to subsume clinical psychology into religion, one can make a good case that modern therapeutic endeavors are forms of the ancient *cura animarum*, that pastoral task of healing mental/emotional pain and indicating paths of self-development.

I use the word "matrix" to underscore a sense of the primordial source from which all mind and feeling derive. To a great extent in technological civilization, we have lost our healing integration with mother earth. On the positive side, I am searching for insight, both reflective and experiential, that will help up re-integrate ourselves into the therapeutic dimension of nature. Therefore, this essay leaves much unsaid on the subject of ecology. I am not addressing the great ethical issues about ecological pollution and the economic-political systems that engineer such destructiveness. Nor will I propose specific modes for psychotherapy and pastoral counseling to integrate ecological consciousness into concrete practice. My goal is more modest.

I want to "circumambulate" the ecological matrix, to get glimpses of its potential for religious-psychological therapy. My presupposition is that the journey to this center, this central experience, becomes an indispensable initiation, a kind of baptism for working toward a sane ecological ethics and holistic psychotherapy. It is more like getting a taste of the living vision that undergirds the writings of Teilhard de Chardin, Thomas Berry and Erazim Kohak. It doesn't matter whether one disagrees with such thinkers on this or that point. What counts is a more primordial thing, a sensing of our role in what Loren Eiseley calls the "immense journey" of the whole evolutionary project of the planet. Here critical intellectuals may bite their lips, anticipating sentimental romanticism. We academics are rightly suspicious of romanticizing away the hard facts of planetary wreckage and its calculating or stupid directors. But "romantic" is also a salvageable word because it implies love. We need to learn to love the natural world and ourselves as a part of it.

Our path around the matrix will be interdisciplinary, seeking touchstones of ecological spirituality in a variety of fields from philosophy and literature to religion. I am interest in tracing what might be called an experience of ecological psychospirituality. Put another way, I want to see how many lines cross through a circle that might be termed an ecologically transcendent experience. Religious experience can be treated in traditional theological terms. But religiousness, as an experience of deep inwardness and transcendence in life, cannot be confined to conventional categories and fields. In the broad sense of religion as a "re-ligio," a tying back to primordial

---

[4]Bianchi 67-82.

roots in the earth, the experience of "deep ecology" is a religious sentiment or experience. In imitation of nature, therefore, we will not be linear; we will search for touchstones by walking in circles.

A final caution before examining touchstones of nature-oriented psychospiritual experience concerns omissions and possible exaggerations. In this presentation, I am focusing on the positive dimensions of what we might call nature mysticism. I am leaving out nature's negative aspects (at least for human well-being) such as floods, hurricanes, and disease. Also I am not addressing what might be seen as the more violent animal interactions in the natural world. Further, I do not pretend to give an exhaustive account of any particular touchstone, such as that of ecofeminism. I am not distinguishing, for example, between different schools of nature-oriented feminists; nor am I saying that any of these schools are beyond criticism. It would, furthermore, be an exaggeration to say that the nature experiences I elicit will cure all forms of mental-emotional disturbance. It may require a reasonably healthy sense of self to profit from the therapeutic dimensions of nature. A person with a seriously damaged sense of self may need some form of the traditional modes of psychoanalysis or psychotherapy to be able to turn outward toward the ecological realm for further growth.

Some Philosophical Resources

The work of David R. Griffin and others to construct post-modern visions on the basis of process philosophy offers an intellectual structure for psychospirituality in an ecological framework. This philosophy could also be listed under religious studies, as process theology, but I want to focus on the underpinnings for supporting an ecological perspective. Philosophical-historical considerations like Griffin's may seem removed from our more psychological topic. Philosophical writers tend to speak in abstract conceptual rather than therapeutic terms. But this wider intellectual outlook positions the therapeutic in a broader context, clarifying the long journey that has removed us from a sense of unity with nature. To understand our alienation from the ecological matrix, we need to appreciate the influence of Cartesian dualism and Newtonian mechanism. Moreover, I would submit that philosophical language, though conceptual, can be passionate and deeply engaging.

We might draw together lines of this post-modern philosophy as material for meditation. Away from the classroom or counseling office, a process-supported ecological vision would incline us to contemplate a world of dynamic events embodying creative power and a degree of freedom. The panexperientialism of process thought endows all creatures with some subjectivity, breaking down the view of human subjectivity over against a world of mere objects. Humans become part of a newly enchanted nature where respect is owed to the interrelational and intrinsic values in all beings. It cherishes the priority of the organic over the mechanistic, relationships over things, persuasion over coercion, internal becoming over locomotion.

As this philosophy moves toward reflection about God, its naturalistic theism envisions divinity as the soul of the world; a God immersed in a process of co-creativity with all entities. God as poet of the world [5] responds with love, sympathy and persuasion, respecting the pluralism of creation. The divine is closely related to life as a transformative cosmic power [6] graciously enhancing our trust in emergent possibilities in each new situation. We are not only co-creators in freedom with God, but shapers of value and novelty. This philosophic meditation could sketch wider parameters for developing a nature-oriented psychospirituality.

Erazim Kohak extends the philosophical meditation into a naturalist morality. He invites us to re-establish a moral order of nature of which humans are a part. He sees the development of Western thought as a systematic depersonalization of ourselves and the world around us. The fundamental insight of his vision concerns authentic relations between beings based on mutual respect and empathetic understanding issuing from a fundamental order of moral law rather than from individual or collective utility.[7] Kohak's perspective is not at all naively anti-utilitarian or anti-instrumentalist. He understands the need for compromises in our relationship with nature. Nor does he advocate some simple naturalism in which human artifacts are excluded. In one sense, our technology is itself an extension of nature through the evolution of the human mind. Yet he invites us to a more profound philosophical contemplation, to realize that:

> The impersonality of our world is no more than a mask of a real world, a personal world. . . . The forest with its creatures, the boulders, the entire world of nature . . . are not a senseless, impersonal aggregate of matter in motion. The world . . . has a life, a rightness and an integrity of its own.[8]

Kohak calls for a re-personalization of our relationship with the inanimate and the animate world for their sake as well as for a deeper personalization of the human community in the process. His very method of philosophizing is located within sensuous meditations on the New England countryside:

> It seems to me so urgent that philosophy should ever return down the long-abandoned wagon road . . . not to speculate but to see, hear, and know that there is still night, star bright and all-reconciling, and that there is dawn, pale over Barrett Mountain . . . .[9]

---

[5]David R. Griffin, *God and Religion in the Post-Modern World* (New York: SUNY Press, 1989) 142.

[6]John B. Cobb and Charles Birch, *The Liberation of Life* (Cambridge: Cambridge University Press, 1981) chap. 5.

[7]Erazim Kohak, *The Embers and the Stars* (Chicago: University of Chicago Press, 1984) 210.

[8]Kohak 211.

[9]Kohak 217.

Kohak's themes and method become psychotherapeutic as they graphically and sensuously lead the contemplative soul beyond the important but limiting conflicts of life to experience herself in a realm where she senses a true belonging to God in nature. He makes philosophers speak not from a distant Olympus, but from the ecological matrix whence all reflection evolved.

The Literary Naturalists

There is another group whom we can call literary naturalists and latterly "deep ecologists," who open up possibilities for psychological and spiritual growth. Henry David Thoreau expressed a nineteenth century naturalist spirituality that extended from the transcendental ideas of his mentor and friend, Ralph Waldo Emerson to Walt Whitman's lyrical naturalism to the intrepid John Muir uncovering sacred landscapes in the West.

Thoreau's famous phrase emphasizes the therapeutic dimension of living contemplatively close to nature: "I went to the woods because I wished to live deliberately, to front only the essential facts of life, and see if I could not learn what it had to teach."[10] The creatures of Walden became teachers for him: "Sometimes, in a summer morning . . . I sat in my sunny doorway from sunrise till noon, rapt in a revery, amidst the pines and hickories and sumachs, in undisturbed solitude and stillness . . . ."[11] He reminds us that the majority of people lead lives of quiet desperation. Sometimes his experience takes on directly religious expression:

> I have penetrated to those meadows on the morning of many a . . . spring day, jumping from hummock to hummock . . . when the wild river valley and the woods were bathed in so pure and bright a light as would have waked the dead. . . . There needs no stronger proof of immortality.[12]

Whitman is a poet of great ecological sensibility, yet the shelves of literary criticism on Whitman seldom refer to his obvious naturalism. The focus is either on his own personal history or on political and cultural themes. This is noteworthy since it indicates what is of importance to the student of the poet. It shows that the kinds of questions we ask of texts powerfully determine the outcome. Let us listen to verses from Whitman's *Song of Myself* for the experience of union with nature. The poem opens with the poet choosing the outdoor atmosphere over perfumed interiors:

> The atmosphere is not a perfume. . . .
> It is for my mouth forever. . . . I am in love with it,
> I will go to the bank by the wood and become undisguised and naked, I am mad for it to be in contact with me.

---

[10]Thoreau 90.
[11]Thoreau 111.
[12]Thoreau 317.

The smoke of my own breath. . . .
My respiration and inspiration. . . . the beating of my heart
    . . . . the passing of blood and air through my lungs. . . .
                                          (stanza 2, 11 4ff.)

Whitman's sense of unity with nature can hardly be more intimate than his linking of respiration and inspiration. Again, he finds laws of ancient meaning that attach him to a flying geese:

The wild gander leads his flock through the cool night
Ya-honk he says, and sounds it down to me like an invitation,
The pert may suppose it meaningless, but I listening close,
Find its purpose and place there toward the wintry sky. . . .
I see in them and myself the same old law.   (stanza 14, 11 1ff.)

The poet plunges naked into the sea in an experience of loving union:

You sea! I resign myself to also--I guess what you mean,
I behold from the beach your crooked, inviting fingers,
I believe you refuse to go back without feeling of me,
We must have a turn together,
I undress, hurry me out of sight of the land,
Cushion me soft, rock me in billowy drowse,
Dash me with amorous wet, I can repay you
Sea of stretch'd ground swells,
Sea breathing broad and convulsive breaths,
Sea of the brine of life and of unshovell'd yet always-ready graves,
Howler and Scooper of storms, capricious and dainty sea,
I am integral with you, I too am one phase of all phases.
                                          (stanza 22, 11 1ff.)[13]

John Muir manifested a similar spirituality in the journals of his western journeys. In *Travels in Alaska*, he wrote: "The grandeur of these forces (the glaciers) and their glorious results overpower me and inhabit my whole being."[14] He saw his vocation in part as that of a prophet, trying to awaken others to the primordial experience of their connection with the natural world. "I care to live only to entice people to look at Nature's loveliness."[15] Like Thoreau, Muir occasionally speaks of his nature mysticism in traditional religious terms, as when he describes the Alaskan auroras as "the most glorious of all the terrestrial manifestations of God."[16]

---

[13]Walt Whitman, "Song of Myself," *Leaves of Grass* (New York: The Modern Library, 1966).

[14]John Muir, *Travels in Alaska* (Boston: Houghton Mifflin Co., 1915) v.

[15]Muir v.

[16]Muir vii.

Contemporary naturalists, more acutely aware of our devastating encroachment on nature, speak with passionate intensity about our unity with earth and our uses of it. One of the most eloquent of these writers, John Hay, reminds us that our own worth cannot be divorced from the natural world. "We cannot live in the full use of earth and earth's complex, expectant, vast experience and deny it at the same time. Worth is defined by participation."[17] But this intellectual message is joined in Hay with a mystic sense arising out of his own experience:

> When I look out on the rippling landscape and breathe the lasting air, walking in the right of earth and sun, I am a central part of the globe, humanly claimed, and I also depend on a reservoir of knowing and being forever incomplete. Buried deeper than our microscopes can see, there is a well of flux and motion, incomparable elaboration, a consuming joined with a proliferation, out of which all things are born. . . ."[18]

Where Hay envisions the spiritual experience of our birthing in nature, Annie Dillard leads us to rebirth or conversion in nature. She echoes Ezekiel in urging us to go alone up into the gaps of the earth:

> The gaps are the thing. The gaps are the spirit's own home, the altitudes and latitudes so dazzlingly spare and clean that the spirit can discover itself for the first time like a once-blind man unbound. The gaps are the clefts in the rock where you cower to see the back parts of God; they are the fissures between mountains and the cells the wind lances through, the icy, narrowing fjords splitting the cliffs of mystery. Go up into the gaps. If you can find them; they shift and vanish too. Stalk the gaps. Squeak into a gap in the soil, turn, and unlock--more than a maple--a universe. This is how you spend this afternoon, and tomorrow morning, and tomorrow afternoon. *Spend* the afternoon. You can't take it with you.[19]

Dillard tells us that we ignore the earth and its potential for psychospiritual growth. We distract ourselves from entering into this spiritual pedagogy by confining ourselves to what Thomas Merton called the "itsy-bitsy statutes" of daily routine. But we end up impoverishing ourselves by rejecting the sometimes hard noviceship of Gaia; we cut ourselves off from the experience that Dillard voices: ". . . I go my way, and my left foot says "Glory," and my right foot says "Amen": in and out of Shadow Creek, upstream and down, exultant, in a daze, dancing, to the twin silver trumpets of praise."[20]

---

[17]John Hay, *In Defense of Nature* (Boston: Little, Brown and Co., 1969) 208.
[18]Hay 209.
[19]Annie Dillard, *Pilgrim at Tinker Creek* (New York: Harper Magazine P, 1974) 269.
[20]Dillard 271.

The Scientific Naturalists

If the literary naturalists, through their artistic gifts, open us to insights about psychospirituality, scientific naturalists also alert us to the tenuous relationship between environment and human becoming. After Rachel Carson's *Silent Spring* launched the contemporary epoch's ecological awareness, Rene Dubos, the renowned biologist, challenged us to look hard at the relationship between technological civilization and the destruction of our habitat. He reminded us that young people raised in ugly and unhealthy environments will be crippled intellectually and emotionally.[21] Loving nature does not mean escaping the city for the countryside, but it demands in our era the humane transformation of urban settings. Dubos pointed out that our institutions are not designed to help people enjoy the good life, but to make them more efficient, productive tools of commerce. Conservation for Dubos meant a balance among the multiple components of nature, including the human component. In this perspective, he underlines the theme of this essay about psychotherapeutic becoming and natural surroundings:

> Since environmental factors profoundly condition most aspects of daily existence, and in particular the biological and psychological development of children, the most urgent need in urban planning is a better knowledge of what human beings require biologically, what they desire culturally, and what they hope to become. In this . . . the know-how is less important than the know-why. . . ."[22]

In a more recent study of urban nature, Rachel Kaplan underscores the importance of landscape, parks and gardens for city dwellers. Subjects of the study testified that natural beauty united with architectural quality contributed to a sense of mental tranquility and inner peacefulness.[23] The solitude and stillness of these urban settings led to mental satisfaction and emotional serenity. View of trees and water also contributed to improved psychological states. Gardening in urban settings, sometimes coupled with bird watching, gave participants a sense of involvement in cultivating life and in being needed.[24] Subjects of the study spoke of their sensory pleasure in gardening and they related an experience of fascination about working in an enclosed natural space that is enticingly open to mystery. Unfortunately, such experiences are in very short supply for many in the modern city. Such lack of access to hands-on involvement in nature "may be significantly detrimental to psychological health," notes Kaplan.[25]

---

[21]Rene Dubos, *So Human an Animal* (New York: Charles Scribner's Sons, 1968) 194.

[22]Dubos 237.

[23]Rachel Kaplan, "The Role of Nature in the Urban Context," *Behavior and the Natural Environment* (New York: Plenum Press, 1983) 157.

[24]Kaplan 153.

[25]Kaplan 158.

Writing just after World War II, the conservationist, Aldo Leopold, was a precursor of the contemporary ecological movement. In his concept of a "land ethic," he urged us to curb the mutual destruction of human and natural communities. He told us that we abuse the land as a commodity rather than appreciate it as a community. For Leopold, a land ethic meant an enlarging of the boundaries of community to include soil, water, plants and animals.[26] He advocated an extension of social conscience from people to land. Leopold also emphasized the importance of wilderness conservation. It is easy today to forget that all culture originated from wilderness. Wilderness was and is the diverse "raw material" out which humans fashion the artifact of civilization. "The rich diversity of the world's cultures reflects a corresponding diversity in the wilds that gave them birth."[27] The diversity of ecosystems in the wild has been greatly reduced by the incursions of human civilization. This is tragic for the wilderness itself with its intrinsic values of interconnected genera and species. But depletion of the wilds also stymies human welfare; the "shallow-minded modern" no longer understands "why the raw wilderness gives definition and meaning to the human enterprise."[28]

A recent longitudinal study on the importance of wilderness [29] for human psychospiritual development offers some suggestive results. The study was based on the decade-long Outdoor Challenge Program in which participants kept journals about their experiences in wilderness situations. Those involved in the project reported a deeper appreciation of tranquility, peace and silence. These outcomes are related to a more integrated sense of self-identity and a greater feeling of personal wholeness. Wilderness fostered a contemplative environment conducive to a higher achievement of self-integration. Finally, the participants noted a quality of oneness with the universe, an experience akin to transcendent or religious modes of consciousness. The researchers, after acknowledging William James' reflection on oneness with the world in *The Varieties of Religious Experience*, speak of it as "a spiritual dimension of human experience, to which psychology has given relatively little attention."[30]

These touchstones of ecological awareness in various fields indicate a deep human need and longing for an intimate connection with the rest of creation. The passage from *The Little Prince*, quoted at the start of this essay, encapsulates this frequently hidden desire for regaining a relationship with our ecological matrix. The fox, who represents the natural world, tells the Little Prince that the intimacy of friendship cannot be bought. He invites the Prince

---

[26]Aldo Leopold, *A Sand County Almanac* (London: Oxford UP, 1949) 204.

[27]Leopold 188.

[28]Leopold 201.

[29]Steven Kaplan and Janet Frey Talbot, "Psychological Benefits of a Wilderness Experience" in Irwin Altman and Joachim Wohlwill, *Behavior and the Natural Environment* (New York: Plenum, 1983) 163-203.

[30]Kaplan and Talbot 200.

to tame him. The French *apprivoiser*, however, does not connote the dominance of "tame" in English. Rather, it expresses a shared experience of understanding and appreciation.

Just as such companionship with the animal realm stimulates psychospiritual wholeness, the opposite outcome is graphically portrayed in Colin Turnbull's anthropological study, *The Mountain People*. The Ik, a hunter-gatherer tribe in the Kidepo Valley of Kenya, was excluded from its mountain land which was taken over for a national park. The movement of the Ik to much less hospitable terrain contributed to a profound change in their personal and social relations. Turnbull describes a radical swing from a society of cooperation in their original milieu to a grouping of depressed individuals who demonstrated mistrust, skepticism and hostility in the hostile terrain to which they had been confined.[31] Although such major psychological upheavals cannot be reduced to a single cause, the case of the Ik provides a dramatic lesson about the link between habitat and psychospiritual states. St. Exupery's positive example of human relations with nature and Turnbull's negative one lift up the reciprocal relationship between ecological habitat and human becoming. These examples highlight the value of the ecological matrix for both religion and psychology. In both areas, unfortunately, self-realization has focused too narrowly on ego fulfillment or at best, improved relationships with immediate family or intimates.

Against these tendencies, Arne Naess, the Norwegian philosopher, introduced the term, "ecological self."[32] To identify self-realization with ego shows a vast underestimation of human potential. Naess urges us to enlarge our notion of self to embrace all animate and inanimate reality in the sense of the Buddha's injunction to care, feel, act with compassion. Naess also counsels us to avoid moralism in educating people toward this deeper sense of ecological self. Rather he advises us to appeal to a person's inclination toward beauty rather than to his/her morals to act in ecologically ethical ways.

> If reality is experienced by the ecological Self, our behavior *naturally* . . . follows norms of . . . environmental ethics. . . . We need the immense variety of sources of joy opened through increased sensitivity toward the richness and diversity of life.[33]

Deep ecology, therefore, invites us beyond intellectual and ethical concepts to actually experience our ontological identification with an evolutionary process. For some people this felt awareness may follow from theoretical pursuits or social involvement relating to ecological causes. But a more experiential change perspective is exemplified in John Seed's comment: "`Iam

---

[31]Colin M. Turnbull, *The Mountain People* (New York: Simon and Schuster, 1972) 256.

[32]Arne Naess, "Self-Realization: An Ecological Approach to Being in the World," *Thinking Like a Mountain*, eds. John Seed et al. (Philadelphia: New Society Publishers, 1988) 20.

[33]Naess 29.

protecting the rain forest' develops to `Iam part of the rain forest protecting myself. I am that part of the rain forest recently emerged into thinking.'"[34]

Ecofeminism

Another important touchstone of ecological psychospirituality is found in the contemporary womanist movement. Ecofeminism explores the relationship between women and nature. On the negative side, ecofeminists relate the abuse of the earth to the oppression of women who have been linked throughout history with nature. Carolyn Merchant's magisterial work, *The Death of Nature*, expands on this negative theme as it developed in the religion, politics and culture of the sixteenth and seventeenth centuries. During this period, a worldview and a science emerged that "by reconceptualizing reality as a machine rather than a living organism, sanctioned the domination of both nature and women."[35]

Woman and nature came to be seen as symbols of disorder, needing to be controlled and exploited by patriarchal dominance, as in the instance of witch-hunting. The machine metaphor led to exaggerated dualisms of body and soul, of nature and humanity. Technological society furthered the "new image of nature as female to be controlled and dissected through experiment (which) legitimated the exploitation of natural resources."[36] Merchant also discusses communal and utopian movements that were partly inspired by organic worldviews. In these systems, women and nature fared better in terms of respect and freedom. But such movements were peripheral to the dominant thrust of hierarchical patriarchy with its oppressive dualisms. This negative reading of modern history from an ecofeminist perspective provides a context for appreciating both the need for ecological spirituality and the difficulty of attaining it in an age still deeply influenced by patriarchal and mechanistic traditions.

But the ecofeminists also underscore positive dimensions of women's experience for building a nature-oriented psychospirituality. A key aspect of ecofeminism is the experience of interconnectedness among all beings. Susan Griffin's poetic prose expresses this sense of unitary relationship with nature. Addressing the earth, she writes:

Now my body reaches out to her . . . and I learn at no instance does she fail me in her presence. She is as delicate as I am; I know her sentience; I feel her pain and my own pain comes to me . . . I open my mouth to this pain, I taste, I know . . . why she goes on . . . in drought, in starvation, with intelligence does she survive disaster. This earth is my sister; I love her daily grace, her silent daring, and how loved am I. . . .[37]

---

[34]John Seed, "Beyond Anthropocentrism," in Seed et al. 36.
[35]Carolyn Merchant, *The Death of Nature* (San Francisco: Harper and Row, 1980) xxi.
[36]Merchant 189.
[37]Susan Griffin, *Woman and Nature* (New York: Harper and Row, 1978) 219.

Interconnection fosters compassion and identification with others in the natural and the political worlds. Starhawk emphasizes this point, reminding us that a sense of interconnection links us to the people in South Africa, as well as to the eagles and the whales.[38] It is particularly noteworthy that many ecofeminists express their ideas about interconnectedness in ways that join intellect and emotion in the written statement. This method of expression itself becomes a holistic way of communicating.

Another trait of ecofeminism is its vision of immanence. According to Rosemary Reuther, an ecological feminist theology of nature must rethink the hierarchical chain of being and of command. This view saw in a descending order of value beings of transcendent spirit at the top and entities of spiritless matter at the bottom.

> "The God/ess who is primal Matrix, the ground of being new-being, is neither stifling immanence nor rootless transcendence. Spirit and matter are not dichotomized but are the inside and the outside of the same thing."[39]

New developments in physics that indicate a continuum between matter and energy offer confirming metaphors for this immanent penetration of spiritual and material reality. In nature, energy shifts from visible to invisible patterns and back again. For Starhawk, the Goddess is embodied in human, animal, plant, and mineral communities and their inter-relationships. This is akin to Lovelock's Gaia thesis, imaging the world as a living, responsive, and adapting entity.[40]

If one cultivates a sense of immanent value, sources of inner power are discovered. A person thus empowered can reach out with greater responsibility toward others. Moreover, the ecofeminist perspective criticizes typical forms of power relationships obtained in society at large. These are external arrangements of dominance over others rather than networking, immanent relationships of mutual respect and consensus.

Ecofeminism brings its own contributions to an ecological spirituality. These tie in closely with Naess' "deep ecology" in which a person realizes his/her embeddedness in nature, thereby gradually overcoming alienation from other forms of life and developing reverence for all beings. Psychological and religious forms of therapy would be incomplete without careful attention to ecofeminism's spirit and mandate.

Finally, ecofeminism insists on ritualizing its spirituality, not merely intellectualizing it. Felt convictions need to be acted out in rituals of song, meditation, dance and the other arts. Nature is dynamic, physical, and

---

[38]Starhawk, "Feminist, Earth-based Spirituality and Ecofeminism," *Healing the Wounds: The Promise of Ecofeminism*, ed. Judith Plant (Philadelphia: New Society Publishers, 1989) 178.

[39]Rosemary R. Reuther, "Toward an Ecological-Feminist Theology of Nature," in Plant 178.

[40]James Lovelock, *Gaia* (New York: Oxford University Press, 1987).

emotional. Our senses and feelings must be actualized in an ecological spirituality. Spirit, body and earth need to touch and savor.[41]

Ecospirituality and Religions

As we move more explicitly into the area of religions, let us first consider touchstones of psychospirituality from two traditions removed from the European heritage, those of native American Indians and of Taoism. Our discussion of these important traditions will be very brief and partial in its coverage. This inadequacy will be compounded by the problem of how much we can appropriate healthier ecological outlooks from traditions not our own. Yet despite such limitations, we cannot afford to ignore the richness of these spiritual cultures for shaping a healing ecological vision for western humanity. Through study and especially meditation and practice, there is a way of crossing over into foreign traditions and returning to one's own with benefit.

One of the first differences between native American spirituality and the European heritage concerns our notions about the sacred and the profane. We can, of course, point in both traditions to moments that are considered more sacred in a community's myth and ritual. But in general, native tribes understand religious experience as surrounding us all the time in relationships between humans and between humanity and nature. Religion in the European perspective has tended to place the sacred in transcendent realms that are more removed from the ordinary life of earth. For example, the Navajos "would say that there is probably *nothing* that can be called nonreligious."[42] Religion is viewed as a network of reciprocal relationships between humans and the processes operating in the world of nature. Health is a good example. We often conceive of the recovery of health as a compartmentalized activity involving doctors and medicines. The Navajos would consult a healer who uses not only medicines but also rituals for putting one back in step with natural cycles. Regaining health, therefore, for the native American is a holistic, religious process. This process is a kind of "reciprocation" [43] at the heart of all activity in the world. The human and the natural realm exist in a network of incessant mutuality and compenetration, a sacred process, whether the activities be ritual dance, rug weaving, or moccasin making.

This kind of reciprocity leads to a sense of moral appropriateness regarding animals and the land. What is appropriate has been fashioned by the imaginative cultural experience of the tribes over generations. Thus a Navajo man whose family was in dire economic conditions would not hunt for animals while his wife was close to birthing. ". . . It is inappropriate that I

---

[41]Seed 97ff. Joanna Macy and Pat Fleming describe the rituals of the Council of All Beings worship.

[42]Barre Toelken, "Seeing with a Native Eye: How Many Sheep Will It Hold?" *Seeing With a Native Eye*, ed. Walter H. Capps (New York: Harper and Row, 1976) 11.

[43]Toelken 17.

should take life just now when I am expecting the gift of life."[44]

The Indian does not primarily view nature as an objective commodity to use or study. The native vision of the natural world is more complex, seeing the physical dimension of nature as also a sacred reality. The Indian cultural imagination about relationships with soil, plant, and animal life resonates with a sense of the sacrality of place. A key example of this is the Four Corners area in the southwest where Mt. Huerfano joins four western states. For the Indians this place is embedded in mystery, as a mythic locus for the origin of all things. This landscape is sacred because of its nearness to the source of life's beginnings; creation stories flow naturally from earth as matrix of all creatures.[45] Chief Luther Standing Bear of the Lakota Sioux expresses this Indian participation mystique with the earth:

> The Lakota was a true naturalist--a lover of nature. He loved the earth, the attachment growing with age. The old people came literally to love the soil and they sat or reclined on the ground with a feeling of being close to a mothering power. It was good for the skin to touch the earth and the old people like to remove their moccasins and walk with bare feet on the sacred earth.[46]

If we wanted to incorporate some of this attitude into western psychospirituality, we would need, among other things, to re-vision our education systems as they form our consciousness of nature. The objective approach of the botanist would have to be complemented by a new education of imagination in children and adults. They would have to appreciate the object as also a subject in a mutually interactive energy field with themselves. This is difficult for the contemporary mind, caught between a scientistic reductionism and a wariness about exaggerated romanticism. Yet a solution lies in neither extreme. We can learn to live a dialectic between wonder and scrutiny, a polarity akin to Paul Ricoeur's "second naivete." We can find ways of not only educating the critical scientist but also of drawing out the nature mystic in each of us. The earth can become a place of psychospiritual centering for us.

These Indian themes of reciprocity and appropriateness are reflected in thoughts attributed to Chief Seattle in an 1854 address concerning the selling of Indian lands. He rebukes the new settler for whom "One portion of land is the same . . . as the next, for he is a stranger who comes in the night and takes from the land whatever he needs. The earth is not his brother but his enemy, and when he has conquered it, he moves on."[47] The words attributed

---

[44]N. Scott Momaday, "Native American Attitudes to the Environment," in Capps 44.

[45]Beldon C. Lane, *Landscapes of the Sacred* (New York: Paulist Press, 1988) 48.

[46]Lane 51.

[47]"Chief Seattle's Message," in *Seed* 69. A graduate student and colleague, Rebecca K. Gould, pointed out to me that the text of Chief Seattle was actually written a hundred years later by an American script writer and attributed to Seattle. See *Environmental Ethics*, 1989:

to Seattle remind the new settler about the familial reciprocity between natives and the land:

> What is man without the beasts? If all the beasts were gone, men would die from a great loneliness of spirit. For whatever happens to the beasts soon happens to the man. All things are connected. You must teach your children that the ground beneath their feet is the ashes of our grandfathers. . . . Teach your children what we have taught our children, that the earth is our mother. Whatever befalls the earth befalls the sons of the earth. If men spit upon the ground, they spit upon themselves. This we know. The earth does not belong to man; man belongs to the earth. This we know. All things are connected like the blood which unites one family. All things are connected.[48]

Gwaganad, a native of the Queen Charlotte Islands in the Canadian Northwest, brings a sense of reciprocity to an intimate linking of physical and spiritual experience. Both in the gathering of food and in fishing, Gwaganad describes an experience of intense respect for land and water. "I was taught to respect the food that comes from the land . . . everything had a meaning. In gathering the food--the nearest I can translate--I can say to gather food is a spiritual experience for me."[49] She relates the keen sense of anticipation during the months leading to the harvest of herring roe:

> It's a spiritual thing that happens. . . . My body feels that it's time to spawn. . . . I get a longing to be on the sea. I constantly watch the ocean surrounding the island. . . . My body is kind of on edge in anticipation. Finally the day comes when it spawns. The water gets all milky around it. . . . I share this experience with all the friends . . . this wonderful feeling on the day that it happens, the excitement, the relief that the herring did indeed come this year. And you don't quite feel complete until you are right out on the ocean with your hands in the water harvesting the kelp, the roe on kelp, and then your body feels right. . . . And it's not quite perfect until you eat your first batch of herring roe on kelp. . . . your body almost rejoices in that first feed. . . . If you listen to your body it tells you a lot of things. . . . If you put something right in it, your body feels it. Your spiritual self feels it.[50]

This earthy sense of reciprocity and appropriateness climaxes in the vision of the Oglala Sioux, Black Elk, when he sees the whole hoop of the earth from a high place in the center of the world. The experience of kinship with the earth, manifest in the mountain and the great tree, leads him to a sense of social oneness. The awareness of unity with the earth opens the way to an ethical vision of union in diversity among the peoples of the earth:

195-96.

[48]Seattle 71.

[49]Gwaganad, "Speaking for the Earth: The Haida Way," in Plant 77.

[50]Gwaganad 78-79.

Then a voice said: 'Behold this day, for it is yours to make. Now you shall stand upon the center of the earth to see, for there they are taking you." . . . Then I was standing on the highest mountain of them all, and round about me was the whole hoop of the world. And while I stood there I saw more than I can tell and I understood more than I saw; for I was seeing in a sacred manner the shapes of all things in the spirit, and the shapes of all shapes as they must live together like one being. And I saw that the sacred hoop of my people was one of many hoops that made one circle, wide as daylight and as starlight, and in the center grew one mighty flowering tree to shelter all the children of one mother and one father. And I saw that it was holy.[51]

The Taoist contribution to psychospiritual development resembles native American wisdom. The Chinese worldview of Taoist masters stresses organic process, intrinsic relations and a dynamic, holistic understanding of nature. Although the Taoist cosmos is impersonal, it is not inhuman. Humans are intrinsic to the constant transformation process of the world. The whole context of this process, which always remains beyond human ken, is called Tao. The Tao has also been referred to as an emerging pattern of relatedness [52] whose particular instances (*te*) participate and develop in the wider context of Tao. Thus Taoism envisions a world of particulars in their environing conditions, interpenetrating and interdependent without loss of distinctions, a simulataneous multiplicity and relativity immersed in a unifying mystery.

The human operation by which the particular is forever developing in its wider context is called *wu-wei*, sometimes spoken of as dynamic nonaction. This is not a passive concept, but rather a way of responding with an awareness that enables one to maximize the creative possibilities of self and environment.[53] In *wu-wei*, the particular event authors itself in deference to the needs of its environment, while calling on environing circumstances to defer to its integrity. "*Wu-wei* as 'making' is irrepressibly participatory and creative."[54]

Water is a chief Taoist symbol for the dynamic context of Tao, *te* and wu-wei. Water symbolizes both definiteness (as used in measurement) and fluidity (as a metaphor for a realm of indeterminate creativity). Another symbol of Taoist harmony is the circular depiction of yin and yang. Yet all of these concepts are returned to the natural. When they have been incorporated into a person's way of visioning the world, there is no need to constantly refer to theory.

The story is told of a Taoist master and a disciple trudging through the snow when a rabbit sprang across their path. "What would you say of that?" the master asked. "It was like a god!" the disciple answered. Since the master

[51]Black Elk, *Black Elk Speaks* (New York: Pocket Books, 1972) 35-36.

[52]Roger T. Ames, "Putting the *Te* Back into Taoism," *Nature in Asian Traditions of Thought*, eds. J. Baird Callicott and Roger T. Ames (New York: SUNY Press, 1989) 136.

[53]Ames 140.

[54]Ames 138.

was unimpressed with the answer, the disciple returned the question: "Well, what would you say it was?" "It was a rabbit!"[55]

Taoist insights foster an ecological spirituality because of their commitment to the interdependence of polar categories. This precludes the human/nature dualism that has so long dogged Western thought. The person is always understood as a being-in-environment. "Under this conceptual framework, personal cultivation and cultivation of one's environment are coextensive. To reduce nature to a 'means' is not only to compromise the creative possibilities of nature, but also to impoverish one's own."[56] The Taoist notion of polarity rather than dualism requires that we foster the environment not as other, but as a dimension of ourselves. Taoist spirituality integrates a sense of divine energy into the transformative process of promoting one's personhood by the quality of one's contributions to the significance of the world.[57] Transformation of self and world through enabling, noncoercive participation is alluded to in these lines from the *Chuang Tzu*:

> Without praises or curses,
> Now a dragon, now a snake,
> You transform together with the times.
> And not willing to act unilaterally,
> Now above, now below,
> You take harmony as your measure.[58]

Christianity presents an ambiguous record on ecological spirituality. From Lynn White's strong critique of Christian theology for its anti-ecological religiousness [59] to the recent work of Thomas Berry, the negative appraisal continues. In general, Christianity is criticized for its other-worldly outlook that removes religiousness from the natural world to focus on issues of personal salvation that transcend the world. The Christian religion is also criticized for its anthropocentrism and its oppressive subordination of nature. Yet the negative assessment of Christian influence has been complemented since Lynn White's essay by a number of works upholding the positive potential of Christian theology for shaping an ecological spirituality.

Perhaps the leading study in this revisionist quest is Paul Santmire's *The Travail of Nature*; his subtitle, *"The Ambiguous Ecological Promise of Christian Theology"* characterizes his sweeping investigation of theologians from the

---

[55]Huston Smith, "Tao Now: An Ecological Testament," *Earth Might Be Fair*, ed. Jan G. Barbour (Englewood Cliffs, NJ: Prentice-Hall, Inc., 1972) 78.

[56]Ames 142.

[57]Ames 143.

[58]Ames 134.

[59]Lynn White, Jr., "The Historical Roots of Our Ecologic Crisis," *Science* 155 (1967): 1203.

New Testament times to the present.[60] Santmire finds two great motifs conflicting in Christian theology: the spiritual motif of ascent away from earth and the ecological motif in the metaphors of fecundity and journey that call Christians toward a this-worldly spirituality. Authors underscoring the promise of Christianity and Judaism for developing an ecological religiousness[61] usually stress such themes as creation, incarnation and sacramentality in an ecological vein. For purposes of this essay, I want to highlight a few themes from these thinkers to support the ecological matrix of psychospiritual development.

Thomas Berry, building on the evolutionary cosmic vision of Teilhard de Chardin, sets the stage for the spiritual and psychotherapeutic task. In his call for a new religious orientation, he maps three great shifts in western history in ways of mediating the numinous. In the premodern period, such mediation took place according to a hierarchical model from the transcendent divine to earthly humanity. In the modern period of scientific enlightenment, mediation of the numinous takes place on the inter-human plane. In this regard, think of various therapeutic enterprises of the past century which stress the intrapsychic and the interpersonal. Berry sees humanity poised on the verge of a third phase of mediating the numinous through human-earthly processes. The new phase does not exclude the previous mediations, as I understand it, but subordinates them to the religious experiences of the earth community as our primary loyalty.[62] Our intrinsic participation in the great drama of earthly evolution becomes a primary source of divine revelation. In this underlying thrust of his thinking, Berry reminds us that in "reinventing the human" in an ecological perspective, we are cycling back to recapture the earliest human experiences of the divine which emerged from awe and wonder at natural processes.[63]

If we apply Berry's vision to the psychological and spiritual healing process, we might say that the counselor's task becomes in part one of weaning us from negative dimensions of our cultural coding toward living in greater unison with our genetic coding. The therapeutic endeavor would partially consist in curing us of the cultural illnesses of greedy competition and heedless consumerism, both individual and corporate. Berry speaks of the destructive dream of enlightenment rationalism which leads to salvation

---

[60]H. Paul Santmire, *The Travail of Nature* (Philadelphia: The Fortress Press, 1985).

[61]Jurgen Moltmann, *God in Creation* (San Francisco: Harper and Row, 1985); George S. Hendry, *Theology of Nature* (Philadelphia: Westminster Press, 1980); Jay B. McDaniel, *Earth, Sky, Gods & Mortals* (Mystic, CT: Twenty-Third Publications, 1990); John Carmody, *Ecology and Religion* (New York: Paulist Press, 1983); John Hart, *The Spirit of the Earth* (New York: Paulist Press, 1984); see Thomas Berry's appreciative critics in *Thomas Berry and the New Cosmology* (Mystic, CT: Twenty-Third Publications, 1988); for a Jewish revisionist version, see Jeremy Cohen, "On Classical Judaism and the Environmental Crisis," *Tikkun* 5.2 n.d. 74-77.

[62]Thomas Berry, *Thomas Berry and the New Cosmology*, 5-26.

[63]Thomas Berry, *Dream of the Earth* (San Francisco: Sierra Club Books, 1988) 39.

through accumulation of things and control over human and natural others (read "objects").[64]

Can the religious psychotherapist or counselor believe that he or she has accomplished a humanly therapeutic function without working to re-establish in themselves and in their clients Berry's functional relationship with the earth process? Our therapies are still too anthropocentric, too narrowly confined to immediate personal or interpersonal issues without putting these in the wider context of a "functional cosmology," of a mystique or spirituality of deep reverence for our broader habitat. Without such a focus, we may be trivializing psychotherapy and religious counseling. We need to develop new therapeutic rituals that help us to participate in the liturgy of the universe. We might find that such therapies and the archetypal revisioning underlying them help us resolve our inner rage against earthly existence.

Alerting us to the sensual and earthy dimension of the mystical tradition may be one of Matthew Fox's most important contributions.[65] He points out Julian of Norwich's incarnational spirituality in her vision of God lodged in our very sensuality and in the divine's motherly embrace of our bodiliness.[66] Meister Eckhart can teach us to see the world itself as the great sacrament of God; he tells us to penetrate things to find God.[67] Eckhart teaches that the body is in the soul, turning around a traditional notion of the soul imprisoned in matter. His sense of the body being in the soul reveals the sacredness of the physical itself, the interpenetration of body and soul within a continuous sacred energy. The earthly spirituality of mystics can lead us toward a consciousness diaphanous to the world of nature, as the true home of our religiousness. Moreover, the poetic intensity of mystical writings can inspire a new level of spiritual experience for persons in therapeutic or retreat situations.

In the end, an ecological psychospirituality might be judged escapist in a world of multiple social evils. It might be seen as a luxury in a time when so many people around the world struggle to survive each day. But such a conclusion would be a serious misinterpretation. For many of our social ills are the result of anti-earth mentalities of exploitation and oppression. In as much as we rape and hoard the resources of earth, in as much as we see humankind as alienated from a companionship with (not just stewardship of) creation,[68] we perpetuate and expand public evils. The criterion of social

---

[64]Berry, *Dream* chap. 15.

[65]Hildegard of Bingen, *Book of Divine Works*, ed. Matthew Fox (Santa Fe: Bear & Co., 1987); Matthew, introduction and commentaries, *Breakthrough: Meister Eckhart's Creation Spirituality in New Translation* (Garden City: Doubleday & Co., 1980).

[66]Matthew Fox, *Original Blessing* (Santa Fe: Bear & Co., 1983), chap. 3.

[67]Fox, *Original Blessing,* chap. 6.

[68]Michael J. Himes and Kenneth R. Himes, "The Sacrament of Creation," *Commonweal* CXVII.2 (1990): 42-49.

justice is intrinsic to a wise ecological consciousness. We must not only be willing to struggle against individual actions that destroy the environment, but also against greed-driven corporate abuses of nature.[69]

When we experience ourselves deeply as companions of nature rather than as an individualistic species apart, we will be more attuned to support ecological legislation and work in the public sphere for a healthy earth. To embrace again the ecological matrix of our psychospiritual well-being calls for a profound reordering of values. We might want to mitigate the "only" in Thomas Berry's remarks, but they sum up my general theme: "Our survival concerns should address not only humanity in its physical reality but also the survival of our own being in our deepest spiritual, imaginative, creative capacities. Only if we have a beautiful world can we have a beautiful mind and a beautiful soul."[70] Listen to St. Exupery's fox and seek friendship with him: ". . there is no shop anywhere where one can buy friendship, and so men have no friends anymore. If you want a friend, befriend me." Befriend the earth.

[69]Kirkpatrick Sale, "The Trouble With Earth Day," *The Nation* (April 30, 1990): 594-98.
[70]Thomas Berry, "Finding Heaven on Earth," *New Age* (March/April 1990): 50.

SCHILLEBEECKX'S CREATION-BASED THEOLOGY AS BASIS FOR AN ECOLOGICAL SPIRITUALITY

Dorothy A. Jacko

It is my contention that *theology*, not psychology, is the only appropriate foundation for developing a holistic Christian spirituality. Attention to psychology certainly is necessary in spirituality but its role is that of an adjunct discipline which enables one to explore and better understand the human person, the subject of spirituality, as the initial step of a larger theological process of reflection.[1]

But, some may object, spirituality is not identical with theology--reiterating an unfortunate conception of spirituality as totally distinct from theology which occurred in the late Middle Ages when theology became increasingly speculative (a matter for the universities) and thus more and more separated from the daily living of Christian life in the plenitude of its mystical and practical dimensions. In our day, happily, this misleading and harmful separation has been overcome and the unity of theology and spirituality has been restored once again, particularly in the varieties of liberation theologies emerging in both Third and First Worlds. In these contemporary theologies, spirituality is clearly and simply "the following after Jesus", which in its daily living of the Christian life is both the precondition for theological reflection and its live practical expression.[2] It is this indissoluble unity between theology and spirituality, as the intertwined theoretical and practical dimensions or moments of Christian living, that is presumed in this paper. Theology is spirituality "under reflection" and spirituality is theology "in action."

---

[1] The notion of utilizing other human disciplines to "explore the terrain" as a preliminary step prior to theological reflection, properly speaking, is Schillebeeckx's. For a summary of his understanding of the relationship between the human sciences and theology, see "Interdisciplinarity in Theology," *Theology Digest* 24 (1976): 137-42. His clear distinction between the two kinds of discourse is important and necessary to maintain the distinctiveness and irreducibility of theology as the "discourse of faith."

[2] Important contemporary theologies which show the unity of spirituality and theology include Jon Sobrino, *Christianity at the Crossroads* (Orbis, 1978); Leonardo Boff, *Jesus Christ Liberator* (Orbis, 1978); and Edward Schillebeeckx, *Jesus in our Western Culture: Mysticism, Ethics and Politics* (SCM Press, 1987).

Having acknowledged my hidden polemical interest, I should like now to turn to the work of the eminent Catholic theologian, Edward Schillebeeckx, in order to borrow from it several elements which, I believe, can be assembled into a workable framework for developing a comprehensive contemporary and theologically grounded ecological spirituality. The five elements I have selected, along with the role each would play in an ecological spirituality, are as follows:

1. The subject of spirituality: the human person in ecological relationship.
2. The *locus* of spirituality: creation (i.e., the world).
3. The content of spirituality: mystical, political and ecological action.
4. The norm and criterion for spirituality: Jesus of Nazareth,"creation as God intends it to be."
5. The goal of spirituality: a new creation.

Having named these elements, allow me now to say a few words about the meaning and function of each in Schillebeeckx's theological synthesis and to identify some directions for an ecological spirituality to which they point.

The Subject of Spirituality:
The Human Person in Ecological Relationship

While older forms of spirituality tended to define the human person primarily in vertical terms of relationship to God, more recent twentieth-century spiritualities have sought to balance this vertical tendency by elaborating the horizontal dimension of human interpersonal relationships as the fundamental arena in and through which one's relationship to God is lived and expressed. Yet these newer approaches, though helpful in presenting a more dynamic and relational view of spiritual life, remain largely within an anthropocentric view of reality. It is precisely this anthropocentrism and its unwitting contribution to the destruction of the ecosphere which is being challenged by today's ecological movement and which sets the agenda for theology/spirituality in the 1990s and beyond.

Schillebeeckx's theology provides a foundation for a spirituality which avoids the dangers of anthropocentrism by describing the human person--the subject of spirituality--not only in dynamic and relational, but also ecological and eschatological categories. Firmly rejecting all *a priori* definitions of humanity inherited from past philosophies,[3] he proposes instead a list of seven anthropological constants, which "point to permanent human impulses and orientations, values and spheres of value, but at the same time do not provide us with directly specific norms or ethical imperatives in accordance with which true and livable humanity would have to be called into existence

---

[3]"We do not have a pre-existing definition of humanity--indeed for Christians it is not only a future, but an eschatological reality," Schillebeeckx writes in *Christ: The Experience of Jesus as Lord* (Seabury Press, 1980) 731. The historicity of creation makes it impossible to posit *a priori* definitions since creation will become itself definitively only in the eschaton.

here and now."[4] At the outset, these anthropological constants make explicit three important realities about human existence: 1) its radical historicity; 2) the complexity of the human task in history; and 3) the inescapable need for human commitment to the historical task.

Of the seven constants which structure the human task in history, the first is most obviously related to our topic of an ecological spirituality. It is the relationship of persons to their own corporeality and by means of their bodies to the wider sphere of nature and the ecological environment. This primary relationship sets the human task in every age: 1) to respect the limits--human physical and psychological ones as well as the limits of nature and of the cosmos; 2) to engage in aesthetic and enjoyable converse with nature; and 3) to utilize technology in a humanizing and ecologically respectful manner.

The practical implications for a contemporary ecological spirituality deriving from this first constant are manifold. They include the renouncing of all relationships of exploitation, domination, manipulation, violence and aggression; a respect for the needs and limits of one's own body-mind-spirit as well as for those of the cosmos; a new mode of thinking which respects the "interconnected web of all being"[5]; a critical stance toward science and technology which asks at whose and at what expense so-called advances in science and technology are being made; an affirmation of not only human freedom and reason but of imagination, instinct and love, of the need for contemplation and playfulness as well as for work and productivity.[6] The refusal to live ecologically, Schillebeeckx cautions, results in the destruction of the natural environment, hence in the erosion of the basis of human life itself.

Anthropological constants two and three identify the interconnectedness of human beings with one another and with social and institutional structures. Personal identity is inextricably bound up with relationship to others, as the human face in its directedness towards others reveals, Schillebeeckx notes in constant number two. In the free, loving affirmation of the other in interpersonal relationship, one achieves one's own identity and affirms, thereby helping to create, the other. But the other of one's concern in Schillebeeckx's view is not only the "privileged other" or the others of one's

---

[4]Schillebeeckx, *Christ* 733. In other words, these anthropological constants point out the direction and delineate the parameters of the human task in history; i.e., they offer general ethical norms for living but do not posit *specific* universal and timeless norms for human action. The latter must be worked out painstakingly in each new time and place. For Schillebeeckx's discussion of the anthropological constants, see *Christ* 731-43.

[5]The concept of the "interconnected web of all being" is an important one in contemporary feminist writings, a concept they borrow from native American religions. See the various articles collected in *Weaving the Visions*, especially Part 4, for discussion of the implications of this concept for contemporary spiritualities.

[6]Schillebeeckx lists these final implications in his discussion of the first anthropological constant. See *Christ*, 736.

immediate personal interest but includes *all others*, especially the underprivileged others--the poor, the despised, the oppressed, the violated of the earth. The inescapable social dimension of personal existence is the theme also of constant number three, which spells out the relationship of humans to social and institutional structures. This deep structure of human life calls for the building of structures and institutions which make possible and support human freedom and the realization of human values to the benefit of all peoples.

The constitutively social nature of human existence holds many implications for a contemporary ecological spirituality. Most obviously, it renders invalid any approach to spirituality which is purely privatistic (concerned only with God and me), interior, or "exclusively spiritual" in content. Positively, it calls for a commitment of one's life to an active involvement in the building of a more just and humane world, a habitable world wherein all of God's creation may move toward, and already enjoy in some preliminary way, the well-being, wholeness and happiness which God intends for all of creation. Although these two constants speak specifically about human society, because the anthropological constants taken together form an irreducible synthesis, they are informed by the wider ecological relationships between humans and the entire cosmos delineated in the initial constant. It therefore is legitimate to extend their concerns beyond human society in itself to include the disadvantaged and oppressed of other species and the endangered cosmos itself within the realm of one's concern for and commitment to the communitarian life and well-being of the whole.

Fourth, Schillebeeckx's anthropological constants underline the radical historical and geographical conditioning of peoples and cultures by reason of their immersion in time and space. This fact grounds humans solidly within their own period of history and posits for them their unique task in history. This constant reminds us that spirituality always must be a continuing effort to embody the specific life-promoting values which emerge as those of greatest need and priority within each historical context. During the latter part of the twentieth century in a highly industrialized and technological society whose habits and practices are endangering the life of the cosmos itself, the primary values which are rapidly emerging and coalescing are the interconnected values of an ecological consciousness. To be concerned about developing an ecological spirituality, therefore, is not to capitulate to the latest fad but to be sensitively attuned to reading the "signs of the times" as Jesus proclaims we must do and as Vatican II reminds us of the need to do.

The twin anthropological constants of the mutual relationship between theory and practice and between the religious and para-religious consciousness of humans provide for permanence and change, the two essential dimensions of human life and culture. Unless human beings wish to opt for a kind of "spiritual Darwinism", an instinctual struggle for the survival of the fittest, Schillebeeckx asserts, they must choose to combine theory and practice in an ongoing project of building a permanent culture which is increasingly worthy of humanity and which brings salvation for all creation.

The emphasis on the mutual relationship between theory and practice which is central to all contemporary liberationist theologies[7] rescues spirituality from the old dualisms, dichotomies, dilemmas and hierarchies which plagued older spiritualities: contemplation vs. action, prayer vs. work, spiritual exercises vs. secular activities, love of God in competition with love of neighbor. If one's spirituality encompasses the whole of one's way of being/living in the world, then moments of contemplation, worship and reflection prepare for and lead to faith-filled action, which in turn leads back to and provides the experiential basis for contemplation and worship. To say this is not to reduce prayer and liturgy to some strictly utilitarian function which enables persons to work better and harder, but to acknowledge that human life is an integral unity of contemplation and action, both of which are indispensable to the living of a full Christian, indeed any human, life. A hierarchy of "privileged religious moments/actions" cannot be set over against less important and therefore dispensable times of "secular work".[8]

Finally, in speaking about "para-religious consciousness," Schillebeeckx is naming the utopian element of human consciousness--that dimension of our humanness which is able to envision totally new, yet unborn, possibilities for a better world on behalf of all creation. What is imaginable is indeed possible; thus this visionary capacity creates the initial step of a process which includes as a second step the work of devising the necessary strategies for the implementation of the vision here and now in history. While all human beings have this imaginative utopian capability, those who profess to live an explicitly Christian spirituality see it as their means of involvement in God's salvific process in history, their participation in the furthering of the kingdom of God in and through their own histories.

The preceding delineation of the human subject in the dynamic, relational, ecological and eschatological categories of Schillebeeckx's anthropological constants has already suggested in broad terms the directions in which a Christian ecological spirituality would need to move. To elaborate the theological content of such a spirituality more fully, however, the paper will now turn to a brief discussion of the remaining elements of the framework.

---

[7]For a helpful and clear exposition of the interrelationship of theory and practice in the hermeneutic circle, see Juan Luis Segundo, *The Liberation of Theology* (Orbis, 1976), chapter one.

[8]In saying this, I am not denying--nor would Schillebeeckx--that the intense and focused times of communion with God in contemplation, prayer and liturgical celebration can be "privileged times" of grace but am merely underlining the indispensability and importance of the rest of human life and action.

The Locus, Content, Criterion, and Goal of an Ecological Spirituality

First, a few words about the locus or place where one's spirituality is lived. In his efforts to undo the harmful dualisms and hierarchies which have plagued past theological reflections and distorted Christian spiritualities down to this day, Schillebeeckx's theology increasingly has emphasized the fact that it is in creation (the theological word for world) that God's salvific process is at work. Like his original master, Thomas Aquinas, Schillebeeckx utilizes the Christian doctrine of creation as the foundation for his entire theological enterprise and has over the several decades of his writings translated this key doctrine into contemporary historical terms.

In Schillebeeckx' perspective faith in creation means acknowledgment of the indissoluble bond which exists between God and world by reason of creation. In the act of creation, God simultaneously constitutes the world in its own reality (i.e. distinct from God), yet graciously pledges to remain intimately near to it as its foundation, support and goal.[9] For the believer, there is no such thing as a "neutral" world apart from God. Everything in creation thus becomes a possible mediation of God's saving presence; indeed it is only in and through the created world that human beings can meet God in this life, for they have no other world in which to live and no other way of encountering God except through the world's mediation. It is in the world that grace becomes a tangible reality, proffered as free gift of God but requiring concrete human response. Wherever people of good will respond to God's gratuitous offer in loving and liberating deeds, there God's salvation becomes a reality--whether they consciously recognize this or not.

So indispensable is the world in God's salvific process that Schillebeeckx writes, in a play on Cyprian's famous (or infamous!) dictum, "outside the *world*, there is no spirituality."[10]   For the purposes of this discussion, we might take the liberty of a further adaptation of Cyprian's statement and say that from the vantage point of concrete Christian life, "outside the world, there is no spirituality." For God's grace, i.e. God's saving presence, is not restricted to some privileged sphere of interiority but is mediated through the whole of reality of which humans are a part. To seek God "alone" or "directly" in Godself is to chase after a void, Schillebeeckx cautions.

Is this to suggest that spirituality is nothing more than "worldly activity"--deeds of charity or compassion, socio-political action or the promotion of ecological causes--to the exclusion of contemplation, prayer, and liturgy? Indeed not, for to do so would be to replace the false dualisms of the past with an equally false monolithic reduction of life to pragmatic deeds. As will become more clear in the following paragraphs, both are indispensable. To

---

[9]Schillebeeckx offers a clear, concise and systematic development of the meaning of creation in his essay, "I Believe in God, Creator of Heaven and Earth" published in *God Among Us: The Gospel Proclaimed* (Crossroad, 1983), 91-102.

[10]"God, the Living One," *New Blackfriars*, 62 (1981), 366.

formulate the relationship between overtly religious action (mystical-liturgical) and implicitly religious ones (all deeds which contribute to the liberation of creation), I borrow the language Schillebeeckx uses to speak about the distinctions-in-relationship among world or history, religions, and theology.

If the world is the place where God's salvation is being made a reality, then the only *locus* for the living of an authentic Christian spirituality is solidly in the world in commitment to the furthering of God's salvific process which is occurring there. But just as this salvific process which is taking place in the world has need of religions to name and celebrate this process as coming from God and has need of theology to reflect critically on the manner of human participation in it, so every authentic spirituality needs its moments of "making salvation", its times of naming and celebrating it in joyous and grateful affirmation and its periods of reflecting in honest and self-critical awareness.[11] The process is all of a piece, all three activities--action, prayer and theological reflection--contributing their indispensable parts to the living of one's own holistic spirituality.

With this synthesis, we have already moved into the third component of an ecological spirituality: its content, which is both mystical and political-ecological activity.[12] Because human beings live not in the eschaton of fully reconciled relationships but in a history broken by massive suffering and injustice, a life of Christian love must find expression not merely at the personal or interpersonal level, but also in the larger sphere of socio-political life. Given the new consciousness of massive innocent suffering in our time, Schillebeeckx writes, a political form[13] of love of neighbor has become "one of the historically urgent forms of present-day holiness, the historical imperative of the moment . . . today's "kairos" or moment of grace."[14] Since, as already has been seen, God's presence to human beings in history is not directly immediate, but always a "mediated immediacy",[15] it is only through their engagement in the world, i.e., by working to transform the history of suffering (non-salvation) into a history of salvation, that they encounter God. And because there is a mutually shaping process between human beings and the socio-political structures in which they live, engagement in God's salvific

---

[11]For Schillebeeckx's discussion of the distinction between the reality of salvation which occurs in the world and religion and theology, see *Christ*, 365-66.

[12]While Schillebeeckx speaks of the unity of "mysticism and politics", it is in keeping with his intentions to add the word "ecological" to this phrase because of the cosmic relationships he outlines in the first of his anthropological constants, as has already been noted.

[13]The word "political" in Schillebeeckx's theology does not have the narrow bipartisan meaning it generally has in North American usage but refers to the whole realm of societal and cultural concerns.

[14]"Jerusalem of Benares? Nicaragua of de Berg Athos?", *Kultuurleven*, 50 (1983) 386. For the development of this topic in English, see especially *Christ* 804-21 and *Jesus in our Western Culture: Mysticism, Ethics and Politics* (SCM Press, 1987).

[15]See *Christ* 810-11.

process in the world cannot proceed merely at the personal level, but must include the simultaneous transformation of structures and institutions.[16] The latter involves the two-fold task of protesting against all unjust, dehumanizing and ecologically destructive structures and of working in positive ways for the building of more just, humane and ecologically sound ones.[17]

The intransigency of suffering which never can be fully overcome within history, however, requires that faith and love be strengthened and hope nourished through more immediate encounter with God in prayer and liturgical celebration. In a still unreconciled world, writes Schillebeeckx, the sacraments serve as both "anticipatory, mediating signs of salvation" and "symbols of protest serving to unmask the life that is not yet reconciled."[18] Sacramental liturgy serves not only to affirm but to nourish and keep alive human hope. As the place where Christians become most pointedly aware of the gulf between God's purposes for the world and its present reality, liturgy summons people to liberating action in the world, or else it is meaningless, he states. Liturgy is thus the point of integration or intersection between the mystical and political dimensions of Christian life.[19]

In his most recent writings, Schillebeeckx links the mystical and political dimensions of Christian life even more closely. Defining mysticism as "an intensive form of religious experience or religious love" and politics as "an intensive form of societal engagement," he points out that places of intense suffering and injustice are today the privileged *loci* for the experience of God. Precisely in their simultaneous experience of God's absence from situations of oppression and intense experience of God's presence in their opposition to injustice, many contemporary people come to a new experience of the transcendent; a mystical experience of God as the heart and soul of every true liberation. "The experience of God is the ensouling accompanying moment of concrete deeds of liberation, in which simultaneously this praxis is exceeded: It is the active witness of the God of justice and love."[20] In short, "Mysticism is essentially not just a process of knowledge but a particular way of life--a way of salvation."[21] Ultimately, therefore, it is the praxis of liberation which is decisive in faith life. Yet the inseparable bond between the mystical and

---

[16] Schillebeeckx analyzes the interrelationship between interior freedom and external structures, among other places, in "God, Society and Human Salvation," *Faith and Society* (Acta Cong. International Louv., 1976) 80-93. The intertwining and mutual shaping of the two counteracts the persistent theological assertion that if human beings attend to "conversion of heart," more just institutional structures and relationships will emerge automatically.

[17] The devising of strategies for accomplishing these tasks require the use of human reason and imagination; faith provides not a blueprint for life but the certainty that God wills a just and humane world in which all of God's creatures may live.

[18] *Christ*, 836.

[19] *Christ*, 836.

[20] *Jesus in our Western Culture* 74.

[21] *Jesus in Our Western Culture* 67.

political-ecological dimensions of life remains, for "without prayer or mysticism politics quickly becomes grim and barbaric; without political love prayer or mysticism becomes sentimental and irrelevant interiority."[22]

The final two elements of the framework for an ecological spirituality offered by Schillebeeckx's theology concern the norm or criterion and the goal of such a spirituality. In classical spiritualities, based on the "high Christology" which dominated theological thought throughout most of the Church's history, the goal of spirituality was seen to be the intimate union between the soul and Christ--a "Christ mysticism"--by means of which the process of personal spiritual transformation was effected. This internal transformation, made external by the imitation of Christ's life in one's own life, then issued forth in a life of charity toward one's neighbor.[23] Informed by modern biblical exegesis, contemporary theologies have recovered the importance of the Jesus of history, thereby refocusing and unifying the living of spiritual life at the concrete external level as the praxis of "following after Jesus," and showing that it is precisely in this following of him that one comes to intimate knowledge of and union with God and Jesus. In this shift of direction and focus to which Schillebeeckx's theology makes an important contribution, Jesus is seen not as the goal of spiritual life but rather as its norm and criterion.

What does it mean concretely to say that Jesus is the norm and criterion of spiritual life? In accord with the consensus of contemporary biblical scholarship, Schillebeeckx affirms that the center and heart of all that Jesus proclaims and enacts in his public ministry is the coming Kingdom of God. The concept of God's kingdom, with its origins deep within Jesus' own Jewish tradition with its tumultuous history of disaster and suffering, announces that God's own self will come to reign in history, setting right all wrongs, ending all injustices, putting a definitive end to all evils. In his preaching and public ministry, Jesus does not simply proclaim the kingdom as an event of some distant future time and place, but in his every deed embodies and enacts God's future coming as humanity's salvation already in the here and now. Rooted deeply in his own profound experience of God as *Abba*, loving father, Jesus' preaching and deeds, in their unbreakable and mutually reinforcing unity, reveal God as loving creator who opposes all evil in willing the salvation of all creation. Jesus' kingdom praxis "liberates and makes glad," enabling all who in accepting faith come into contact with him to experience God's saving love as healing, restoring, reconciling even now in their everyday lives. His is a praxis aimed at the wholeness of others, not at a self-serving

---

[22]"Jerusalem of Benares?" 338.

[23]While classical spiritualities were capable of producing deep holiness, as attested by the great saints of the Christian tradition, by making love of neighbor the result or "fruit" of spiritual life, the danger always existed of placing love of neighbor in competition with or secondary to the pursuit of God.

"holiness" as with some sectarian groups within the Judaism of his time.[24] Nowhere is this whole-making praxis more dramatically visible than in Jesus' table fellowship with the "sinners and outcasts", of his society, a fact so repugnant to his opponents that it leads eventually to his death.

But this is not all. Jesus also calls followers into discipleship and invites them to share in and continue his own mission of kingdom building down through the ages. Their own salvific experience of God's kingdom breaking into their lives through the words and deeds of Jesus frees and enables the disciples to do exactly what Jesus did--to make the kingdom of God a reality able to be experienced by others in the present through their own liberating praxis. Jesus in his salvific praxis as norm and criterion of Christian life grounds spirituality concretely in history and the specific needs of each historical time just as Jesus, in his kingdom-centered life and ministry, responded in creative fashion to the concrete needs of his own day. Thus for Schillebeeckx, Christological faith is faith in "creation underlined, concentrated, and condensed: faith in creation as God wishes it to be."[25]

By placing Jesus and his saving praxis in history as norm and criterion of Christian life, Schillebeeckx's theology is able to direct spirituality toward the ultimate goal of life, the making of a new creation. By translating into current historical categories Irenaeus' understanding of creation as the inauguration of a good but yet unfinished process wherein humanity, created in a state of infancy, must progress toward full maturity in history,[26] Schillebeeckx brings the whole of Christian life into eschatological perspective, opening it out toward the future. Guided by the biblical vision of "a new heaven and a new earth" in which "every tear shall be wiped away,"[27] Christian spiritual life becomes nothing less than the engagement of one's whole being in the completion of creation as God would have it. Their personally experienced freedom from sin and guilt, despair, alienation and egotism brought by the salvific encounter with Jesus sets Christians free for ethical commitment to righteousness and peace, for the fashioning of a new world in which the

---

[24]For a discussion of the distinction between wholeness which is the object of Jesus' praxis and the holiness pursued by some other groups within the Judaism of his time, see Elizabeth Schussler Fiorenza, *In Memory of Her* (Crossroad, 1983) 118-30.

[25]"I believe in Jesus of Nazareth: the Christ, the Son of God, the Lord", *Journal of Ecumenical Studies*, 17 (1980) 20.

[26]Western theology in the past has been dominated by the Augustinian view that humanity was created in a state of original perfection but fell from its glorious state through catastrophic sin at the beginning. Salvation in this perspective consists in the return to original perfection. By contrast, Irenaeus sees humanity as created in a state of immaturity and incompleteness and in need of growing gradually into the perfection which God intends for it. In this view, salvation is the completion, not merely the restoration, of creation. For a description of the contrast between the two theological perspectives, see John Hick, *Evil and the God of Love*, Revised ed. (Harper and Row, 1978) 211-15.

[27]Rev. 21:1,4.

healing and making whole of every aspect of creation becomes a possibility.

It is this healed and completed creation, effected through graced human action in history, to which God will give a surprising, new and definitive form in the end. Eschatological salvation, gift of God alone, depends upon--indeed is impossible without--the contribution of human beings to creation's completion in history, for it is the "raw material" from which God will fashion it. Eschatological salvation is creation in its definitively fulfilled form, consisting in the final fulfillment of every person in her or his uniqueness, the healing of all societal alienations and the mending of all ecological destruction.[28] It is a creation which has attained the goal which God intended for it from the beginning. The eschatological goal of a new creation thus challenges any conceptions of spirituality directed merely to the transformation of the entire cosmos. If salvation is indeed the making whole of the whole person in all of her or his relationships--which include relationships to society and to the cosmos, as specified in the anthropological constants--then spiritual life can be nothing short of active participation in the entire salvific process.

Conclusion

Because Schillebeeckx makes creation the basis of his entire theological system, his theology seems particularly suited to the development of a comprehensive and contemporary ecological spirituality. On the one hand, its grounding in creation shifts the focus of theological concern from a narrow anthropocentrism by placing human concerns and actions within the larger context of responsibility for the whole of creation. On the other hand, this creation basis keeps his theology firmly grounded in history with a need to attend to its concrete evils and sufferings. It thus seems capable of addressing the new set of concerns raised by the emerging ecological consciousness while retaining the commitment of liberation theologies, to the overcoming of real social and structural injustices. An ecological spirituality must be sensitive both to the requirements of maintaining a healthy ecological milieu which is capable of sustaining all life forms, and to the necessity of replacing with liberating and life-promoting structures the oppressive socio-political ones which inhibit the flourishing of life. Schillebeeckx's comprehensive theological vision seems eminently suited to offer guidance for faith-inspired living which takes both spheres seriously.

In summary, this brief assembling of key elements from the creation-based theology of Edward Schillebeeckx into a framework for a contemporary ecological spirituality has shown that such a spirituality would possess the

---

[28]The biblical vision of eschatological salvation, which Schillebeeckx translates into these terms, is presented in the three metaphors of the resurrection of the body, the reign of God and the coming of a new heaven and earth. See "Jerusalem of Benares?" 346.

following characteristics: it would be relational, respectful of the entire cosmos, contextual, non-hierarchical and non-dualistic, imaginative and future-oriented, world-affirming and world-building, actively committed to doing of justice on behalf of the poor and exploited of all species, contemplative, celebrative, Jesus-normed and liberating of self, others and the earth.

Part Five

ETHICS

AND ECOLOGICAL VISIONS

ENVIRONMENTAL ETHICS
AND CONTEMPORARY MORAL DISCOURSE

James A. Donahue

This essay explores the relationships between environmental ethics and the major themes that concern contemporary Christian ethics. Its purpose is to suggest ways to understand those concerns so as to lead to the creation of an adequate environmental ethic, one committed to preserving and sustaining the life of the planet in all of its manifestations.

Some presumptions underlie my analysis here that derive from both my reading of the present and historical ecological situation and from conceptual commitments that form my outlook on Christian ethics. Among these is the belief that the current environmental crisis is real and that, without some fundamental personal and societal commitment to change, long established ways of thinking and acting threaten the very future of life on planet earth.[1]

There are many reasons why the environmental crisis fails to grab our attention sufficiently and to generate adequate moral response: the inability of individuals to make conscious connections between personal life and social life, making it difficult to develop the idea of responsibility to others[2]; the failure to make connections between past, present, and future making the concept of responsibility to future generations a difficult achievement; a lack of understanding of the story of the evolving cosmos[3]; and the failure of many of the existing categories and conceptualizations in theology and ethics to explain the complex nature of environmental reality.

---

[1]The literature that demonstrates this point is abundant. For a comprehensive analysis and survey of the contemporary state of the environment, see *The Worldwatch Institute Annual Report on the State of the Environment: 1990* (Washington: The Worldwatch Press, 1990).

[2]For an analysis of the relationship between the personal and the social in ethics, see Donald Jones, ed. *Private and Public Ethics* (New York: The Edwin Mellen Press, 1978). Also see my "Careerism and the Ethics of Autonomy," in *Horizons* 15.2 (Fall 1988).

[3]For a thorough analysis of the idea of cosmos in philosophical and theological literature, see Thomas Berry, *The Dream of the Earth* (San Francisco: Sierra Club Books, 1988). Another helpful understanding of the notion of cosmos in theological context can be found in the works of my colleague, John Haught. See in particular his *The Cosmic Adventure* (New York: Paulist Press, 1984).

I agree with both Alasdair MacIntyre and Jeffrey Stout in their assessment of the current state of contemporary moral discourse as in disarray and in need of retrieval and reconstruction.[4] I disagree with their specific proposals for remedying this situation, however. My own contention is that a lack of imagination in contemporary Christian ethics impedes attempts to make the environment an alluring concern and to develop a commitment to responsive action on behalf of the environment. A fruitful avenue for Christian ethics is to develop a renewed understanding of the role of imagination in morality.

This essay is divided into three parts. Part I outlines components necessary for an adequate Christian ethic of the environment. Here I summarize themes or values which must be included in any conceptual framework that attempts to address the complex reality of the environment.

Part II surveys the main conversations occurring in Christian ethics today. The following thematic polarities form the basis of the more significant debates in contemporary Christian ethics: 1) communitarianism versus liberalism as the organizing order for social and political life; 2) the universal and the particular in ethics; and 3) classicism versus revisionism in natural law ethics. Under each polarity I summarize the main issues and indicate what is at stake in this debate for environmental ethics.

Part III proposes in a preliminary way an understanding of imagination that I contend is essential to develop an ethics that is sufficient to meet the demands of an environmental ethic. Imagination provides a way of deciding between the polarities that exist in moral discourse today.

Components of an Environmental Ethic

While a systematic ordering and justification of the components of an environmental ethic is a task that far exceeds the scope of this paper, it is possible to sketch some of the *necessary* components. An environmental ethic in the Christian context is grounded in the realization that all life constitutes the arena of God's creation and activity. We as humans have a responsibility to come to understand our place in that creation and to exercise responsibility toward that created order. Such an ethical system must include:

--A foundational theory of human nature in which all the aspects of and all the participants in the created order possess intrinsic value and worth by virtue of their participation in that order. This takes the value of creation to be intrinsic to it rather than only of instrumental value to humans.[5]

---

[4]The main works of these authors that have generated significant response are: MacIntyre's *After Virtue* (Notre Dame: University of Notre Dame Press, 1981), and Stout's *Ethics After Babel* (Boston: Beacon Press, 1988).

[5]Theologies that would provide this foundation would be those that emphasize the creationist motifs in scripture and in theological tradition. The works of Matthew Fox, while a focus of some dispute in theological circles, attempt to use the creationist motif as a central lens for beginning theological analysis. See his *Original Blessing: A Primer in Creation Spirituality*

--An understanding of the relational ordering of the natural world in which humans by virtue of reason possess a distinctive though not sovereign position.[6]

--An understanding of a cosmic narrative, a story of the patterning and coherence of the evolution of the cosmos, and an understanding that human value and distinction can be realized only in light of our place in this evolution.[7]

--A sense of the intrinsic relatedness of all persons and things -- a "web of relationships."[8] We can know ourselves only in relationship to others with whom we are integrally bound.

--Imagination as central to the ethical task.[9] Imagination bridges facts, senses, insights, intuitions, and reasons and brings them into consciousness in understandable and compelling ways.

--A understanding of the need for "a sense of place;" that is, an understanding of how living in a particular location (in a home, on a parcel of land, or in a community) over time fosters a respect for and obligation to the caretaking of that location.[10]

--A theological foundation that affirms a sense of both the immanence and transcendence of God in the experience of the moral life.

--A sense of the inherent limitations of human existence.

--An understanding of the sacramentality of all existence, that is, the conviction that all living activity points to and is ultimately meaningful only in relation to the source of that life which is God, the ultimate mystery.[11]

Current conversations in Christian ethics will be assessed in light of these components. My task is to examine how close or how far contemporary

---

(Santa Fe: Bear and Company, 1983).

[6]Two natural law works, one in theological ethics, the other in philosophical ethics, are Joseph Fuchs, *Natural Law* (New York: Sheed and Ward, 1965), and John Finnis, *Natural Law and Natural Rights* (Oxford: Oxford University Press, 1987).

[7]The idea of cosmic narrative is developed in some detail in the works of Thomas Berry and John Haught.

[8]The ideas of relationship and responsibility as central categories for theological ethics derive in large part from the work of H. Richard Niebuhr. See in particular *The Responsible Self* (New York: Harper and Row, 1963). The use of the term "web of relationship" is taken from a superb article by William French, " Nature and the Web of Responsibility: Reflections on a Mother's Death," in *Second Opinion* 10 (March 1989).

[9]In the last section of this paper I contend that the idea of imagination is receiving some attention in theological ethics today and that the most promising work in this area can be found in Philip Keane, *Christian Ethics and Imagination* (New York, Paulist Press, 1986); Kathleen Fischer, *The Inner Rainbow* (New York: Paulist Press, 1983); and Sabina Lovibond, *Realism and Imagination in Ethics* (Minneapolis: University of Minnesota Press, 1983).

[10]For a development of the idea of place as an important aspect of one's sense of being in the world, see Wendell Berry, *Standing by Words* (Berkeley: North Point Press, 1986).

[11]For an introduction to the idea of sacrament in Christian theology, see Bernard Cooke, *Sacraments and Sacramentality* (Mystic: Twenty-Third Publications, 1983).

Christian ethics is from incorporating these insights in order to provide an adequate environmental ethic.

Contemporary Moral Discourse: The Critical Conversations

1. *The communitarianism/liberalism debate.* The publication in 1971 of John Rawl's *A Theory of Justice* precipitated a most serious debate among social and political philosophers about the nature of political, economic, and social organization in Western democracies.[12] This debate has long concerned Christian ethicists as well.[13]

The main lines of division among social ethicists focus on the degree to which the atomistic individual is seen as the primary locus of political and social organization, proponents of liberalism asserting that the individual is prior to the social group in political and social organization, communitarians asserting that the individual is understood only as defined in relationship to the social whole. David Hollenbach summarizes the main contentions of both liberals and communitarians in the far reaching discussion in social ethics. Concerning liberal theorists he says:

> There are a number of common assumptions (among liberal theorists) about the appropriate normative standpoint toward social and political activity and institutions:
> 1. They take as the fundamental norm of social morality the right of every person to equal concern and respect.
> 2. They are committed to organizing the basic political, economic, and social structure of society in a way that will insure that society is a fair system of cooperation between free and equal persons.
> 3. They are especially sensitive to the pluralism of modern moral and political life. Because free and equal persons hold sometimes conflicting philosophical, moral, and religious convictions about the full human good, an effort to implement a comprehensive vision of the good society through law or state power is excluded. Such an effort would violate some person's right to equal concern and respect. This perspective is summarized by affirming that the right is prior to the good.
> 4. Because persons cannot be said to deserve the circumstances of their birth, such as special talents or economic advantages, the tendencies of these circumstances to lead to disproportionate outcomes must be counteracted by appropriate societal intervention.[14]

Hollenbach summarizes the assumptions held by communitarians:

> 1. The human person is essentially a social being. A person's communal roles, commitments, and social bonds are constitutive of selfhood.

---

[12]John Rawls, *A Theory of Justice* (Cambridge: Harvard University Press, 1971).

[13]The literature in this debate is vast. For a comprehensive overview of the main ideas and points of dispute, see David Hollenbach, "Liberalism, Communitarianism, and the Bishop's Pastoral Letter on the Economy," in *The Annual of the Society of Christian Ethics: 1987* (Washington: Georgetown University Press, 1987).

[14]Hollenbach 21.

2. The determination of how persons ought to live, therefore, depends on a prior determination of what kinds of social relationship and communal participation are to be valued as good in themselves. Therefore the good is prior to the right. In fact, the very notion of rights, as it functions in liberalism, denies the constitutive role of community in forming the self.

3. Human beings do not know the good spontaneously, and they cannot know it either by deeper and deeper introspection or by philosophical analysis of selfhood apart from the ends the self ought to pursue. Therefore, if we are to know how persons should live and how communities should be organized we must be schooled in virtue. That is, we must serve as apprentices in a community with a tradition that has taught it virtue.

4. How society as a whole ought to be organized will depend on a vision of the integral good of the whole community, that is, the common good. But because of the deep pluralism of modern social life, we lack a civic community with the traditions and virtues that are needed to teach us what the common good is. Therefore, for the time being, we must concentrate on learning those virtues in communities that are smaller than humanity as a whole or than a nation, that is in local and intentional groups that do share a vision of the human good.[15]

At first glance this conversation is not specifically about the nature of the environment. Yet any action or response (for example social policy) vis a vis the environment will depend on some form of social, economic, and political organization. Moreover, the way that a civic community is organized greatly affects the way what is valuable and important in a society is perceived.

One of the most significant issues in this debate from the perspective of environmental ethics is the theory of value that undergirds both the liberal and communitarian positions. Both polarities value the individual but there are different conceptions of the individual in each. In liberalism the self is the center of the moral world and of the world of social consciousness. Freedom, autonomy, individual rights, and self-interest are conceptually prior to other and more communal considerations such as altruism, participation. The self in liberalism is atomistic, autonomous, and independent from other selves in the social world.[16]

In communitarianism the self comes to full realization and valuation through participation and solidarity with the group.[17] In that I take the environment to be a reality other than the self to which the self must respond (or in some ways the "object" that the self has created), its parameters extend beyond the self to the other, whether that other be individual persons, other creatures and things of the earth, or other social groups. Communitarianism

---

[15]Hollenbach 21-22.

[16]A critique of the idea of the self in liberalism is articulated in a very powerful and engaging way in Robert Bellah's much discussed book, *Habits of the Heart* (Berkeley: University of California Press, 1985). For a collection of responses to this important work, see *Soundings* LXIX.1-2 (Spring/Summer 1986).

[17]An excellent articulation of the communitarian perspective can be found in David Hollenbach's *Claims in Conflict* (Washington: Georgetown University Press, 1978).

seems *in principle* more capable conceptually of including considerations of the entirety of planetary life (the other, the cosmos) than liberalism.

In communitarianism the common good takes precedence over the preferences of the individual: the good of the person has to fit within the concern for the common good of all creation. The problem with communitarianism is the potential for authoritarianism (in Roman Catholic natural law),[18] sectarianism (in Hauerwas, MacIntyre), or the lack of full recognition and respect for the uniqueness of the self. The issue at stake in communitarianism is the degree to which the individual is intrinsically valued in him/herself. Rights theory is an attempt to provide a way of dealing constructively with these issues, although this has historically tended to shift easily into subjectivism and individualistic autonomy.[19]

From an environmental standpoint the test of a theory of value is its ability to view the self as constitutively part of a larger whole. Thus, since on liberal premises the purview of the self is limited to what best promotes the self in terms of advancement and individual enhancement, it is difficult to ground an adequate environmental ethic. Since an environmental ethic must include not only individual persons, but all creatures of the earth, future generations, and the world of future cosmic evolution and possibilities, communitarianism is more poised for construing the part-whole, self-other relationship that is essential for such an ethic than is liberalism.

2. *The Universal and the Particular in Ethics.* The dominant debate in Christian Ethics today is between ethicists whose insights derive from the competing theological outlooks of foundationalism and non-foundationalism (or confessionalism). Douglas Ottati summarizes these two views:

> "For foundationalists true beliefs are based on foundations, and foundations in turn are either self-justifying or irrefutable. . . . Theological foundationalists interpret Christian believing in relation to universally held facts, principles, structures. . . . Foundationalists tend to think that unrelieved pluralism threatens relativistic chaos. For them, a fundamental task of Christian theology is to show how Christian believing connects with a common ground that will help to order public life in a cosmopolitan age."

Non-foundationalists, on the other hand, hold that the search for any universally self-justifying and irrefutable foundations is eventually futile. Human reasoning and experience, they say, are polymorphic functions of specific communities, and only specific communities provide practices, assumptions, commitments and language which people share. Non-

---

[18]An insightful discussion of the role of authority in Roman Catholic theology and natural law ethics is found in T. Howland Sanks, *Authority and the Roman Catholic Church*, and Charles Curran, *Dissent* (Kansas City: Sheed and Ward, 1988).

[19]A representative presentation of rights theory in the liberal tradition can be found in Ronald Dworkin's *Taking Rights Seriously* (Cambridge: Harvard University Press, 1978).

foundationalists theologians eschew universals, and insist that Christian theology should proceed from the inner resources of the Christian community. They tend to think that pluralism (either moral or theological) evidences the particularity of human life and community. For them, the fundamental issue is how the Church can present a distinct alternative to the world's many ways.[20]

These differing theological perspectives lead to very different construals of the task, method, and content of Christian ethics. Foundationalists in general argue that the task of ethics is to search for those universal principles that provide the basis of a common morality. Non-foundationalists contend that an ethics is a product of a particular historical context and a common morality is derivative from particularist moralities.

In this debate Stanley Hauerwas,[21] James McClendon,[22] Alasdair MacIntyre,[23] and Gilbert Meilander[24] argue for the primacy of virtue and narrative in ethics; David Hollenbach,[25] John Coleman,[26] David Tracy,[27] Max Stackhouse,[28] and others argue for the need for a common basis upon which to ground a common morality and to develop a public theology.

One of the most visible forms of this debate focuses on the relationship between an ethics of norms and principles and an ethics of virtue or character.[29] The disputants on this point argue on the one side that ethics is about moral action; doing the right thing involves acting upon those norms derived from some foundational set of understandings or convictions about reality and the nature of the moral life. The virtue-ethicists argue that to be moral means to be schooled in virtue or to possess those qualities of character that represent those excellences of our moral strivings in our pursuance of the

---

[20]Douglas Ottati, "Foundationalism and Non-Foundationalism in Ethics." Unpublished paper delivered at the Christian Ethics Roundtable, Washington, D.C., May 1989.

[21]See particularly his *Vision and Virtue* (Notre Dame: University of Notre Dame Press, 1972), and *A Community of Character* (Notre Dame: University of Notre Dame Press, 1980), and *Truthfulness and Tragedy* (Notre Dame: University of Notre Dame Press, 1978).

[22]See his *Biography as Theology* (Nashville: Abingdon Press, 1974), and *Systematic Theology: Ethics* (Nashville: Abingdon Press, 1986).

[23]MacIntyre, *After Virtue*.

[24]See his *The Theory and Practice of Virtue* (Notre Dame: University of Notre Dame Press, 1986), and *The Limits of Love* (University Park: The Pennsylvania State University Press, 1987).

[25]*Claims in Conflict*.

[26]*An American Strategic Theology* (New York: Paulist Press, 1982).

[27]See his *Blessed Rage for Order* (New York: The Seabury Press, 1975), and *Plurality and Ambiguity* (New York: Harper and Row, 1987).

[28]See his *Ethics and the Urban Ethos* (Boston: Beacon Press, 1972), and *Political Theology and Political Economy* (Grand Rapids: Eerdmann's and Sons, 1987).

[29]A helpful analysis of this issue can be found in two works by Richard Gula, *What Are They Saying About Moral Norms?* (New York: Paulist Press, 1986), and *Reason Informed By Faith* (New York: Paulist Press, 1989).

good. For this latter school, an ethics of being is prior to an ethics of doing; qualities of character are prior to moral action. At the heart of this debate is the idea of narrative and its limits and possibilities. Non-foundationalists contend that an ethic is an historical construction, that it is developed through the cultivation of the virtues in a particular community, and that virtue is best understood in the context of the narrative or story that gives content to the virtue.[30] Any ethic is narrative dependent. Foundationalists criticize a narrative approach for its historical, relativistic perspective and its failure to meet the requirements of universalizability.

From an environmental perspective, the interrelatedness of planetary and cosmological existence makes the dependence of a narrative on the exclusive historical development of a particular community morally problematic. In that the environment is a universal reality, any ethic that is constitutively set apart from other narratives and fails to be integrally connected, *or at least in principle is incapable of interrelatedness with other and all narratives,* must fail the test of an environmental ethics. In this light the criticism by the foundationalists of the confessionalists that a narrative theology is unable to support a "public ethic or theology"[31] is correct. How can the environment, which by its very nature is a public if not cosmological reality, become an intrinsic moral concern in an ethic that derives from a commitment to particularity? Confessionalists like Hauerwas, despite their protestations, are unable to defend their ethic over against the critique of sectarianism and therefore unable to support an adequate environmental ethic.

Yet narrative, at least as a mode of moral analysis without its sectarian thrust, is an essential feature of an environmental ethic. One of the major contributions of a narrative approach to ethics is its capacity to engage the moral agent at a level of involvement that is more compelling than in a foundationalist, rationalist ethic. By its appeal to the imagination and the particularity of the reader's experience, it provides a richer and more textured view of moral agency than does foundationalism. Narratives move us to action in more powerful ways than do rationalist analyses. For this reason narrative is an essential feature of an environmental ethic.

An environmental perspective requires that we examine our existing narratives, understand the consequences of these narratives, and reconstruct an understanding of the development of virtue that can accommodate the demands of a public ethic. Understanding the cosmos through the lens of narrative is necessary.[32] Using a narrative approach we might ask: What is the story of the land, the earth, the cosmos, and the economic order that have

---

[30]This position is best argued in the works of Stanley Hauerwas.

[31]This charge is made most forcefully throughout the works of David Hollenbach and John Coleman.

[32]This point is especially developed in John Haught *The Cosmic Adventure* (New York: Paulist Press, 1986).

created the environmental crisis we are in now? Narrative as a mode of ethical analysis provides a vivid and familiar entry point for developing an understanding of the interrelatedness of the created order.

Other critiques of foundationalism argue against it from an environmental perspective. It is guilty of what Wendell Berry refers to as the problem of abstraction.[33] Its emphasis on the principle of universalizability requires such a generalization of human experience that the moral agent is left distanced from an "immanent" understanding of his or her own humanity. Also, the reductionistic quality to both Kantian and natural law foundationalism tends to reduce human moral experience to either its rationalistic dimensions (Kant) or biological processes (natural law). Both fail to address the multifaceted nature of the moral agent and the natural world. The environment is not simply a rational construct, nor is it merely nature understood as biological processes. Only those moral theories that seek an understanding of the comprehensive nature of moral agency and experience can provide a basis for supporting an adequate environmental ethic.

An environmental ethic requires a narrative approach that avoids the pitfalls of the particularism and sectarianism that have plagued the current proposals for a narrative theology, and one that does not fall into the problems created by an overly abstract and rationalistic foundationalism.

Under the heading of narrative theology might also be included a concern for contextualist theologies[34]. Among these I would include feminist theology and various types of liberation theologies. Criticisms concerning the relationship of the public versus the particular nature of these theologies must be addressed carefully. From the perspective of environmental ethics, these theologies would have to demonstrate that they are capable of accommodating experiences that are more than simply the atomistic experiences of a particular group. It is necessary to demonstrate *how these theologies* reflect possibilities for a universal application, and yet a universality that is not ahistorical and purely formal in its dimensions.

Classicism and Revisionism in Natural Law Ethics

The current ferment in natural law ethics is the source of both confusion and promise for moral theology in the Roman Catholic tradition. The changing state of moral theology has been described as the change from a classicist worldview, composed of static essences, abstract and universal principles, deductive reasoning, pre-established norms, and authority to a post-enlightenment worldview that is historical, dynamic in its understanding of reality, inductive in its method, and open to new data and experience in its

---

[33]Wendell Berry, *Standing by Words*, 178.

[34]This would include most works in Feminist, Black, and Latin American Liberation Theology.

formulations of moral truth.[35] Several strands constitute this ferment, each of which has a significant effect on the way the Catholic tradition analyzes and understands ethical issues.

1. *The Role of Norms in Moral Theology*. In a classicist worldview norms are fixed and pre-determined according to a definition of reality that is immutable and certain because it is communicated by proper authority (the Church, tradition, scripture). Moral responsibility involves the application of these norms case by case (casuistry). In an historical worldview, norms are attempts to capture and realize moral truth and thus constantly need to be formulated and revised according to the changing nature of the historical reality being investigated. The tension here is caused by competing understandings of reality and the nature of the evolving process of moral assessment.

2. *The Meaning of Proportionate Reason*. The debate over proportionalism is a debate over what reasons can be said to be morally justifying for overriding a concrete value.[36] "Proportionate means a formal, structural relation between the premoral value(s) and disvalue(s) in an act. More specifically it means a proper structural relation of the means to the end or of the end to further ends. Proportionate reason, then, is both a concrete value (reason) in the act and its proper structural relation to all of the other elements (premoral disvalues) in the act."[37] At stake in this debate is an understanding of what conditions must apply to make for the moral correctness of an action when the performance of that action involves the performance (or letting happen) of some disvalue.

James Walter, in his insightful essay on the proportionalism debate, asserts that there is a conceptual confusion in the contemporary debate and clarifies this discussion by distinguishing three levels of inquiry: 1) the definition of proportionate reason, 2) the criteria that guide and establish the assessment of proportionate reason, and 3) the modes by which we know that the criteria have been fulfilled.[38]

3. *The Intrinsic/Instrumental Value Debate*. The basic issue in this debate, similar in part to the proportionalism debate, is the degree to which a natural law ethic is committed to consequentialist reasoning that opens the possibility

---

[35]Insightful analysis of the differences between classical and revisionist natural law ethics can be found in Richard Gula, *What Are They Saying About Moral Norms?* (New York: Paulist Press, 1982) 5-25. Also see Charles Curran, *Themes in Fundamental Moral Theology* (Notre Dame: University of Notre Dame Press, 1977).

[36]My interpretation here of the notion of proportionate reason relies in large measure on the work of James Walter. See his "Proportionate Reason and Its Three Levels of Inquiry: Structuring the Ongoing Debate," *Louvain Studies* X.1 (Spring 1984). And see Bernard Hoose, *Proportionalism: The American Debate and Its European Roots* (Washington: Georgetown University Press, 1987).

[37]Walter 32.

[38]Walter 30.

for devaluing persons, things, or actions that are imbued with a sense of value and worth by virtue of their being part of God's creation. Some ethicists[39] claim there is a deontological nature to Christian ethics and argue that an absoluteness to moral norms permits no justifications for overriding them. Revisionists claim that there are reasons that allow for the overriding of some moral values. While all things are imbued with value by virtue of their creation by God, there are times when human reason, God's unique gift to us, requires that we perform those actions that cannot fully realize the absolute good but can only approximate the good in a limited way.[40]

4. *The Understanding of Human Nature*. The most telling criticism of classical natural law ethics is that it tends to view nature in terms of its biological or "physicalist" properties, as opposed to seeing the multiple qualities and characteristics that constitute something's or someone's nature.[41] Sexuality, in perhaps the most vivid example of classicism, is understood and analyzed in light of the physical aspects of sexual genital activity rather than in terms of relationship, emotional development, and human communication. Historically minded natural law theorists see nature in a processive way in light of the many new discoveries that arise in the course of human history.

5. *The Relationship Between Scripture and Ethics*. One of the primary historical failings of Catholic moral theology has been its inability to integrate the moral insights of the natural law with the moral insights from scripture.[42] Compatibility has historically been assumed between the demands of scripture and the demands of the natural law. William Spohn has characterized this relationship as "scripture serving as a moral reminder."[43] With a renewed interest in scripture emerging as a central concern for Catholic theology in general, there are several who see the conflicts between natural law and scriptural imperatives and who assert the primacy of the more prophetic nature of the moral demands of scripture.[44] Catholic ethicists who are nuclear pacifists, for example, suggest that the primary moral commands of scripture absolutely forbid complicity with the development of nuclear

---

[39]See particularly Germain Grisez and Russell Shaw, *Beyond the New Morality* (Notre Dame: University of Notre Dame Press, 1974).

[40]This issue is carefully analyzed in Richard McCormick, S.J., *Doing Evil to Achieve Good* (Milwaukee: Marquette University Press, 1978).

[41]This critique is developed more fully in Charles Curran essay on "Natural Law" in *Themes in Fundamental Moral Theology*, 27-80.

[42]A superb analysis of this issue is found in William Spohn, S.J., *What Are They Saying About Scripture and Ethics* (New York: Paulist Press, 1984).

[43]Spohn 36-53.

[44]This is certainly true of the work of Stanley Hauerwas. An overview of the problems and issues associated with sectarianism and the natural law tradition can be found in James Gustafson, "The Sectarian Temptation," *The Proceedings of the Catholic Theological Society of America Annual Meeting* 1985.

weapons. These critics suggest that the assumption of the easy convergence between scripture and ethics needs to be rethought in a more critical way with greater attention given to the ways that scripture makes demands that are not comfortably realized in human terms.

Classicism, Revisionism, and Environmental Ethics

What is significant in these multiple debates for an environmental ethic? First, the definition of nature in natural law is of utmost importance. On this point the revisionist understanding offers much greater possibilities for accommodating an environmental ethic in that it enlarges the scope of attention in ways that are not done in classical natural law. Human nature must include the human person as a dynamic and not a static reality, historical in all dimensions and in relation to others. The question still exists, however, whether the view of human relationship in revisionism is wide enough to accommodate the range of environmental concerns that is necessary for full environmental awareness. James Gustafson has indicted modern theological ethics for its anthropocentric as opposed to theocentric caste, and it is appropriate to ask whether revisionist natural law is sufficiently cosmological or theocentric in its understanding of nature.[45] Or has revisionist nature become an anthropomorphic projection? I suspect that it has.

Is the historical-mindedness of revisionist natural law mired in an historicism that would prevent it from developing either a sufficiently comprehensive understanding of nature or an accommodation to other views of nature that are born of other cultures or other times? In other words, is revisionist natural law suspect on the same grounds that narrative theology is, in that context, culture, community, and time are the defining marks of a theory of nature, value, and truth? The need for an environmental ethics that can accommodate the unlimited possibilities of the created order demands an historical grounding that is not confined to the particularities of a limited view of history.

Does the concept of proportionate reason sufficiently reflect the intrinsic value of the created moral order or is it a form of disguised utilitarianism? Without offering an "edge of the wedge" argument to dispute this point, one can still ask whether there is a sufficiently critical understanding of reason in revisionist natural law. Is reason reflective only of human (subjective) biases and prejudices; can reason offer possibilities for incorporating, minimally, other human persons or, maximally, those beings in the created order that have a claim to value by virtue of their place in the cosmic narrative?

Has the notion of norm lost its punch in revisionism? Can revisionism generate the norms necessary to meet the challenge of the environmental

---

[45]On this important issue, see James Gustafson, *Ethics From a Theocentric Perspective* Vol. 1. (Chicago: University of Chicago Press, 1981).

crisis? Movement to environmental action will arise only if there is a compelling notion of the *necessary* nature of responsiveness; we must be moved to act because it is perceived as our moral duty. There is a movement to a voluntarist notion of normativity in revisionist ethics by a deemphasis of the deontological or absolutist nature of the moral problem. This development is understandable as a post-enlightenment phenomenon, but serious questions remain about whether or not duty and obligation have become weakened or diminished in their power.

All these compelling concerns must be raised about the classical-revisionist natural law debate. While the move from the rigidity, stasis, and authoritarianism of classical natural law is to be applauded as liberating to the human spirit, from an environmental perspective there remain serious questions: does revisionism merely provide new conceptual categories for creating new environmental catastrophes? or does revisionism hold promise for ushering in a new way of envisioning the environment and of understanding our moral response to it?

The Moral Imagination: Finding a Road through Polarities

Throughout this essay I have been critical of the categories and conceptualizations that we in Christian theology have used to understand the work that we do, the world that we live in, and (with Gustafson) the God that we believe in and worship. I have argued that an adequate environmental ethic requires moving past the existing polarities that permeate our moral conversations. Some recent writings offer promising possibilities for helping us to address the existing deficiencies. I refer specifically to works that analyze the dimensions of the moral imagination. Works that I find particularly helpful for understanding the imagination are Philip Keane's *Christian Ethics and Imagination*, the work of Wendell Berry, Kathleen Fischer's *The Inner Rainbow*, Sabina Lovibond's *Realism and Imagination in Ethics*, and William Spohn's essay on narrative theology in *Theological Studies*.

These works are significant for an ethics of the environment because each sees the imagination as a way of holding in tension the polarities that permeate our contemporary moral discourse and contends that imagination allows us to envision possibilities for construing our world and our ethics in new and constructive ways. Some examples illustrate the possibilities.

In an instructive review and critique of the literature on the use of parable and narrative in Christian Ethics,[46] William Spohn alludes to a notion of imagination that "grasps the whole which the parts must fit." He cites Sabina Lovibund's work on imagination and finds similarities between her ideas and the "part-whole" structure of H. Richard Niebuhr's theology and

---

[46]William Spohn, S. J. "Parable and Narrative in Ethics," *Theological Studies* 51.1 (March 1990).

ethics. The idea of imagination as providing a mode of apprehension of the "whole" has obvious significance for an environmental ethic. This understanding permits a person to hold within a "holistic" understanding points of tension and disagreement, while also allowing these "partial claims" and divergences to be submitted to some more comprehensive reference point for resolution or action. In an environmental ethic, the cosmos, understood as the arena of God's creation, serves as the "whole" or larger reference point which the parts must "fit." This understanding of how moral imagination works requires further exploration.

The work of Wendell Berry is finally receiving the kind of critical attention that it well deserves from intellectuals.[47] While there is much about imagination in Berry's writings that provides essential insights for an environmental ethic, there are two points that I will mention, one of them methodological, the other substantive.

Methodologically, Berry's use of metaphors for capturing the relationships between different realities provides a way of understanding how two realities, seemingly dissimilar and separate, reflect an essential connectedness among objects and experiences. Berry's use of marriage[48] and farming[49] as metaphors for the relationship to the land and the responsibility of community demonstrates that human activity entails a necessary connection among people, events, and environment, within the drama of human existence. With the necessity of this connection comes a realization of the moral responsibility to respond. Theologies like that of Sally McFague[50] would also be consistent with this methodological insistence on the use of metaphor for understanding Christian ethics.

Substantively, Berry's development of the necessity of having a sense of place is essential not only for construing our relationship to the earth, but also for leading to a basis of action to take responsibility for one's home, for where one is. In associations like this imagination and will become linked and lead to moral action. If the imaginative construal of reality is compelling, the will becomes engaged. This thesis, of course, requires further defense.

Kathleen Fischer's *Inner Rainbow* offers some intriguing insights for an environmental ethic. Fischer uses the image of an inner rainbow to help in understanding the imagination:

> As sunlight is reflected and refracted by a curtain of falling rain, it produces a bow or arc of prismatic colors--a rainbow . . . . It is a potent symbol . . . . It is the bridge which joins God and earth, the sacred and the secular, bringing them into unity in our lives. The imagination enables us to live in multi-leveled, multi-colored truth, and

---

[47]For a comprehensive review of the work of Wendell Berry, see Bill McKibban, "Today's Prophet of Ecology," *The New York Review of Books* 37.10 (1990): 30-35.

[48]Wendell Berry, *The Country of Marriage* (New York: Harcourt Brace Jovanovich, 1975).

[49]Wendell Berry, *Farming: A Handbook* (New York: Harcourt Brace Jovanovich, 1974).

[50]See particularly her *Models of God* (Philadelphia: Fortress Press, 1987).

to receive the truth which is pervaded by mist and mystery. It is also the human power that opens us to possibility and promise, the not yet of the future . . . . The imagination involves the total person, on many levels, and calls for participation. . . . The power of the imagination to hold multiple dimensions of truth in unity relies on analogy, a style of language and thought which illumines the meaning of one thing by reference to another.[51]

The thesis here is similar to the one found in Spohn and Lovibond: imagination as a mode of perception enables us to see a more comprehensive reality as the grounding for our ethical actions, and to see by analogy and by juxtaposition connections and relationships among ideas, insights and objects, as well as persons. A sound environmental ethic requires exactly such connections.

Philip Keane's *Christian Ethics and the Imagination* explores the way that a renewed understanding of imagination can help to enliven moral discourse in contemporary Christian Ethics. His primary insight is that a mode of theology that is non-discursive provides a way to conceive of theology and ethics which is richer and better able to capture the full dynamics of moral experience.[52] He argues that a narrative theology and a hermeneutic theology provide a new foundation for moral theology. This argument implies that the environment cannot be captured sufficiently in a strictly propositional theology or an ethics of norms and principles but requires the presence of creative imagining. As I have demonstrated throughout this essay, on this point he is absolutely correct.

Conclusion

The gap between the current conversations in Christian Ethics and an adequate environmental ethic is wide. There is much unfinished business. My analysis here suggests that the resources for bridging this chasm exist in the current bodies of literature in Christian Ethics, although in inchoate form. The task of reconstructing our moral outlooks in the service of the environment will require the willingness of Christian ethicists to critically assess the categories they employ, and the implications of their insights in light of their effect on the cosmic moral order. Without this reconstruction Christian ethics runs the risk of assisting in the demise of the order that God has bestowed on us.

---

[51]Kathleen Fischer, *The Inner Rainbow: The Imagination in Christian Life* (New York: Paulist Press, 1983) 1, 17.

[52]Philip Keane, *Christian Ethics and the Imagination: A Theological Inquiry* (New York: Paulist Press, 1984).

CATHOLICISM AND THE COMMON GOOD OF THE BIOSPHERE

William French

The increasing weight and range of humanity's impact on our natural environment requires an ecological broadening of our notion of the "common good." Traditionally Catholic theologians have meant by the "common good," the general good of the local community or the nation-state, as opposed to the private good of the individual. However, Pope John XXIII in *Pacem in Terris* (1963) distinctively emphasized the priority of the good of a broader community, the "common good of the entire human family."[1] He appealed to various "signs of the times" as warrants for his expansion of the common good notion beyond its traditional borders to include now the well-being of the global human community.

Important ecological "signs of the times" have grown more apparent since Pope John's day and seem to require another expansion of our understanding of the common good. Today's "signs" of increasing degradation of the planetary biosphere suggest that a expansion of the common good is needed to include not just the global human family, but the entire planetary biospheric community--that is, both humanity and all of the rest of nature. The burgeoning new data about our alterations of Earth's ecosystems highlights old truths--that we are a part of a natural order and dependent upon its integrity and well-being--and shocks us with new truths--that nature is relatively fragile compared to the power and energy being unleashed by humanity's historically recent technological and industrial advances.

Reevaluating the Revisionist Flight from Natural Law

Humanae Vitae has had a heavy impact upon the ongoing formation of Catholic moral theology. The prominence of the debates generated by it have too often tended to narrow attention to sexual ethical topics where the

---

[1] *Acta Apostolicae Sedis* 55 (1963): I have drawn from the text of the encyclical found in David J. O'Brien and Thomas A. Shannon, eds., *Renewing the Earth: Catholic Documents on Peace, Justice and Liberation* (Garden City, NY: Image Books, 1977) 124-70. Hereafter, cited in text as PT with section numbers.

magisterial affirmation of natural law reasoning has remained most prominent. This led many to associate the natural law heritage primarily with rigorous condemnations of artificial birth control, homosexuality, and all forms of non-procreative sexual activity. It energized methodological debates regarding the status of moral absolutes and the existence of intrinsically evil acts.

In partial reaction revisionist thinkers increasingly substituted a personalist centered methodology focusing upon the value of the full human person and their relationships in place of natural law reasoning. This allowed the revisionists to interpret sexual activity in a broader framework of human relationships and thus to overcome some of the perceived rigidity and narrowness of the physicalist mode of reasoning employed in the encyclical. For many revisionists little seemed at stake in jettisoning the natural law heritage because, in addition to its association with narrow physicalism, important movements in contemporary philosophy were dismissing the static metaphysics of the "classicist" worldview even as many theologians called for more dynamic, biblically based moral categories, perspectives, and paradigms.

Concurrently, other moralists attempting to affirm both the magisterial condemnation of artificial modes of contraception and the adequacy of natural law methodology tended to interpret natural law as a set of claims about the universal, i.e., transcultural, moral principles supported via judgments of practical reason. John Finnis, for example, has elaborated an influential account of the natural law as a "set of basic practical principles" which are grounded in the methodological standards of practical reasoning which enable us to "distinguish sound from unsound practical thinking."[2] While he seeks to locate his approach in close convergence with the natural law system of Thomas Aquinas, Finnis consistently appropriates the deontological elements of Thomas' system without the broader ontological claims about the order of creation which supported Thomas' analysis of the findings of right reason. In Finnis' account, as Lloyd Weinreb has recently put it, we get a "natural law without nature."[3]

Prominent also in recent moral theology has been an accommodation to rights theory and a stress on social justice concerns framed usually as a concern for the promotion for full human rights.[4] The influence of Liberationist concerns has helpfully increased a sensitivity to human rights and the need to transform oppressive social and economic systems. At the same time that the American Bishops' Pastoral Letters on war and peace and the U.S. economy (*The Challenge of Peace*, and *Economic Justice for All*) have

---

[2]John Finnis, *The Natural Law and Natural Rights*(Oxford: Clarendon Press, 1980) 23.

[3]Lloyd Weinreb, *Natural Law and Justice* (Cambridge: Harvard University Press, 1987) 108-17, 122-26.

[4]See generally David Hollenback, S.J., *Claims in Conflict: Retrieving and Renewing the Catholic Human Rights Tradition* (New York: Paulist Press, 1979).

achieved some public notoriety, the general public continues to associate Catholic moral theology with emphases upon human dignity and rights in the social sphere and the right to life in the procreative sphere. Human rights are important claims to affirm but such claims are hardly distinctive contributions of the Catholic tradition. Rather the stress on human rights is the primary contribution of Western liberal culture and political thought and the Church's prominent usage of rights theory illustrates an important accommodation that the Church is making to modern culture.

Many in the animal welfare movement wish to emphasize "animal rights" in order to ground strong claims about human duties regarding nonhuman sentient life. But there are major difficulties in centering environmental ethics in a rights-based model. Rights claims have been used historically to focus attention on the value of discrete individuals, whereas ecology as a science stresses an understanding of individual animals, plants, and natural entities within their multiple relationships in dynamic biospheric communities or ecosystems. Rights claims certainly have their place in environmental ethical reasoning, but their usage must be balanced out by a prior emphasis upon the need to defend the integrity of the whole ecosystem. This requires some sort of aggregative ethical principle and that is what the natural law tradition's focus on the common good provides.

The recent emergence of our burgeoning ecological problems throws into prominent relief the increasing relevance of the distinctive Catholic tradition of natural law reasoning with its long held stress upon the priority of the common good. Because nature is now threatened, many are coming to take seriously the normative implications of the biospheric orderings and ecological structures which condition life on this planet and set necessary constraints upon certain sorts of human action.

Despite the movement among many Catholic moralists to distance themselves from the natural law tradition or reinterpret it along deontological lines, there may yet be great vitality left in the tradition of natural law reasoning. The emphasis of that tradition upon the priority of the common good over private or lesser goods seems to be especially relevant today as we seek to account for our participation within the broader biosphere and to understand our responsibilities of protecting its integrity and well-being.[5]

---

[5]The traditional Catholic moral focus on the common good corresponds closely to the emerging critique in political theory of the individualistic excesses of liberalism. This communitarian approach, spearheaded by Michael Sandel, Roberto Mangabeira Unger, and Michael Walzer among others, raises telling arguments for the need to recover the priority of the community and its well-being. See Michael Sandel, *Liberalism and the Limits of Justice* (New York: Cambridge University Press, 1982); Roberto Mangabeira Unger, *Knowledge and Politics* (New York: Free Press, 1975); and Michael Walzer, *Spheres of Justice* (New York: Basic Books, 1983). See also Amy Gutman, "Communitarian Critics of Liberalism," *Philosophy and Public Affairs* 14 (1985): 308-22. Similarly the common good tradition coheres rather closely with the focus in much recent feminist literature upon the self as inextricably relational and

Descriptive "Wholes" which Frame and Shape Moral Evolution

How broadly or restrictively we draw the circumference of the aggregate, community, totality or "whole" under question is critical in moral analysis. The horizon of what we take to be the relevant "community" sets a boundary or limit to our moral consideration and assessment. The definition of the range of the human beings and other entities which are held to make up the "community" becomes a basic moral judgment, for it determines just which classes of human beings and other entities will be given moral consideration and which will not. The description of the "whole" or "community" holds great normative weight, for it conditions where moral attention will be directed and which questions, concerns, and values will demand or require a response.

The practical significance of the choice regarding the correct interpretive framework of moral analysis is well illustrated by the early debates which raged in Catholic moral theology regarding the legitimacy of organ donorship. Concerned in part to check certain types of radical medical experimentation seen so recently in the outrages of Nazi medicine, Pope Pius XII emphasized that the traditional "principle of totality" held that one's bodily organs and members are meant to serve one's total physical health and integrity for as parts they are to serve the whole of one's body. They have no meaning or finality outside the organism. The part "is entirely absorbed by the totality of the organism to which it is tied."[6] This implied to many moral theologians that it was impermissible to make use of the new medical advances allowing the donation of a kidney to another person. Many continued to classify such a gift as an act of mutilation and thus illicit. Over time, however, the dominant interpretation among Catholic moralists has understood that construal of the totality was too restrictive in narrowing the finality of the kidney to the service of physical health, for this failed to do justice to the complexity of the human persons involved in relationships and community. Catholic personalist oriented moralists, like Martin Nolan, argue that the integrity to be served is not the restrictive biological one but rather a much broader total good, namely that of the person "achieved in self-outpouring in community."[7] Where the traditional physicalist/totality position describes and evaluates kidney donorship as mutilation, the broader personalist perspective redescribes and reevaluates it as an act of charity and courage, to be applauded and respected, not condemned. The different discernment of the totality or whole to be considered generates a different fundamental description of the act and thus a different moral evaluation.

---

participating within familial and communal webs of relations. See Carol Gilligan, *In a Different Voice* (Cambridge: Harvard University Press, 1982) and Jean Grimshaw, *Philosophy and Feminist Thinking* (Minneapolis: University of Minnesota Press, 1986), 162-86.

[6]Martin Nolan, "The Principle of Totality in Moral Theology," *Absolutes in Moral Theology?*, ed. Charles E. Curran (Westport, CT: Greenwood P, 1968) 232-36.

[7]Nolan 243.

The choice of our framework of interpretation of the common good is as fundamental in social and political spheres, as is the question of what is the morally relevant totality in the medical sphere. A traditional understanding of the common good as the good or well-being of the local community or nation rightly highlights our responsibilities to serve the good of the others to whom we are bound. Problematically such a notion does little to encourage sensitivity to our responsibilities to others outside our community or to other human communities. By restricting the meaning and finality of our acts to our community, we cast the moral terrain beyond the borders into deep shadow. In this region the rule of force and the threat of anarchy hold away.

In what follows I will argue that the "signs of the times" point to our common membership in the biospheric community and that this term "community" is rightly used. Late in the twentieth century it is clear that among the various commons we owe allegiance to is the planetary biosphere as a whole upon whose integrity and well-being the health of all lesser common goods depends.

Many think of our emerging ecological threats as analogous in magnitude to the peril posed by the nuclear arms race. This analogy, however, fails to catch the positive dynamism of the short-term economic, political, and social interests which fuel the practices which promote ecological degradation. Nuclear warfare is not an inevitable outgrowth of our national life or of our relations with other nations. But increasingly severe ozone depletion, species extinction, acid rain and other types of pollution, jungle destruction, soil erosion, and (perhaps) global warming are inextricably tied to fundamental industrial, technological, and agricultural processes which sustain the vast productivity of our modern economies and fulfill in some measure the popular expectations regarding consumption patterns which mark the "good life." While almost no community or group save perhaps some bizarre terrorist organization understands their interest to lie in promoting nuclear war, every national community sees its well-being tied to expanding economic growth and resource consumption.[8] Powerful corporate and personal incentives drive us, fueling practices and life-patterns which promote environment degradation.

It is for this reason that Hans Jonas holds the threat of processive ecological degradation to be genuinely more pressing than that posed by our nuclear arsenals. As he argues,

> . . . averting the [ecological] disaster asks for a revocation of the whole life-style, even of the very principle of the advanced industrial societies, and will hurt an endless number of interests . . . . It thus will be much more difficult than the prevention of nuclear destruction, which after all is possible without decisive interference with the general conditions of our technological existence.[9]

---

[8]See Herman Daly and John Cobb, Jr., *For the Common Good* (Boston: Beacon, 1989).

[9] Hans Jonas, *The Imperative of Responsibility: In Search of an Ethics for the Technological Age*, trans. Hans Jonas with David Herr (Chicago: University of Chicago Press, 1984) 202.

Rationality as the Traditional Ticket for Moral Consideration

Human-centered ethical traditions and modern technological practices mitigate against any easy acceptance of the expansion of the common good to include the good of the nonhuman biosphere as well as that of the human community. Deep traditions in philosophy and theology have polarized humanity and the rest of nature and restricted inherent value and dignity to humans based upon claims about our unique capacities of rationality. Often the animal species have been employed as conceptual foils in our reflections on human nature. Thus those characteristics that distinguish us from the animals have been highlighted--reason, language, tool-making, and self-consciousness--as the essence of what it means to be human, while those characteristics which we share with animals--our embodiment, our patterns of instinctive behavior, our physiological finitude--have been downplayed. In this way philosophers have often minimized our rootedness in, and connectedness to, nature, and theologians have often stressed our disassociation with, absolute superiority over, the rest of creation. God's grant in Genesis of dominion over the rest of nature, thus has often been construed as an authorization of domination, conquest, and the unchecked use of nature.

The tendency to draw a strict moral dualism between humanity and the rest of nature can be seen in both Thomas Aquinas' and Immanuel Kant's influential ethical systems. Both felt that because animals lack rationality it is proper to use them as instruments to serve human well-being and interests. For Thomas animals lack "mastery" over their action. Animals thus exist for the sake of humans and are appropriately "subject to slavery."[10] In Kant's *Foundations of the Metaphysics of Morals* he argues similarly that rational beings are designated persons, while merely natural nonrational beings, namely animals, are properly things. Persons by virtue of our rationality are "ends-in-themselves" and have rights due us because of our intrinsic worth, but animals "have only a relative worth as a means," that is as a means to the furthering of the interests of rational beings who are true ends.[11]

This view has strongly shaped modern ethical theory and has led most ethicists until quite recently to affirm that human life has a monopoly upon intrinsic value and consequently on rights. In the work of many theorists, however, we can see a tension between their desire to acknowledge that we do owe animals certain obligations of care and their affirmation of moral categories and models which simply cannot include in any central and coherent way questions of the moral value of animal life. W.D. Ross, for example, accepted that we have a duty to animals to avoid causing them needless suffering. Yet he held that "we should probably say the animals have

---

[10]Thomas Aquinas, *Summa Contra Gentiles*, trans. Vernon J. Bourke, 4 vols (Notre Dame: University of Notre Dame, 1975) 3: 115-16.

[11]Immanuel Kant, *Foundation of the Metaphysics of Morals*, trans. Lewis White Beck (Indianapolis: Bobbs-Merrill Co., 1959) 46.

not rights" because they are not the sort of creatures who can make "claims" upon agents.[12]

Similarly John Rawls in his magisterial account of justice stresses that there are limits to his theory and that he has given no account "of right conduct in regard to animals and the rest of nature." Tension is manifest between his affirmation that "we are not required to give strict justice" to creatures lacking "the capacity for a sense of justice" and his acceptance that we have "duties of compassion and humanity" to animals which require that we not be cruel to them or that we do not destroy a whole species. He states:

> I shall not attempt to explain these considered beliefs. They are outside the scope of the theory of justice, and it does not seem possible to extend the contract doctrine so as to include them in a natural way. A correct conception of our relations to animals and to nature would seem to depend upon a theory of the natural order and our place in it. One of the tasks of metaphysics is to work out a view of the world which is suited for this purpose; it should identify and systematize the truths decisive for these questions. How far justice as fairness will have to be revised to fit into this larger theory it is impossible to say.[13]

Rawls published this in 1971, the year after the first Earth Day celebrations. While no thinker can be expected to include every issue for coverage in their project, the ecological "signs of the times" since 1971 suggest that our relations with nature can no longer be allowed to remain in the conceptual shadows on the margins of our ethical theories. If our relations with nature do not fit coherently into the currently reigning models of moral reasoning, then this is more a sign of the inadequacy of our models than of the appropriateness of giving only marginal importance to the question of the moral status of our relationships with nature. The emerging ecological "signs of the times" seem not to compel us to get on with the task noted, but not engaged in, by Rawls, namely that of situating our theories of justice, rights, and responsibility coherently within a broader framework of reasoning about the "natural order and our place in it." The Catholic natural law heritage, with its elaboration of ethical claims backed by an explicit framework of metaphysical affirmations, may well provide important resources for this enterprise. Obviously, as the citation from Thomas illustrates, the natural law heritage gave priority to the whole or common aggregate within a framework of claims dominated by an anthropocentric value theory. Clearly a flat-footed appropriation of Thomas' system will not provide the resources we need for a contemporary ecological ethic. As I argue later, we need a critical retrieval of Thomas's focus upon the participation of individuals within social and natural wholes, divorced somewhat from his anthropocentrism, and filled out and balanced by the powerful theocentric and biocentric themes which pervade his *Summae*.

---

[12]W.D. Ross, *The Right and the Good* (Oxford: Clarendon Press, 1930) 50.
[13]John Rawls, *A Theory of Justice* (Cambridge: Harvard University Press, 1971) 512.

Pacem in Terris (1963)

Pope John XXIII appeals to the "signs of the times" in a prominent fashion for the first time in the social encyclical tradition to support his argument for the need to expand our notion of the common good to that of the "universal common good" which he defines as the good of the "entire human family" (PT 139-46). He employs a rough method of correlation to guide his application of the moral doctrines of the natural law tradition to the concrete problems needs made manifest by an examination of the signs of the times. We face the challenge of vast cultural, economic, and political revision, he holds, because the spheres of human endeavor "must all be adjusted to the era of the atom and of the conquest of space . . ." (PT 156).

The encyclical is quite traditional in its use of natural law reasoning to appeal in the introduction to the order of the universe and the order "imprinted in man's heart" (PT 1,5). Likewise it remains traditional in Part I, where it examines the "order between men" in terms of natural rights, and in Part II, where it focuses upon the "common good" within a political community or state. His analysis becomes quite innovative, however, where for the first time in the social encyclical tradition he argues at some length that we now need to recognize the interdependence of all the world's national communities and their joint participation in the "universal common good," the "universal family of mankind" (PT 132-39, 145). Just as the common good of any polity requires the guardianship and coordination of a government, so too the "world-wide dimensions" of our historical problems demand some sort of "supranational or worldwide public authority" (PT 138).

In the pope's words, because of "the far-reaching changes which have taken place in the relations within the human community," the "universal common good" is threatened by "problems that are very grave, complex and extremely urgent . . . ." His conclusion is that "at this historical moment the present system of organization and the way its principle of authority operates on a world basis no longer correspond to the objective requirements of the universal common good" (PT 134-35).

Since *Pacem in Terris* it has become increasingly plain that any substantial agenda for peace on earth must also require a concerted effort of human restraint to achieve peace with the earth. The signs of the times suggest that John XXIII's expansion of the common good is itself inadequate because it is too restrictive. The universal common good may no longer be thought of in purely human-centered terms as the universal family of mankind. John XXIII rightly saw that the problem with the traditional analysis of the common good which took the local or national community as the relevant framework for moral analysis and standard of action left the relationship between national communities to be adjudicated by raw force. Given the vast increase in human technical and military power, moral and political anarchy can no longer be allowed to control international relations. *Pacem in Terris* rightly attempts to overcome this anarchy by pointing out the necessity of discerning a broader community in which all the nations and peoples participate. This reconstrual of humanity as a universal community attempts to broaden our moral and political loyalties beyond the horizon of our local and national communities by providing a new, more expansive moral framework for assessing our obligations and responsibilities.

Since 1963 "signs" have appeared which suggest that even Pope John's understanding of the common good as the good of entire human family is itself too truncated today to provide firm moral guidance in an ecologically imperiled age. Rather it is the good of the entire biosphere today which is the morally relevant aggregate that needs to be highlighted and responded to, for it is this entire aggregate that is threatened. Our problems have become truly global in scope. When the common good is restricted to the good of humanity, then our dependence upon, and moral obligations owed to, the rest of the nonhuman natural world are easily forgotten. In an anthropocentric account of the common good, moral consideration is restricted to human life and moral analysis remains focused upon human relations. Human relations, however, with nonhuman living beings--elephants, snaildarters, and trees--with living systems--the Amazon jungle, a marshland--or with non-living natural entities, like soil or the ozone layer, remain beyond the border of moral consideration, and thus are neatly ceded to the regime of techne, the rule of raw force guided by utilitarian goals of efficiency and production.

The inadequacy of anthropocentric construals of the common good has not been manifest so graphically before because the range of our ability to transform and destroy nature had been severely limited by the relative weakness of our earlier technological and industrial capabilities. Now in a rush all that has changed. In *Pacem in Terris* John XXIII rightly situates the social question in its global social context. Today we must understand further that the global social question is situated within a global ecological context. The liberation of peoples and the promotion of justice and equity will mean little if we continue to ignore our fundamental responsibilities to the planetary community of the biosphere.

The Greening of Recent Papal Thought

Pope John Paul II has long been influenced by the perspectives of the personalist movement in philosophy and Catholic theology. Accordingly he has in *Laborem Exercens* (*On Human Work*, 1981) stressed the dignity of the human person and his or her freedom to transform the earth through work and the use of technology and industry.[14] However, more recently in the encyclical *Sollicitudo Rei Socialis* (*On Social Concern*, 1987) he articulates sharp limits to our use and transformation of nature because "when it comes

---

[14]Pope John Paul II, *Laborem Exercens* (Washington, D.C.: United States Catholic Conference, 1981).

to the natural world, we are subject not only to biological laws but also to moral ones . . . ."[15] This document is the first in the social encyclical tradition to give any sustained attention to ecological issues. While it argues that industrial and economic development cannot "exclude respect for the beings which constitute the natural world . . . ." (SRS 34), the dominant focus of the encyclical is an affirmation of the world-wide social and economic development of peoples. Only three and a half sections out of a total forty-six are developed specifically to ecological issues.

While *Sollicitudo Rei Socialis* remains caught in the pro-transformationist and pro-development bias exhibited in so much of recent Catholic personalist thought, other magisterial documents have begun to push more deeply and consistently for industrial, technological, and economic restraint in order to protect the biosphere. Both the Filipino and the Indonesian Bishops have recently written pastoral letters on ecology which get beyond the developmentalist framework of *Sollicitudo Rei Socialis*.[16]

In the recent World Day of Peace message of Pope John Paul II titled "Peace With God the Creator, Peace With All of Creation" (January 1, 1990), we have the most extensive papal statement ever on ecological issues.[17] The letter begins with this statement: "In our day there is a growing awareness that world peace is threatened not only by the arms race . . . but also by a lack of due respect for nature." He writes of the "sense of precariousness and insecurity" we feel in contemplating these new worldwide environmental problems and notes that "a new ecological awareness is beginning to emerge which . . . ought to be encouraged . . . ." (PWC 1) He stresses the integrity of nature and says that the "earth is ultimately a common heritage . . ." (PWC 7-9). Ecology stresses, the pope holds, that there is "an order in the universe which must be respected" and he charges us to "preserve this order for the well-being of future generations" (PWC 15).

Our responsibilities for the common good include, he argues, an "obligation to contribute to the restoration of a healthy environment." Christians must realize "their responsibility within creation" and "their serious obligation to care for all of creation" (PWC 15-16). While employing common good language, the pope does not seem to wish to expand the category to include in direct fashion the good of the nonhuman participants in the biosphere. By common good he seems to understand solely the good of humans. It is because our well-being is dependent upon the well-being of the environment that we are charged to protect the environment. An "updated

---

[15]Pope John Paul II, *Sollicitudo Rei Socialis* (Washington, D.C.: United States Catholic Conference, 1987) section 34. Hereafter cited in text as SRS with section numbers.

[16]Catholic Bishops conference of the Philippines, "What is Happening to Our Beautiful Land? A Pastoral Letter on Ecology," *CBCP Monitor* 9 (1986): 16-19,22,27,30-33.

[17]John Paul II, "Peace With All Creation," *Origins* 19 (1989): 465-68. Hereafter cited in text as PWC and page numbers.

charter of human rights" must include, he believes, the "right to a safe environment" (PWC 9). While he holds that the earth is a common heritage, he approvingly cites *Gaudium et Spes*, (para. 69) where it states that "God destined the earth and all it contains for the use of every individual and all peoples" (PWC 8). While he states that "merely . . . better management or a more rational use of the earth's resources" is not a radical enough solution to our moral crisis, still we should push for "a more internationally coordinated approach to the management of the earth's goods" (PWC 5,9). This emphasis upon human rights and the "goods of nature" suggests that while we are to "keep ever alive a sense of fraternity" (PWC 16) with nonhuman beings and natural entities, their value is still derived from their resource value to present and future generations of humans. The pope speaks of the "aesthetic value of creation" in its "deep restorative power" to bring "peace and serenity" to humans who contemplate its beauty (PWC 14).

Pope John Paul II in this document examines the implications of the ecology crisis for the common good of the human family, but he does not explicitly extend the concept of common good beyond the human community to elaborate a sense of human and nonhuman nature's common participation in a universal community of the planetary biosphere. His anthropocentric interpretation of the common good restricts the boundary of the moral community deserving of direct moral consideration to the class of human persons. Ecologically enlightened human self-interest then becomes the primary moral argument for environment protection. Moral concern is extended to the non-human world but only insofar as its well-being can serve human well-being. While the pope does argue that we should care for all of creation because God cares for all of creation, the dominant argument in the document for a care for nature remains our care for human value and rights.

This human-centered view of the common good, I will argue, fails to go far enough because it does not provide a strong enough challenge against the anthropocentric moral tradition which has for so long helped us enjoy easy consciences even as we have proceeded to exploit, develop, and destroy many species and ecosystems of the biosphere. On the other hand, the Catholic tradition does not support the view of biocentric equality in which human life is of no more value than other forms of life.

Shallow or Deep Environmentalism

A number of environmentalists have begun to distinguish "shallow" from "deep" ecological views. Shallow ecology is anthropocentric and restricts intrinsic value solely to the community of rational human agents. This position can generate strong arguments for environmental protection, but only on the grounds that the well-being of nature is critical to the well-being of the human, who alone has inherent value and is alone deserving of direct moral consideration. Care for nonhuman nature in this approach is derived from our fundamental moral concern for the well-being of present and future human life. The value of animal species and individual animals, of tress and whole ecosystems, remains instrumental, construed as containing solely resource or commodity value for human use and enjoyment.

Against this human-centered ethic, some theorists are arguing for "deep ecology," an ethic which holds that while humans have inherent value, such value also runs deeply throughout the nonhuman living species of the community of the biosphere. Animals and ecosystems have inherent value in themselves, independent of their usefulness to humans, that demands direct moral consideration for them in their own right. Animals and plants may certainly have important resource value to humans, but that sort of value does not exhaust their moral worth or exhaust the moral consideration due them. Deep ecology, with its affirmation of inherent value in animals and the rest of the natural world which is independent of their potential service of human ends, presents a potent moral check against the easy conceptual objectification and thingification of the rest of the nonhuman biosphere.

A critical area of contention lies in the emphasis by many deep ecologists upon the biocentric equality of species, which leads them to refuse any claim that some species have "greater or lesser intrinsic value than others."[18] This position is taken primarily as a moral check against human destructive interference with other species. Yet this is coupled often with the claim that it is permissible for humans to reduce biospheric richness and diversity when vital human interests are at stake. As Naess puts it, in these situations humans have "overriding obligations towards their own kind."[19] This tendency among some of the deep ecology movements to push claims like biocentric equality, and then to bring in through the back door principles about priorities which acknowledge that human vital interests take precedence over animal interests, generates confusion regarding how we should interpret their use of the term "equality." At least some seem to mean this more as a general metaphysical or ecological principle to inform in a broad way our moral perspectives about the biosphere, and not as a strict ethical claim meant to determine decision and action in concrete cases involving conflicts of interests between and among different species.

While a biospheric expansion of the common good tradition may join deep ecology in affirming that all of creation with all of its life forms has inherent value, still the Catholic common good tradition will distinctly break with deep ecology where the latter continues to insist upon biocentric equality claims which can be read as implying that a human, a rodent, and a tree have equal moral worth.

---

[18]Arne Naess, "The Deep Ecological Movement: Some Philosophical Aspects," *Philosophical Inquiry* 8 (1986): 15.

[19]Naess 14,22. See generally his articles "The Shallow and the Deep, Long-Range Ecology Movement: A Summary," *Inquiry* 16 (1973): 95-100 and "A Defence of the Deep Ecology Movement," *Environmental Ethics* 6 (1984): 265-70.

Conceptual Resources for an Ecologically
Expanded View of the Common Good

There is a distinct convergence between the stress of the emerging ecological sciences upon humanity's participation in the general community of the biosphere and Catholicism's traditional stress upon the common good. Aldo Leopold once observed in *A Sand County Almanac*, an early ecological classic: "Ethics are possibly a kind of community instinct in-the-making." "All ethics," he states, which have "so far evolved rest upon a single premise: that the individual is a member of a community of interdependent parts. . . . The land ethic simply enlarges the boundaries of the community to include soils, water, plants, and animals, or collectively: the land."[20] Such an expansion of our notion of community can draw upon moral and theological resources deep within the Catholic heritage of thought. There are many such resources and I will only briefly note three here: 1) the Noachic Covenant in Genesis, 2) the Stoic Cosmopolitan tradition, and 3) Thomas Aquinas' stress upon Creation.

1. *Ecological Covenant with the Rainbow as a Sign*. Some theologians have so stressed God's mighty acts in history of liberating the Israelites that they forget to give due emphasis to the fact that the Exodus was not just a journey into freedom, but a journey into freedom *in a good land*. Likewise while we have long tended to emphasize God's special covenant to Israel, and broadly to all of humanity created in the *imago Dei*, scholars and pastors have been much slower to give proper weight to the general covenant to all of creation which God announces to Noah after the flood subsided. This covenant, God announces, is "between me and you and every living creature that is with you, for all future generations . . . . (Gen. 9:12). Instead of stressing creation and fall as a completed thematic unit, now some scholars are suggesting that it is better to interpret creation, fall, flood story, and new covenant together as a textual whole whose movement builds toward the elaboration of a universal and an ecological covenant.[21] The Noachic covenant serves as an important scriptural resource for grounding a biospheric expansion of our notion of the community whose good should be served and protected.

2. *The Stoic Cosmopolitan Tradition*. The stress upon the priority of the common good over that of the individual originated in the West in ancient Greece where political theory arose out of the experience of citizenship within the polis. Plato in *The Republic* holds: "Our aim in founding the State was not the disproportionate happiness of any one class, but the greatest happiness of the whole," for a State so ordered "to the good of the whole" will be more

---

[20]Aldo Leopold, *A Sand County Almanac: With Essays on Conservation from Round River* (New York: Sierra Club/Ballantine, 1966) 239.

[21]Bernhard W. Anderson, "Creation and Ecology," *Creation in the Old Testament*, ed. Bernhard W. Anderson (Philadelphia: Fortress Press, 1984) 157. See also Walter Brueggemann, *The Land* (Philadelphia: Fortress Press, 1977) 1-14.

likely to be one of justice.[22] This stress on the priority of the whole over the parts becomes in Aristotle's hands a major theme in his metaphysics, ethics, and political theory. At the beginning of the *Nicomachean Ethics*, Aristotle describes politics as the "master art," for it aims at not just the good of the individual but the "finer and more godlike" good of a "nation" or city-state.[23] Again in the *Politics* Aristotle holds "the state or the political community" is the highest community which "embraces all the rest." Therefore the good to which it aims is a good "in a greater degree than any other . . . ."[24]

With the breakdown of the autonomy of the polis and the rise of great empires under Alexander the Great and later the Romans, Stoic thought employed this parts/whole analysis to expand the "common good" from the well-being of the polis to that of the entire universe, the cosmopolis. Politics was recast in the image of a larger order, the order of nature, understood now as a community ruled and guided by divine reason. As Cicero describes this cosmopolis: "Again, they hold that the universe is governed by divine will; it is a city or state of which both men and gods are members, and each one of us is a part of this universe; from which it is a natural consequence that we should prefer the common advantage to our own."[25] As Marcus Aurelius states in *The Meditations*: "If we have intelligence in common, so we have reason which makes us reasoning beings, and that practical reason which orders what we must or must not do; then the law too is common to us and, if so, we are citizens; if so, we share a common government; if so, the universe is, as it were, a city--for what other common government could one say is shared by all mankind? From this, the common city, we derive our intelligence, our reason and our law . . . ."[26]

The Meditations illustrate a tension that runs throughout the Stoic conception of the universal community. Stoicism, in linking political theory to claims about the order of the universe, stressed both the individual's membership in the universal human community and also their membership in the natural universe which was also construed, at least at times, as a vast community. Thus when Aurelius emphasizes the importance of serving the common good, typically he refers to the common good of human society; but he does insist on understanding human society as a part of the universal natural order whose ordering patterns must be respected and served. For

---

[22]B. Jowett, trans., *Republic* by Plato vol.1 of *The Dialogues of Plato*, 2 vols. (New York: Random House, 1937) 682-83. (in this specific text page 682)

[23]Aristotle, *Nicomachean Ethics*, trans. Martin Ostwald (Indianapolis: Bobbs-Merrill, 1962) 1094a26-1094b10. (in this text pages 4-5).

[24]Benjamin Jowett, trans., *Politics*, by Aristotle, in *The Basic Works of Aristotle* ed. Richard McKeon (New York: Random House, 1941) 1252a1-6. (in this text page 1127)

[25]Cicero, *De Finibus*, trans. H. Rackham (London: William Heinemann, 1921) III,XIX,64. (in this text page 1127)

[26]Marcus Aurelius Antoninus, *The Meditations*, trans. G.M.A. Grube (Indianapolis: Hackett Publishing, 1983) IV,4. (in this text 26-27)

Marcus Aurelius, while political and ethical norms are tied to the service of the common good of humanity, this community is always understood as a participant within a greater whole, namely, the natural universe. While this cosmological expansion of the frame of reference for political and ethical reflection had great appeal in Hellenistic and Roman society, many political theorists have since argued that by expanding the notion of citizenship to that of the community of the universe, the Stoics attenuated the force of traditional notions of political allegiance and moral obligation. Some charge that the Stoics by grafting the order of politics and ethics onto the cosmic order, confused social and natural categories and contexts and thus weakened the bite of traditional political and ethical terms.[27] While there is much merit in this critique, one could counter it today by arguing that humanity's technological advance has expanded our powers so greatly that we can no longer afford to accept a dualism between the ethical and social disciplines which guide human decision and action and the scientific disciplines which attempt to discern the makeup of the natural cosmos within which we live and act. It is critical for ethics, social theory, and reflections upon state security to be informed closely by the findings of sciences which chart the biospheric constraints which set distinct limits to human action.

3. *One Medieval Appropriation: Thomas' Stress on Creation*. The Stoic stress upon the primacy of the common good continued to have a broad influence upon Christian theologians in the medieval period. Thomas Aquinas developed the most comprehensive treatment of the notion of the common good and in this section I will focus upon his views. Thomas used this notion both to refer to the common good of all creation under God and more specifically to the common good of the citizens of a particular society or state. By drawing analogies between God's government of the universe and a human ruler's authority over the state or political community, Thomas' thought achieved an architectonic power and breadth of vision unmatched in medieval or modern Catholic thinking. While Thomas, in describing the eternal law, does state that "the whole community of the universe is governed by Divine Reason,"[28] most modern Catholic commentators and moralists have focused upon Thomas' political and social thought which elaborates the common good in the context of natural and human law ordered to the good of a particular human community or state. This is most forcefully displayed in the Treatise on Law in the *Summa* and this work has come to be regarded among Catholic theorists generally as the authoritative text describing the common good.

Thomas distinguishes various types of law, and contemporary notions of the common good have generally derived from Thomas' accounts of natural

---

[27]Sheldon S. Wolin, *Politics and Vision* (Boston: Little, Brown and Co., 1960) 81.

[28]Fathers of the English Dominican Province, trans., *Summa Theologica*, by Thomas Aquinas; 5 vols (Westminster, MD: Christian Classics, 1948, reprint 1981) 2:996; 1a, 2ae, q.91, art.1.

and human law. Law, Thomas states, "is a rule and measure of acts, whereby man is induced to act or is restrained from acting."[29] "Every law," he argues, "is ordained to the common good," the "last end" of action.[30] Later he says that human law must be "ordained to the common good of the state," and he quotes Isidore who held that "law should be framed, not for any private benefit, but for the common good of all the citizens."[31] Just laws are distinguished from unjust ones by whether they serve the common good or not.[32] Because social conditions change, Thomas holds that "human law is rightly changed, in so far as such change is conducive to the common weal."[33]

In Thomas' analysis of the virtue of justice, he argues that an individual is related to the community as a part is to the whole. Justice "directs man to the common good" and thus is properly called a "general virtue."[34] "The common good is the end of each individual member of a community, just as the good of the whole is the end of each part."[35] Likewise Thomas holds in his work *On Kingship* that the service of the common good distinguishes just governments from the unjust. The further a government departs from the common good, the more unjust it becomes.[36]

Given the prominent attention accorded to the Treatise on Law by modern Catholic theologians and ethicists, it is not surprising that Thomas' notion of the common good has almost universally been interpreted as an ethical-political principle, which it indeed is. However, if we attend to Thomas' use of the common good concept elsewhere in the *Summa*, especially in his Treatises on the Creation, the Work of the Six Days, the Divine Government, and in various passages in the *Summa Contra Gentiles*, we find the concept also employed as cosmological-ecological principle suggesting that all species, including the human, are parts which participate within the greater whole of the universe.[37] God as Creator and Sustainer is the good common to all that exists and is the highest good. After God the highest good

> ... among created things, is the good of the order of the whole universe, since every particular good of this or that thing is ordered to it as to an end . . . and so, each part is found to be for the sake of its whole. Thus, among created things, what God cares for most is the order of the universe.[38]

---

[29] Aquinas q.90,art.1,2:993.

[30] Aquinas q.90,art.2,2:994.

[31] Aquinas q.95,art.4,2:1016, and q.96,art.1,2:1017.

[32] Aquinas q.96,art.4,2:1019-20.

[33] Aquinas q.97,art.2,2:1023.

[34] Thomas Aquinas, *Summa Theologica*, 2a,2ae,q.58,art.5,3:1432.

[35] Aquinas art.9,ro3,3:1434.

[36] Dino Bigongiari, ed., *On Kingship*, by Thomas Aquinas in *The Political Ideas of St. Thomas Aquinas* (New York: Hafner Press, 1953) 182; chap.3, para.24.

[37] Aquinas, *Summa Contra Gentiles* book 3,part 1,ch.64,para.9,3:212.

[38] Aquinas para.10,3:213.

The vastness of God's goodness cannot be participated in, nor adequately represented by, any one creature or type of creature, even humanity. "For goodness, which in God is simple and uniform, in creatures is manifold and divided; and hence the whole universe together participates in the divine goodness more perfectly, and represents it better, than any single creature whatever."[39] The best universe is one filled with the maximum diversity and richness of creation. This includes the common good of particular human communities, but they participate in the greater whole or community of creation whose common good includes theirs. As Thomas puts it: "the principal good in things themselves is the perfection of the universe; which would not be, were not all grades of being found in things."[40]

Clearly a dominant organizing principle of Thomas' ethical system is a claim about the absolute superiority of rational human life over all lesser creatures. Thomas is impressed with the special status of rational beings made in the *imago Dei* and capable of enjoying genuine friendship with God. He draws directly upon the Aristotelian/Stoic dictum that "plants are for the sake of animals and animals exist for the sake of human beings" to argue that God rules intellectual creatures for their own sake, while ruling non-intellectual creatures and objects for the sake of the intellectual creatures. He elaborates a strict hierarchical value scheme holding human life as having value in itself while animal and plant life hold only instrumental value as resources to be used their service of human ends.[41]

Our emerging ecological concerns, however, provide the hermeneutical impetus to discern a second organizing principle in Thomas' ethics, namely his stress on the good of the order of the universe, the common good, that is, of the community of creation. While this theme is often overwhelmed by Thomas' anthropocentrism, still it elaborates an important holistic creation-oriented vision which converges with important insights of contemporary ecological analyses.

Thomas does not believe that God loves irrational creatures with "the love of friendship," but he does hold that God loves them with "the love of desire."[42] Much is made of Thomas' stress that only angels and humans are created in the *imago Dei*, but few commentators have taken seriously his claim that other creatures bear a "likeness of a trace" of their Creator. [43] God is "the likeness of all things . . . ."[44] "In all creatures there is found the trace of the Trinity . . . ."[45]

---

[39]Aquinas, *Summa Theologica* 1a,q.47,art.1,1:246.

[40]Aquinas q.22,art.4,1:124.

[41]Aquinas, *Summa Contra Gentiles* Book 3, Part 2, chs.111-12,4:114-19.

[42]Aquinas, *Summa Theologica* 1a,q.20,art.2,ro.3,1:115.

[43]Aquinas q.93,art.6,1:473.

[44]Aquinas q.57,art.2,1:284.

[45]Aquinas q.45,art.7,1:238.

A powerful sense of God's presence throughout creation sustaining it in being pervades Thomas' theology. "God loves all existing things."[46] God conserves all things in being "by continually pouring out existence into them."[47] Likewise, Thomas stresses, in ways which are closely compatible with contemporary ecology, the fundamental relationality of all creatures as well as the participations of parts within greater wholes or communities. "Therefore all beings apart from God are not their own being, but are beings by participation."[48] In his discussion of the creation of angels, he argues that they probably were created at the same time as corporeal creatures. As he continues: "This stands in evidence from the relationship of creature to creature; because of the mutual relationship of creatures makes up the good of the universe. But no part is perfect if separate from the whole."[49]

This expansive theme of Thomas' notion of the common good intended by God's government of the entire realm of creation offers rich resources for charting our responsibilities in an age beginning to acknowledge the gravity of the ecological problems we are promoting. Clearly we cannot simply drag various passages from Hebrew Scripture, Stoic texts or Thomas' *Summae* out of their historical and textual settings and expect a direct correspondence to our current historical concerns. However a creative and critical retrieval of some of the concerns, insights and elements of these traditions, I believe, offers us important resources for critically responding to the ecological "signs of our times" by expanding the traditional understanding of the common good to a biospheric horizon. This is really not such a new thing for it simply requires that we revivify a sense of close kinship with creation and understand ourselves, our communities, our nations, and the entire human species as participating within a broader community whose common good we must responsibly defend. Modern theologians have stressed God's action in history. But in an age like ours wherein humanity's power for action and destruction has grown so powerful, it is important to recall the insights of traditions which understood that God acts in both history and in nature and which discerned that human action in history and culture occurs enfolded within an environing biosphere sustained by God's loving energy.

---

[46]Aquinas q.20,art.2,1:115.
[47]Aquinas q.104,art.3,1:514.
[48]Aquinas q.44,art.1,1:229.
[49]Aquinas q.61,art.3,1:303.

Part Six

ECOLOGICAL AWARENESS

IN EASTERN RELIGIONS

THE BUDDHAHOOD OF THE GRASSES AND THE TREES: ECOLOGICAL SENSITIVITY OR SCRIPTURAL MISUNDERSTANDING?

William Grosnick

Because one of the functions of cosmological myth is to articulate the place human beings occupy in the material and spiritual universes, most of the world's great religious traditions have major ecological implications--they provide basic frameworks for understanding how human beings fit into the rest of the natural world. Mahayana Buddhism is no exception. It is a fundamental tenet of Mahayana cosmology, for example, that human beings do not stand alone in the spiritual universe--a whole array of gods, demigods, animals, ghosts, and hell-dwellers are co-participants in the scheme of things, and like human beings are even capable of attaining Buddhahood. This belief not only influenced the forms of popular religious poetry (even today, Zen monks drink the water with which they have washed their food bowls and dedicate it to the relief of hungry ghosts,[1] and Tibetan Buddhist pilgrims take their animals with them to sacred pilgrimage sites so that those animals might share in the merit); it also had important ecological implications. For example, Mahayana Buddhists consider it wrong to kill animals even for food, since they are beings who, like themselves, are destined for Buddhahood. And they show enormous respect for non-human life. Perhaps the most striking example of this is found in the practice of the eccentric Japanese Zen Master Ryokwan, who was once observed on a warm winter day carefully picking the lice out of his underwear, placing them on a piece of paper to warm them in the sun, and then returning them to his chest as the day cooled.[2]

---

[1]Jiyu Kennett, *Selling Water by the River: A Manual of Zen Training* (New York: Random House, 1972) 33.

[2]D. T. Suzuki, *Zen and Japanese Culture* (Princeton: Bollingen Series, 1959) 372. One of Ryokwan's poems reads:

O lice, lice / If you were the insects / Singing in the autumn fields,
My chest (fudokoro) would really be / For you the Musashino Prairie.

But as extensive as this traditional Mahayana respect for the non-human world was in other parts of Asia, it was eclipsed by the Buddhism of Japan, which for centuries held that even nonsentient things like grasses and trees, or even non-living substances like rocks and land, were capable of Buddhahood. This idea of the Buddhahood of the nonsentient became a major subject of scholarly debate in Japanese Buddhist monastic circles from the ninth century on, and probably reached its point of greatest popularity during the Muromachi period, when it became a major theme in Noh drama. However, by the time that the doctrine of the Buddhahood of the nonsentient found popular expression in Noh drama, the orthodox Buddhist idea of nonduality that gave rise to the doctrine had been amalgamated with some non-Buddhist ideas from the more animistic Japanese Shinto tradition. This was perhaps understandable, since the primary concern of the authors was dramatic impact rather than philosophical clarity or doctrinal orthodoxy. But the original Buddhist significance of the doctrine may have been lost.

As it appears in Noh plays, the doctrine of the Buddhahood of the nonsentient is generally expressed through the dramatic attainment of Buddhahood by a plant of some sort. During the 14th and 15th centuries, the most prominent theme of Noh dramas was the attainment of Buddhahood by the ghost of some historical person, and the substitution of the spirit of a plant for the ghost of a person was merely a variation of this larger theme. Of the approximately 240 plays in the present repertoire, 11 have protagonists who are the spirits of plants such as the banana, the plum, the moonflower, the cherry, the iris, the wisteria, the willow, or the maple, or else the spirits of insects like the butterfly, or even the spirits of nonliving substances like the snow.[3]

In most of these plays the protagonist appears in the first half of the play in the guise of a young woman (or, on rare occasion, a white-bearded old man), who meets a travelling Buddhist monk and falls into a discussion of the doctrine of the attainment of Buddhahood by the grasses and the trees. When the monk asks the young woman her name, she tells him that if he will spend the night under a certain tree or flower, she will reveal her identity to him. In the second half of the play, as the monk sleeps, she appears in his dream as the spirit of the plant in question, and, after praising the virtues of the plant she represents, performs a dance to celebrate her attainment of Buddhahood, accompanied by a recitation of the chorus. When the monk awakens, he finds the blossoms or leaves of the plant strewn about him on the ground.[4]

The plants and other things that were chosen to be the protagonists of these plays seem to have been specifically chosen because they represent

---

[3]Donald H. Shively, "Buddhahood for the Nonsentient: A Theme in Noh Plays," *Harvard Journal of Asiatic Studies* XX, 1 & 2 (June, 1957) 136.

[4]Shively 137.

certain Buddhist themes, such as the important Buddhist theme transitoriness. Perhaps the line from Buddhist scripture most widely quoted in Noh drama is the declaration from the *Nirvana Sutra*, "Shogyo-mujo"--"All things are transitory." The spirits of the various plants discover enlightenment as they recognize their own fragile nature. The delicate blossoms of the cherry and plum, the frail butterfly, the falling leaves of the maple tree, all last but for a moment, and in the temperate Kyoto climate, snow melts upon falling and the tropical banana plant succumbs to the first frost. As metaphors for the transitoriness of life, the protagonists were admirably chosen.

The authors of the Noh plays also took poetic advantage of other qualities of plants to express Buddhist themes. In *Teika,* the clinging quality of vines is used as an expression of the persistence of romantic attachments. In the play a monk comes upon the tomb of Princess Shokushi, which is overgrown with a vine which contains the spirit of her former lover. The attachment that the two lovers had for one another is what prevents their attainment of Buddhahood.[5] In the second part of the play the monk refers to the *Lotus Sutra,* telling the princess:

> In this Wonderful Scripture
> Even the grasses and the trees are not omitted,
> So part from the vine which has this attachment for you
> And enter Buddha Way.[6]

There are other important metaphorical uses of plants. The banana plant, the protagonist of *Basho,* the most popular of the plays on the Buddhahood of the grasses and the trees, is a recurrent metaphor used in Mahayana sutras to illustrate the hollowness or emptiness of things, for when banana leaves are removed one by one from the outside of the plant, nothing is found to remain at its core. (The author of *Basho* compounds this image of insubstantiality nicely in the play, by adding dream imagery to it. At one point the deuteragonist monk asserts, "As I contemplate it, this transient world is like a dream about banana leaves").[7]

Although the authors of the Noh dramas show considerable aesthetic sensitivity in choosing these various plants as metaphors for existence, when it comes to citing scriptural support for the doctrine of the Buddhahood of the nonsentient, the authors sometimes show an amazing disregard for the figurative use of language. For example, one chapter from Mahayana literature that is frequently cited as scriptural support is the "Medicinal Herbs" chapter of the *Lotus Sutra,* in which one finds a metaphor likening the Buddha to a great rain cloud which "rains down on all grasses and trees,

---

[5]Shively 155.
[6]Shively 155
[7]Shively 143.

shrubs and forests, and medicinal herbs,"[8] providing life-sustaining moisture to them all, without distinction. The sutra declares that in similar fashion the Buddha universally proclaims the Dharma, without making any distinction between different kinds of people, whether noble or base, moral or immoral, or of right or of wrong understanding.[9] The authors of the Noh plays seem to choose to ignore the obvious metaphorical intent of the *Lotus Sutra,* and take this chapter to mean that the Buddha rains his teaching down upon the grasses and trees as well as human beings. At one point in the play *Taema,* for example, the protagonist asks a monk, "Is not what you were just reciting the Chapter on the Parable of the Plants?'" The monk replies, "It is. In this Wonderful Scripture even the grasses and the trees are not omitted."[10]

The verse from Buddhist scripture that is most often cited in support of the idea of the Buddhahood of the grasses and the trees, and the verse that is most important for understanding the genesis of the doctrine, is a verse which both Buddhist commentaries and Noh plays erroneously attribute to a sutra known as the *Chuingyo (Antarabhava Sutra):*

> When a single Buddha attains the Way
> And contemplates the Dharma-realm,
> The grasses, the trees and the land
> All becomes Buddha.

This verse, or at least the second half of it, appears in virtually every Noh play that deals with the subject of the Buddhahood of the nonsentient,[11] and was also a focal point of Buddhist commentarial works. The passage can be traced back to writings of the 12th century Tendai commentator Shoshin, a critic of the idea of the Buddhahood of the nonsentient, who quotes it in his *Shikanshiki.*[12] It can also be found in a text of uncertain date which Shoshin virulently criticized, the *Kankoruiju,* so there is little doubt that the verse existed prior to Shoshin.[13] The *Kankoruiju* is one of many anonymous Tendai commentaries which, during the 12th century, were composed from a body of short epigrammatic Buddhist verses then in wide circulation, verses that were probably originally passed from teacher to pupil during the esoteric initiation

---

[8]Leon Hurvitz, tr., *Scripture of the Lotus Blossom of the Fine Dharma* (New York: Columbia University Press, 1976) 102.

[9]Hurvitz 107.

[10]Shively 155.

[11]Shively 140.

[12]Miyamoto Shoson, "'Somoku-kokudo-shikkai-jobutsu'-no-busshoronteki-igi-to-sono-sakusha," ("The Authorship of the Phrase, 'The Grasses, Trees, and Land All Attain Buddhahood' and its Significance to the Buddha-Nature Theory") *Indogakubukkyogakukenkyu,* IX, 2 (1961) 265a.

[13]Miyamoto 265a.

rites of Tendai *mikkyo*.[14] So the original author of the verse probably never can be determined, although scholars have discovered some passages in the writings of the ninth-century Tendai *mikkyo* Master Annen which may have served as prototypes:

> The *Chuingyo* says, "When Shakyamuni Buddha attained the Way, all the grasses and trees without exception became the six foot tall Buddha-body and proclaimed the Dharma."[15]
>
> The *Chuingyo* says, "Shakyamuni Buddha attained the Way, and in all the lands, sentient and nonsentient beings alike had the six foot tall body and all proclaimed the Dharma."[16]

It would appear from these prototypes, as well as from the verse itself, that what is being spoken of is the enlightenment of a Buddha, and not the enlightenment of a particular plant or other nonsentient object. This is suggested by the fact that all the phrases begin with a reference to a Buddha "attaining the Way." It is a Buddha whose enlightenment is being described, and the references to the grasses and the trees "becoming Buddha" or "proclaiming the Dharma" seem to be intended more as descriptions of what a Buddha experiences in enlightenment than as statements of the capacity of nonsentient things for attainment.

Nevertheless, it also seems clear that, to the authors of the various Noh plays, the verse "When a single Buddha attains the Way, and contemplates the Dharma-realm, the grasses, the trees, and the land all become Buddha," meant that the grasses, trees, and land were all capable of attaining Buddhahood because they had the mental apparatus necessary for it--in short, because they all had souls. This is suggested first of all by the basic dramatic structure of the plays themselves, which shows the spirits of plants talking and acting like human beings, sharing the human longing for liberation, and experiencing the joy of redemption. It is also suggested by some of the arguments presented in the plays, arguments aimed at convincing the audience that plants have spirits. The following passage from *Mutsura* argues that plants have hearts (*kokoro*, a word that also means "minds") because they seem to know what to do at the different seasons of the year:

> The grasses and the trees through the four seasons,
> Each in accordance with its proper time,
> Display differing appearances of flowers and leaves.
> Who can say that they do not have hearts?[17]

---

[14]Tamura Yoshiro, *Tendaihongakuron* (Tokyo:Iwanamishoten, 1976) 521-23.

[15]*Taisho Shinshu Daizokyo* 75, 84c.

[16]*Taisho* 75, 436b.

[17]Shively 150.

In *Taema,* a play in which a cherry tree mysteriously blooms with the color of the lotus, the flower traditionally associated with the Buddha, it seems to be argued that because the cherry blossoms have hearts, they have the capacity for future Buddhahood:

> It is said that because its blossoms have hearts
> It blooms the color of the lotus.
> That is indeed very fine.
> As the grasses and trees and land will become Buddha
> The hearts of the blossoms are dyed with that color and fragrance.[18]

The notion that plants might have souls and therefore be capable of spiritual attainment probably derived more from the influence of Japan's native Shinto tradition than it did from Buddhism. For while Buddhists traditionally tolerated animistic folk beliefs, they seldom indulged in much metaphysical speculation regarding souls; indeed, the *anatman,* or "no-self" doctrine of Buddhism is of such central significance to the religion that when Buddhists address the issue of "souls," it is generally to deny their existence.[19]

Shinto is not a very metaphysical religion either, but the ancient texts of Japan provide abundant evidence that Japanese folk belief traditionally held that plants and other natural objects were animated by spirits which enabled them to act in very human ways. The *Nihongi* (II,2) speaks of a time when the stones could speak and had to be silenced,[20] and some of the prayers (*norito*) indicate that tree trunks and blades of grass could also speak.[21] The *Manyoshu* recounts stories of mountains struggling with one another.[22] And what is perhaps most important, the ancient texts speak of the spirits or *kami* that animate plants. The *Kojiki* (I,vi) mentions a tree-*kami,* Kukunochi-no-kami, who is the son of the creator pair Izanami and Izanagi.[23] Other plant-*kami* mentioned in the *Nihongi* and *Engishiki* are the female spirits of the grass (Kayanohime) and the rice plant (Toyoukehime-no-kami).[24] Still other *kami* are the spirits of the fire (Goshinka) and the mountains (Sanrei).[25] The natural world is alive with spirits.

These animistic notions seemed to have increased in popularity by time of the composition of Muromachi period Noh plays. Saka Shibutsu's

---

[18]Shively 156.

[19]See, for example, the arguments against the idea of a soul contained in the Pali Buddhist canon, such as those found in Henry Clarke Warren, *Buddhism in Translations* (New York: Atheneum, 1972) 129-52.

[20]Jean Herbert, *Shinto* (London: George Allen and Unwin, Ltd., 1967) 477.

[21]Kato Genchi, *A Study of Shinto, the Religion of the Japanese People* (Tokyo, Zaidan Hojin Meiji Seitoku Kinen Gakkai, 1926) 32.

[22]Herbert 472-73.

[23]Herbert 492.

[24]Kato 17.

[25]Miyamoto 263b.

fourteenth century diary of his pilgrimage to the main Shinto shrine at Ise speaks of the worship of a sacred cherry tree called "Sakura-no-miya" in the precincts of the Ise shrine itself.[26] There was a wealth of legends concerning the spiritual powers of plants and the magical effects of poetry upon them. One Muromachi legend surrounding the poet and statesman Sugawara no Michizane (845-903) was that when he was driven from government and sent into exile, he so longed for his plum tree in the capital that he composed a poem to it. The poem so affected the tree that it uprooted itself and flew to his side, planting itself at Anrakuji, henceforth being known as the "Flying Plum."[27]

That these animistic Shinto ideas would permeate Noh drama was perhaps inevitable, for Noh itself originated out of the Shinto tradition. The first Noh stages were built within Shinto shrines, facing the main object of worship. The Noh drama began as a Shinto ceremony at the sacred Yogo pine tree at the Kasuga shrine in Nara. In this ceremony, the power of a *kami* supposedly descended on a dancer, who then let the god guide his movements. This dance later developed into the climactic second act dance found in all Noh plays.[28] (The conjoining of the two most ecstatic moments of the two religions--the moment of enlightenment from Buddhism and the moment of god-possession from Shinto--must have produced a powerful effect on the Muromachi audience).[29]

Nevertheless, awe-inspiring as the Noh plays might have been, the animistic idea that plants had spirits was precisely what had led many earlier Buddhist commentators to reject the notion of the attainment of Buddhahood by the grasses and the trees. Opposition to the notion of the Buddhahood of the grasses and trees can be found as early as the fifth century in the writings of such Chinese monks as Seng-jou, Seng-liang, and Chih-tsang,[30] and later continued in the writings of the ninth century Hua-yen Master Cheng-kuan.[31] In the 12th century, a Japanese Tendai monk named Shoshin went against the prevailing trend of his school by fiercely criticizing the notion of the Buddhahood of the nonsentient. Shoshin's basic argument was that Buddhahood is the result of spiritual practice, and without mind, important Buddhist practices like the aspiration for supreme, perfect enlightenment (*bodhicitta*) would be impossible. Since nonsentient beings were by definition without mind, it was absurd to speak of their attainment of Buddhahood.[32]

---

[26]Kato 11.

[27]Shively 158.

[28]Donald Keene, *No: The Classical Theatre of Japan* (New York, 1966) 28.

[29]The *Lotus Sutra* contains many passages which suggest that ecstatic dancing was also found in early Mahayana Buddhism.

[30]Miyamoto 285b.

[31]Miyamoto 275b.

[32]Miyamoto 271a-73a.

Like many Chinese commentators before him, Shoshin cited the *Mahaparinirvana Sutra* as scriptural support for his position. The *Mahaparinirvana Sutra* is the sutra which introduced into Mahayana Buddhism the notion of the universal Buddha-nature, the idea that all beings possess the capacity for enlightenment. One verse frequently cited by detractors of the idea of the Buddhahood of the nonsentient asserts that only sentient beings can attain enlightenment: "The sentient being is himself the Buddha-nature. Why? Other than by a sentient being, supreme, perfect enlightenment cannot be obtained."[33] Another draws a seemingly absolute distinction between the capacity for enlightenment--the Buddha-nature--and those things which lack consciousness: "What are not the Buddha-nature are nonsentient things like the tiles of walls. What is distinct from such nonsentient things is termed 'the Buddha-nature.'"[34]

It is instructive to note, however, that those Buddhist thinkers and commentators who accepted the idea of the Buddhahood of the grasses and the trees did not try to argue that nonsentient things had minds. Instead, they took as their starting point the middle path doctrine of Buddhism, a doctrine which denies that truth can be expressed in dualisms like sentient-insentient, inner-outer, mind-matter, subject-object, or existent-nonexistent. Like Shoshin, they too quoted the *Mahaparinirvana Sutra,* but unlike Shoshin, who quoted verses which denied Buddha-nature to the nonsentient, they cited verses like the following, which speak of the Buddha-nature as the middle path:

The Buddha-nature of sentient beings is nothing but the middle path.[35]
As the Buddha-nature unites both elements of existence and nonexistence, it is referred to as the "middle path."[36]
As it is neither inner nor outer, it is the middle path.[37]

Referring to the last of these verses, the Tendai Master Annen argued that the verses meant that neither sentient beings (the "inner"), nor objects like the grasses and the trees (the "outer"), alone possess the Buddha-nature, but rather it is all-pervading.[38] The Buddha-nature is something that transcends the distinction between inner and outer. The 10th-century Tendai Master Ryogen argued that if one makes a distinction between the kinds of Buddha-nature possessed by sentient and nonsentient beings, the middle path principle itself would be violated, for one would fall into the error of affirming the duality of the sentient and the nonsentient.[39]

---

[33]*Taisho* 12, 568c.
[34]*Taisho* 12, 581a.
[35]*Taisho* 12, 572a.
[36]*Taisho* 12, 572b.
[37]*Taisho* 12, 572a.
[38]Miyamoto 268a.
[39]Miyamoto 266a.

The thinker responsible for introducing the middle path principle into Tendai thought was the Chinese founder of the school, Chih-yi. He himself did not discuss the idea of the attainment of Buddhahood by nonsentient things, but it is clear that he lay the philosophical groundwork for the development of the notion through his identification of the middle path with all phenomenal existence and his affirmation of the principle of nonduality of subject and object. Chih-yi's perhaps most famous expression of his understanding of the middle path is the phrase, "if ordinary existence is united with the Dharma-realm, if an instant's thought is made one with the Dharma-realm, then there is not a single form or a single scent that is not in the middle path,"[40] a phrase that identifies the middle path with the direct realization of phenomenal reality. The part of this phrase which refers to "uniting with the Dharma-realm" may be the ultimate source of the phrase, "when a single Buddha . . . contemplates the Dharma-realm," in the famous verse which speaks of the grasses trees and land "becoming Buddha." Chih-yi held that from the standpoint of absolute truth (paramartha-satya), mind and its objects (dharmas) were non-dual, and that form and mind were immanent in one another and inseparably bound together.[41] In his treatise, Mahayana Meditation (Mo-ho Chih-kuan), for example, he wrote, "mind is all dharmas and all dharmas are mind."[42] This meant to Chih-yi that when one realized Buddhist enlightenment, one had a direct realization of the sights and sounds of the world, without any sense of being a separate, independent observer of those phenomena. The idea of the Buddhahood of the nonsentient may have already been implicit in this understanding, for if in the moment of realization, the subjective or "sentient" side of experience, is discovered to be identical to the objective or "nonsentient" side of experience, then why should only the sentient side of the identity be credited with the attainment? If phenomena are no different from mind and mind no different from phenomena, why should it be only mind that is capable of realization?

The great Zen Buddhist master of the Kamakura period, Dogen, who was himself heavily influenced by the Tendai thought, gave a more explicit expression to this idea in a couple of the fascicles of his magnum opus Shobogenzo. In the fascicle, "Valley Sounds and Mountain Colors" ("Keiseisanshoku"), he recounts the story of a man named Koji who experienced enlightenment upon seeing the mountains and hearing the sounds of valley streams--directly realizing phenomena in the very way Chih-yi suggested. Dogen then asks a question that implies the enlightenment could as easily be attributed to the "nonsentient" objects of experience. "Was it Koji who realized the Way?" he asks, "or was it the mountains and water?"[43] In

---

[40]Miyamoto 263b-264a.

[41]Tamura 494.

[42]Taisho 46, 54a.

[43]Masutani Fumio ed., Shobogenxo (Tokyo: Kadogawashoten, 1975) I, 141.

another fascicle,"The *Udumbara* Flower" (*"Udonge"*), Dogen makes a very similar statement in analyzing the Zen legend of how Shakyamuni Buddha conveyed his teaching to his disciple Mahakasyapa by holding up an *udumbara* flower: "The holding up of the flower takes place before, during, and after Shakyamuni's attainment of the Way. So it is the *udumbara* flower's attainment of the Way."[44]

Dogen's attribution of attainment to the mountains, water, and udumbara flower is based on the same principle of the nonduality of mind and its objects as was found in the writings of Chih-yi. In a fascicle entitled "The Three Worlds are Mind-Only" (*"Sangaiyuishin"*), Dogen asserted that all the inanimate and natural objects of the world are mind:

> "Mind-only" . . . is walls and fences, tiles and gravel; it is mountains, rivers, and the great earth. . . . Blue, yellow, red, and white are mind; birth, death, coming and going are mind; years, months, days and hours are mind; dreams, mirages, and sky-flowers are mind; splashes, bubbles, and flames are mind; spring flowers and the autumn moon are mind.[45]

In another fascicle, "The Scripture of the Mountains and the Water" (*"Sansuikyo"*), Dogen declared that "outer" things are not necessarily to be regarded as nonsentient, and "inner" things are not necessarily to be regarded as sentient: "The green mountains are neither sentient being nor nonsentient being. One's own self is neither sentient nor nonsentient being."[46]

In the light of the emphasis placed on the nonduality of the sentient and nonsentient in the writings of those Buddhist commentators who affirmed the Buddhahood of the grasses and the trees, it would seem apparent that they would not have interpreted the famous verse, "When a single Buddha attains the Way, and contemplates the Dharma-realm, the grasses and the trees and the land all become Buddha," to mean that the grasses and the trees had spirits. Rather, they would have seen it as a statement of what a Buddha supposedly realizes when he attains enlightenment--namely his own oneness with the world that surrounds him. Because in the moment of his realization a Buddha does not see a distinction between himself and the grasses, trees or land that surround him, those grasses and tress and that land all "become" him, which is to say that they "become Buddha."

What ecological conclusions can be drawn from the medieval Japanese doctrine of the Buddhahood of the grasses and the trees? It would seem that the answer to that question would depend on the level of interpretation of the doctrine of the Buddhahood of the nonsentient at which one is speaking.

At the simplest level, if one takes the doctrine of the Buddhahood of the grasses and the trees as a simple expression of animistic worldview, as an

---

[44]Masutani VI, 209.
[45]Masutani V, 17-18.
[46]Masutani II, 13.

assertion that plants like the wisteria, cherry, or banana, or even the land itself, are really spirits, then the obvious ecological implication is that everything in nature is a living being that must be cared for. From the point of view of orthodox Buddhist "theology," with its emphasis on the "no-self" doctrine, such an animistic view should probably be rejected, but from the perspective of the popular religious imagination that is expressed in Muromachi period Noh plays, there can be little doubt that the grasses, trees, and land were thought of as having hearts, and so were included in the countless number of beings for whose salvation the Mahayana bodhisattva worked unceasingly. Understood in ecological terms, this would mean that the great compassion that a Mahayana bodhisattva was to extend to all suffering beings in any world systems whatsoever, would be extended even further to include the world of plants. In addition to ministering to the denizens of hell, to the "hungry ghosts," to animals, and to human beings, and to the gods and demi-gods, a bodhisattva would also minister to the vegetable and even the mineral worlds. It would be hard to imagine a more universal compassion.

At a more fundamentally religious level, the Noh plays about the Buddhahood of the nonsentient should perhaps be seen as religious dramas which attempt to evoke a sense of the numinous in human life. Whether one calls it mana, or a sense of "the Sacred," there can be little doubt that when the medieval Japanese audience saw the spirits of bizarre and exotic plants like the moonflower or banana plant ecstatically dancing out the joy of their liberation, in a dramatic moment which Noh tradition identified as the moment of god-possession, that audience must have felt a tremendous sense of primordial mystery and power. At this level, the idea of the Buddhahood of the nonsentient is not a metaphysical doctrine, but rather the dramatic expression of a confrontation with the ultimate mystery of life and its meaning--a confrontation that defies any rational explanation. It is perhaps impossible to draw rational ecological conclusions from this fundamentally irrational (or superrational) experience, but if there is an ecological meaning to it, it could only be that the mysterious world of nature which confronts human beings is a sacred reality to be approached with awe and reverence.

Finally, if one views the doctrine of the Buddhahood of the grasses and the trees at the level of orthodox Buddhist philosophy, seeing it as a statement of the Buddhist principle of the nonduality of subject and object that is to be experienced in the moment of enlightenment, then the major ecological implication of the doctrine would be that human beings are really one with the environment that surrounds them. The respect and reverence and care that we owe to the natural world is really respect and reverence and care that we owe to ourselves, for from the point of view the Buddhist understanding of supreme truth, no distinction can be drawn between ourselves and the world around us. This is a theological stance very different from the traditional theological stance taken in the West, where traditional cosmogonic myth not only placed the Creator apart from His creation, but also had Him separate man from the rest of creation and assign to him "dominion over the fish of the sea and over the birds of the air." The Buddhist view places human beings not over nature, but within nature, and nature within them.

There is a current saying in ecological circles that declares, "We are running out of 'out.'" It refers to the rapid disappearances of areas outside of human habitation into which we can safely throw things "out." It is instructive, and perhaps tragically ironic, to note that from the point of view of the Buddhist doctrine of nonduality, there is no such place as "out," and there never has been. Human beings and their environment are inseparable. The outer world--that mythic "outer darkness" to which we have traditionally consigned our waste, our garbage, and all the other evils that we have imagined--is, from the Buddhist philosophy, only a false distinction made by our discriminating consciousness. It does not exist independently of us, a fact that we are perhaps beginning to realize as the wastes that we have "discarded" turn up as part of our lives.

CONTEMPORARY JAINA AND HINDU RESPONSES TO THE ECOLOGICAL CRISIS

Christopher Chapple

During a trip in 1981 to a South Indian industrial facility surrounded by denuded hills and dead trees due to factory pollution, I became intrigued and appalled by the obvious lack of sensitivity to environmental issues in India. How could the country of Gandhian justice, rich with religious perspectives that extol the beauty and value of life, be so oblivious to the harm incurred by unbridled industrialization? Three years later the Bhopal Union Carbide disaster catalyzed a new awareness amongst the Indian population regarding the dangers posed to both humans and the earth by the ravages of pollution.

Having written about the possible contributions that traditional Hindu religious values could make to an indigenous environmental movement within India,[1] I travelled to India in 1989 to investigate organizations and resources on ecological issues that have developed recently. This journey revealed that although the outward appearances of the various institutions with which I established contact seemingly reflect the model for environmental action in the United States, in fact the movement in India is deeply influenced by indigenous perspectives. Ecological leaders of India highly value the transformation of the human psyche as the key to societal reform, placing less emphasis on legislative or governmental action. In what follows, I will begin with a brief survey of traditional Indian attitudes toward what in European terms is called the "natural world." I will then focus the discussion first on the Jaina tradition, due to its longstanding affirmation of respect for life, and then turn to various pan-Indian movements that advocate environmental protection. I will conclude with a discussion of some recurring themes within the Indian perspective.

The civilization of India, the beginnings of which have been dated as early as five thousand years ago, has produced a number of theologies and interrelated cosmologies that include human resources for dealing with the

---

[1]Christopher Chapple, "Ecological Nonviolence and the Hindu Tradition," in *Perspectives on Nonviolence*, edited by V.K. Kool (New York: Springer-Verlag, 1990), pp. 168-177.

natural order. Quite often the traditions of India are associated with escapism and disregard for materiality. However, in my own experience of Indian traditions, several conceptual resources are present that can enhance respect for the environment.

In the Vedic hymns, for instance, we find an intimate relationship between persons and various personifications of the earth, water, thunderstorms, and so forth. The Vedic rituals, many of which are still performed today, serve as a matrix from which human prosperity and blessings may arise. In the somewhat later Samkhya tradition, the five great elements (*mahabhuta*) of earth, water, fire, air, and space, are reverenced as the essential building blocks of physical reality. From the Upanishads and later Vedantic formulations, all things with form (*saguna*) are seen to be essentially nondifferent from the universal consciousness or ultimate reality; any thing with form can be an occasion to remember that Brahman which is beyond form (*nirguna*). In this collective Hindu model, the human order can be seen as an extension of and utterly reliant upon the natural order. Meditation begins with concentration on external objects, a process that reveals that the world is not different from oneself. In the language of Vedanta, the Brahman is inseparable from its individual manifestations. As stated in the *Bhagavad Gita*, the person of knowledge "sees no difference between a learned Brahmin, a cow, an elephant, a dog, or an outcaste" (V:18). From the perspectives of Jainism and Hinduism, the killing of life forms is none other than the killing of our own kin. For an American, the loss of trees and lakes due to acid rain could be regarded with indifference. Aside from environmentalists and romantics, most Americans regard the natural world as an object for consumption or appreciation. To a classically trained Indian, the loss of a lake or a tree is the loss of that which composes oneself.

In addition to the Vedic and Vedantic worldview summarized above, the religious traditions of India have been profoundly influenced by the persistent and prophetic presence of the Sramanic or renouncer schools. Preeminent among these are the Jaina, Buddhist, and Yoga traditions. Whereas Yoga became closely associated with Vedic and Hindu forms (and somewhat preempted by Sankara's monism), and Buddhism departed from India with the advent of Islam (and likewise became somewhat subsumed into the larger Hindu tradition), Jainism retained its purity, both in terms of its world view and its community life. In Jainism, all elements have life: the earth, the water, plants, animals, and humans are all said to possess *jiva* or life force. This *jiva* takes repeated forms from beginningless time; each person in a prior existence might well have been a dog or a frog or even perhaps a clod of earth. Due to the continued accumulation of karma through acts of violence, *jivas* are reborn again and again. In order to stop this senseless, directionless reincarnation (a notion found also in Buddhism and later Hinduism), persons are encouraged to undertake an ethical life to mitigate existing karma and minimize future karma. The asceticism of India is designed explicitly so that in revering and respecting the life of another, one's own life is purified.

Rather like the movements of the radical reformation in the Christian milieu, Jainism has struggled to retain its traditional worldview despite the onslaught of competing social norms. Jainism has campaigned for the "vegetarianization" of Hindus and Muslims throughout Indian history, successfully convincing high caste Hindus to spurn consumption of meat and very nearly converting the Muslim Mughal emperor Akbar to a meatless diet. Using resources and arguments similar to the case made for vegetarianism, Jainism confronts modern issues like nuclear proliferation, ecological ravage, and various dilemmas related to the field of medical ethics, including the use of animals for research and production of medicines, and euthanasia.

The conceptual resources offered by Jainism for coping with the ecological dilemma would essentially be the same as for dealing with animals rights and medical ethics. Jainism holds as its fundamental tenet that all life is sacred, as exemplified in the Acaranga Sutra which states that "All beings desire to live." To harm living beings means that one violates this principle, resulting in the accretion of harmful karma that guarantees further violent action and certain rebirth. In order to extirpate these harmful influences, Jaina society advocates a quasi-ascetic lifestyle for its lay adherents and a rigorously ascetic lifestyle for its monks and nuns. No Jaina is allowed to eat nonvegetarian food or engage in professions that promote violent activity. Monastic Jainas adhere to a variety of vows, depending upon sect, which may include total nudity, total avoidance of bathing, sweeping one's path to avoid killing insects, and so forth.

The Jainas have campaigned against the production of nuclear weapons, the use of animals for product testing, and the unnecessary prolonging of life. On the nuclear issue, Anuvibha, an organization based in Jaipur and somewhat affiliated with the Terapanthi branch of the Svetambara Jainas, has forged links with various Western peace organizations and has conducted international conferences on peace issues.[2]

In an earlier study, I postulated that Jainas would disdain the killing of animals for the enhancement of medical research,[3] arguing that any harm to animals would be carefully avoided. However, I have subsequently discovered that the Jaina community controls the pharmaceutical industry in India and of course is required to adhere to safety and testing regulations. The compromise solution that the Jainas have put into effect combines modern exigency with a very traditional practice. Animals are used for testing but then

---

[2]S.L. Gandhi, International Secretary of Anuvibha, has been a valuable resource for my research on Jainism. The address of his organization is A-12, Anita Colony, Bajaj Nagar, Jaipur, Rajasthan 302015, India.

[3]Christopher Chapple, "Noninjury to Animals: Jaina and Buddhist Perspectives" in Tom Regan, editor, *Animal Sacrifices: Religious Perspectives on the Use of Animals in Science* (Philadelphia: Temple University Press, 1986), 213-236.

are "rehabilitated" through shelters and recuperation facilities maintained by the laboratories. For instance, the pharmaceutical branch of India's Walchand Group of industries uses animals for the production of immunoglobulin but then releases them into the wild, as noted by Dr. Vinod Doctori.[4] This practice is not unlike the ages-old Jaina tradition of constructing animal shelter for infirm animals, allowing them to survive until their natural demise.[5]

In a tradition so highly concerned with the preservation of and respect for life, it is poignant that the manner of death receives a great deal of attention and has great importance. In the Jaina tradition animals are given shelter until death; human death is similarly ritualized. It is not an event to be avoided and postponed; if one knows that death is imminent, it is eagerly embraced.[6] A highly ritualized entry into death is practiced occasionally in Jainism through a fast unto death, in which one consciously "drops" the body as preliminary to reentry into the continuum of life. For highly advanced monastics, rebirth does not occur, but one dwells in an eternal state of energy, consciousness, and bliss unfettered by association with karma.

In some ways, given its *telos*, this religious tradition may seem utterly otherworldly and simply incapable of addressing the issue of environmental destruction. Many have criticized Indian forms of asceticism for the seeming disdain toward the material world. However, the nonviolent ethic of Jainism (*ahimsa*) as embodied by both monastic and lay practitioners, does indeed offer resources for a more ecologically balanced lifestyle. During a visit to Jain Vishva Bharati in Ladnun, a small desert town in Western Rajasthan, I visited with Acharya Tulsi, who has served as the head of the Terapanthi Svetamabara sect since 1936[7]. I inquired as to whether the Jaina religion is responding to the current ecological crisis. His response was very much in the style of traditional Indian pedagogy. He spoke not of political or legislative action (though I did ask him about such matters) but rather referred to his own lifestyle. He showed me what he owns: his white robes, his eating utensils, and his personal collection of books. The latter can only be read with a magnifying glass: copies of the primary Jaina sutras and the original 250 year old document establishing his order have been rendered in tiny print, so as to allow easy transport. The life of a Jaina monk or nun is a life of

---

[4]*Ahimsa: Nonviolence*, Michael Tobias, executive producer, writer, and director, Public Broadcasting Service, 1986.

[5]For a graphic depiction of an animal shelter in Ahmedabad, see the film *Frontiers of Peace: Jainism in India*, directed by Paul Kuepferle and Barry Lynch.

[6]For details on this practice, see my forthcoming article "The Fast Unto Death in Jaina Tradition."

[7]For a complete biography of Acharya Tulsi, see *Acharya Tulsi: Fifty Years of Selfless Dedication*, edited by R. P. Bhatnagar, S.L. Gandhi, Rajul Bhargava, and Ashok K. Jha (Ladnun, India: Jain Vishva Bharati, 1985).

homelessness. While in Ladnun, Acharya Tulsi occupies the corner of a classroom at Jaina Vishva Bharati; there is no place and very few things that he can call his own. In a very direct way, he was in fact showing me the most radical form of ecological lifestyle. He owns no automobile, no house few clothes. *Aparigraha*, one of the five requirements for Jaina living, eschews attachment to any thing.

The work of Acharya Tulsi, in many ways akin to Gandhianism but largely free from an encumbered political agenda, has had a long history in India, and has been used for a variety of causes. On March 1, 1949, he instituted the Anuvrat movement, a series of twelve vows that he has urged persons to take, ranging from the vow of ahimsa: "I will not kill any innocent creature" to the twelfth, which states "I will do my best to avoid contributing to pollution."[8] The premise of this program is that the transformation of society must begin with transformation of the individual. S. Gopalan states that Acharya Tulsi insits "that the ills of society automatically get cured by means of the process of self-purification and self-control."[9] In support of the Anuvrat Movement, Sarvepalli Radhakrishnan, India's philosopher-president, has written:

> There is a general feeling in the country that while we are attending to the material progress and doing substantial work in that direction, we are neglecting the human side of true progress. A civilized human being must be free from greed, vanity, passion, anger. Civilizations decline if there is a coarsening of moral fibre, if there is callousness of heart. Man is tending to become a robot, a mechanical instrument caring for nothing except his material welfare, incapable of exercising his intelligence and responsibility. He seems to prefer comfort to liberty.... to remedy this growing indiscipline, lack of rectitude, egotism, the Anuvrat Movement was started on March 1, 1949. It requires strict adherence to the principles of good life.[10]

The goal of the Anuvrat movement, which has been active for over forty years, is to encourage persons to adapt their lifestyle to effect a more nonviolent world. Gandhi employed a similar technique in his Satyagraha campaigns. The current ecological drive towards bioregionalism, wherein people are encouraged to develop an intimate relationship with their immediate environment, is based on similar approaches. The essential message in both instances is that environmental ravage proceeds from over-consumption that arises from disregard. To minimize consumption is to minimize harm to one's environment.

However stark the life of Acharya Tulsi may be, it does not mandate that all Jainas follow the life of a monk. Jaina laypersons have long been

---

[8]See S.L. Gandhi, ed., *Anuvrat Movement: A Constructive Endeavor Towards a Nonviolent Multicultural Society* (Rajasmand, India: Anuvrat Vishva Bharati, 1987).

[9]Gandhi, *Anuvrat Movement* 33.

[10]Gandhi, *Anuvrat Movement*; as quoted from S. Radhakrishnan, *Living With a Purpose* (Glastonbury, CT: Ind-US, Inc., 1983), a profile of fourteen distinguished personalities.

challenged by the example of the monk to make their own lifestyles less violent, as indicated in the illustration of the pharmaceutical company's release of test animals back into the wild. The legendary frugality of the Jainas also underscores a concern to minimize the diminishment of one's resources. This careful lifestyle has ironically resulted in the accumulation of great wealth on the part of the Jainas. According to some sources, Jainas constitute only one percent of India's population, yet they pay approximately half of India's income tax.[11] Individual Jainas control the automobile, pharmaceutical, publishing, and other industries of India. And yet even the wealthiest of Jains for the most part live simply.

As mentioned earlier, during a trip to India in 1981, I was struck with the damage to the environment incurred in India by its burgeoning industrialization. The level of awareness in this regard was close to nonexistent, much to my consternation and distress. However, when I returned this past winter, a noticeable change had taken place: virtually every newspaper included a daily story on the environmental. Since the Bhopal Union Carbide disaster, two major centers have been established to serve as clearinghouses for environmental issues. In New Delhi the Center for Science and Environment, in addition to other activities, provides a news service that supplies India's many newspapers with stories of environmental and ecological interest. It clips those that appear in print and publishes them in a periodical entitled *Green File*. Although this may seem rather simple, it struck me as a resident of Los Angeles as particularly effective. In the *Los Angeles Times*, the Sierra Club is depicted as a dating service and the portrait painted of environmentalists in feature articles often borders on the absurd. California's "slow growth" movement has been maligned in the press, as well as outspent in referendum campaigns by developers seeking to protect their interests. At the *Newhall Signal*, an editor who suggested that a cluster of cancer deaths might be linked to chemical production in a Los Angeles suburb was dismissed from his post. Clearly, the editorial policies of our regional papers have been shaped by business interests; a parallel form of news control can be found in the *New York Times*' undying support for nuclear energy. One possible reason for the willingness of the Indian press to lend credibility to the environmental cause is that the head of the *Times of India*, the leading daily, Ashok Jain, is himself a member of the Jaina tradition.

While in the city of Ahmedabad, home to many Jainas and the residence of Mahatma Gandhi for two decades, I visited with Meena Rahunathan, special programmes officer of the Centre for Environment Education. The CEE was established in 1984 as part of the Nehru Foundation for Development. It conducts workshops and produces materials that reach over ten thousand teachers per year. It operates a "News and Features Service"

---

[11]*Ahimsa: Nonviolence.*

similar to that of the Centre for Science and Environment. It has initiated rural education program to help stem the destruction of India's remaining forests. It conducts various urban programs, including the promotion of smokeless cooking fires through use of a chulha, a wood or dung burning stove with a damper system that captures smoke.[12] In 1986 it launched the Ganga Pollution Awareness Programme, which has been widely documented in the United States. In cooperation with the School of Forestry of the State University of New York, located in Syracuse, it produces a series of environmental films for children. It has developed interpretive materials for the National Zoological Park in Delhi and for Kanha National Park. Within the city of Ahmedabad, it has installed a permanent ecological exhibit at Gujerat University; maintains a bird sanctuary at Sundarvan, its fourteen acre campus; and has developed exhibits for the Gandhi Ashram.[13]

Another institution that has long been attuned to environmental concerns is Gandhi Peace Foundation in New Delhi. Gandhi's village- based economic model may be seen as an early paradigm for the bioregionalism that many ecoactivists promote today. Gandhi wrote:

> Industrialization on a mass scale will necessarily lead to passive or active exploitation of the villages as the problems of competition and marketing come in. Therefore, we have to concentrate on the village being self-contained.[14]

Gandhi also criticized industrial development in a style quite reminiscent of Thoreau's *Walden Pond*:

> This land of ours was once, we are told, the abode of the Gods. It is not possible to conceive Gods inhabiting a land which is made hideous by the smoke and din of mill chimneys and factories, and whose roadways are traversed by rushing engines, dragging numerous cars crowded with men who know not for the most part what they are after, who are often absent-minded and whose tempers do not improve by being uncomfortably packed like sardines in boxes and finding themselves in the midst of strangers who would oust them if they could and whom they would, in their turn, oust similarly. I refer to these things because they are held to symbolic of material progress. But they add not an atom to our happiness.[15]

Reflecting the influence of his Jaina neighbors and advisors, he proposed a solution to the twin problems of industrialization and alienation by advocating

---

[12]One of the greatest sources of airborne pollutants in India is particulants given off by the burning of cow dung, the prime fuel used for cooking fires. This simple device, if universally applied, would greatly reduce air pollution, particularly in urban areas.

[13]"Centre for Environment Education Annual Report, 1987-88," Nehru Foundation for Development, Ahmedabad.

[14]M.K. Gandhi, *The Village Reconstruction* (Bombay: Bhatatiya Vidya Bhavan, 1966) 43.

[15]M.K. Gandhi, *My Socialism* (Ahmedabad: Navajivan Publishing House, 1959) 34.

that every occupation work at the minimization of violence.

> Strictly speaking, no activity and no industry is possible without a certain amount of violence, no matter how little. Even the very process of living is impossible without a certain amount of violence. What we have to do is to minimize it to the greatest extent possible. Indeed the very word nonviolence, a negative word, means that it is an effort to abandon the violence that is inevitable in life. Therefore, whoever believes in Ahimsa will engage himself in occupations that involve the least possible violence.[16]

In addition to promoting and restating the works of Gandhi, the Gandhi Peace Foundation has engaged in various projects to promote village-based economies. It has encouraged farmers to grow food for themselves in addition to cultivating the usual cash crop. In cooperation with the Centre for Rural Development and Appropriate Technology of the Indian Institute of Technology, the Gandhi Peace Foundation has promoted the implementation of organic farming according to the model of Masanobu Fukuoka, who advocates no tilling or weeding, and no use of fertilizers or herbicides.[17] Although this project is in a rudimentary phase, T.S. Ananthu, a research associate, spoke of the foundation promoting this program elsewhere in India.

Two movements in India have taken direct action in an effort to bring attention to environmental concerns. The Chipko Movement in Uttar Pradesh involves local women saving trees by embracing them, staving off bulldozers.[18] Baba Amte, winner of the 1990 Templeton Prize for progress in religion, has focused resistance to the Narmada River Valley dam project by conducting a vigil unto death in protest of the planned destruction by flooding of over 325,000 acres of forest and agricultural land in western India. The first Asian to win the United Nations Human Rights Award, Baba Amte is best known for his pioneering work on behalf of India's lepers. Following the Bhopal disaster of 1984 that claimed over 3800 lives, he began an environmental campaign, stating that "It is this invisible leprosy of greed and ambition that is turning our world into a wasteland."[19] His style on behalf of environmental causes has taken him to villages directly affected by the Narmada River Valley and other super dam projects, somewhat reminiscent of Gandhian grassroots movements.

We have surveyed three Indian approaches aimed at correcting the current ecological assault: changing one's own lifestyle, as advocated by the

---

[16]Gandhi, *My Socialism* 35.

[17]"The Mohanpur Experiment in Natural Farming: Second Interim Report, June 1988," Gandhi Peace Foundation and IIT, Delhi.

[18]Information on this movement is included in the periodical publication *Worldwide Women in the Environment*, P.O. Box 40885, Washington, D.C. 20016.

[19]Mark Fineman, "A River, A Dam, and an Old Man's Last Battle" *Los Angeles Times* (May 1, 1990, Section H, World Report) 1.

example of Acharya Tulsi; efforts at general education, as seen with the Centre for Science and Environment and the Centre for Environment Education; and the direct action of the Chipko movement and Baba Amte. The Gandhi Peace Foundation seemingly combines all three approaches. Each of these movements is rooted in a uniquely Indian orientation and each has demonstrated a degree of success, though perhaps not easily discernable by Euro-American standards. The purest of models is perhaps the first, held forth by Jaina monastics, who own virtually nothing, who will not even as much as touch a leaf, who tend to stay in the desert so that natural life forms will not be disturbed. The second model and third models, focusing on education and direct action, are perhaps more "Western" in approach, at least on the surface. One notable cultural difference, however, is that there seems to be less concern for legislative lobbying in India. When queried, neither the Gandhi Peace Foundation nor the Centre for Environment Education nor Anuvibha knew of environmental lobbying groups comparable to Greenpeace in India. When pressed on this issue, the standard response was that "In India, people do not pay attention to laws; the consciousness must be changed." This basic orientation has not strayed far from Gandhian and traditional religious models.

In many ways the current lifestyle of India contains elements that support the environmental perspective. Most persons live within a short scooter ride or walking distance to work. Foodstuffs consumed by Indians are comprised of grains purchased in bulk from the market and cooked with vegetables procured from travelling greengrocers who push their carts through virtually every neighborhood all day long. Waste is collected and used for fertilizer.

Yet all of this may soon change. In Delhi, I was served yogurt in a disposable plastic container. Private automobiles have begun to proliferate. The advent of a consumer economy seems to be eroding the possibility for an ecologically sound form of development. Although industrialization and technologization of the subcontinent are modest by American standards, the sheer numbers of people entering into the middle class make it difficult for the same mistakes of Western development to be avoided. One small example is the automobile: India now produces its own small cars, and increasingly they are owned by individuals. By some accounts (and verified by personal experience) the Delhi area has perhaps the most polluted air in the world. Yet these newly produced vehicles have no emissions controls, nor does there seem to be an interest in lobbying for them.

And yet as the general awareness of environmental ravage increases, even here in the United States, the best and most cutting-edge solutions seems to follow the model proposed by Acharya Tulsi in India. It is only when each individual makes a change in his or her lifestyle that a societal leap forward can occur. In America, the seeds of this transformation have been sown; over 80% of the populace define themselves as "environmentalists," indicating that concern for ecological harmony has been widely accepted. Americans now are educating themselves on how to minimize the use of the fabulous technology available to us, from household chemicals to nuclear weapons.

In India, people traditionally have not been divorced from the earth: to think of themselves as separate from the ongoing and all pervasive cycle of life and death would be inconceivable. And yet now India and its religious traditions face the challenges of modernity, technology, consumptionism, and technological ravage; in short, buying into the American dream where the world and one's relationship to it become estranged and objectified. Part of the solution to ecological ravage requires the hard work of scientists, technocrats, and educators, those responsible for inventing and inculcating the values of consumer society. However, we need also to look off the wheel, so to speak; we need to get out of the car to fix it. For this, the example set by the renouncers of India who advocate minimal consumption continues to offer a solution for myriad problems. By attacking the source of human misery through uprooting human attachment itself, a true type of peace that automatically extends to others can be fostered.

Part Seven

SYMBOLS AND METAPHORS
OF NATURE, GOD, AND HUMANITY

ANNE MORROW LINDBERGH'S *GIFT FROM THE SEA*
AS A RELIGIOUS MYTH

Fred McLeod, S.J.

The twentieth anniversary edition of Anne Morrow Lindbergh's *Gift From The Sea* describes her book as exuding "great and simple wisdom (that) has spoken to hundreds of thousands of readers."[1] It recounts in a lyrically pleasing way how she spent a two week summer vacation on a secluded island and received from the sea a curious array of thought-provoking seashells. Five of these speak to her in an evocative way about the different stages of her life. As anyone who has been touched by her work can readily attest to, her account pulsates with a spiritual power that penetrates softly but surely into the core of one's heart in a way that can be both individually enriching and personally transforming.

To reveal the religious undertow coursing beneath this work, I plan first of all to examine the meaning of faith and point out how Anne Lindbergh's longings for personal integrity are really a faith search. I will then discuss the meaning of symbol and myth in general and exemplify symbol in detail from the text, leaving the question of whether *Gift From The Sea* is a religious myth until the end of the paper. Afterwards, I will spend time in probing in what sense we can attribute religious significance to Lindbergh's experiences of being at one with nature. To aid us in this venture, I will set her experiences against the backdrop of the ancient Antiochene[2] view that the human person

---

[1]Anne Morrow Lindbergh, *Gift From The Sea*, Twentieth Anniversary Edition, (New York: Vintage Books, 1975). The quote is taken from the back cover. All future references are taken from this work.

[2]"Antiochean" is broadly understood here as referring to those who adhere to the school of thought prevalent first at Antioch, then at Edessa and later at Nisibis. Those most associated with its theological and exegetical positions are Diodore, John Chrysostom, Theodore of Mopsuestia, Nestorius, Theodoret of Cyr, and Narsai. Its approach is often cited as being in opposition to that taken by the School of Alexandria, especially as regards its emphases upon the humanity over the divinity in Christ and upon the literal over the allegorical method in scriptural exegesis. A similar difference can also be noted in the way it stresses our human body as an integral part of our constitution as God's image, while the Alexandrians tend to emphasize more the spirit and mind as the locus of God's image within us. This difference,

is both the image of God and the bond of the universe. This latter approach will provide us, I believe, a theological insight into the overall general theme of an ecology of spirit. I will conclude with a summary of how *Gift From The Sea* can and ought to be looked upon as a religious myth.

Faith as a search for personal meaning and fulfillment

The English word "faith" is open to diverse interpretations. It is most often understood as accepting the word of another. For our purposes, I want to take it in the sense that Paul Tillich has popularized for our age: as an act of being ultimately concerned.[3] It is an act expressing the free commitment of ourself to someone or something that touches us in the core of our being and that we are firmly convinced will bring us personal fulfillment, if only we can acquire it. It manifests itself whenever we have to choose one value over all others. Or it may simply be present in those situations where we sense that our heart is searching for something more than what we possess at this moment. The classic example of this kind of emphasis is found in St. Augustine's oft-quoted remark that "our hearts are restless, until they rest in Thee (O Lord)."

If faith is approached in this existential way, I think that we can readily discern how Anne Lindbergh's *Gift From The Sea* can be considered to be a work of faith. Though she would seem to have all that any woman could desire--a loving husband whose exploits as an aviator has brought him and her international recognition and acclaim, a well deserved reputation in her own right as a talented writer, and sufficient wealth that has provided her with the freedom to do whatever she wants. Yet she openly confesses at the beginning of her vacation that "the bearing, rearing, feeding and educating of children; the running of a house with its thousand details; human relationships with their myriad pulls"[4] have badly fragmented her life. All of these have impelled her to get away by herself, so that she can seek out a new pattern of living that will renew her inner spirit and empower her to give of herself energetically and purposefully to others.

Lindbergh's introduction and first two chapters abound with examples of her search for personal meaning and integrity. When she gazes upon the channelled whelk, she wonders why the hermit crab has abandoned his shell. This leads her to the realization that "I too have run away. . . [and] have shed the shell of my life, for these few weeks of vacation."[5] It also impresses upon her a vital and pivotal lesson that beach living teaches: the need to shed many things we consider indispensable for our ordinary daily living and to adopt a

---

however, must not be blown out of proportion. For except perhaps for Origen, those adhering to the Alexandrian school of thought also maintained the importance of the material and physical.

[3]Paul Tillich, *Dynamics of Faith* (New York: Harper Colophon Books, 1957), p.1.
[4]Lindbergh 29.
[5]Lindbergh 22.

simplicity of life that fosters a spirit of true inner freedom and peace. While she knows that her whole being is yearning for this, she nevertheless recognizes that she has at hand no easy and convenient answers. She has only the clues that her seashells suggest.

The deep unrest that Lindbergh recounts in her first chapter is clearly indicative of a faith search. Though she may not look upon the desire for more in her life as a hungering for an ultimate goal that supersedes all others, yet the dynamic thrust that powers every faith act is unmistakably present here. It is prodding her to abandon the present shell of her life for a new one that will sustain and fulfill her. It has spurred her to take leave of her family for the seclusion and solitude of a primitive cottage, so that she can work through her feelings and determine how she may attain a singleness of purpose in her life. For she recognizes that, unless she can satisfy the yearnings of her heart, she will surely lack the inner strength to carry out her many duties and commitments.

Symbol and myth as faith expressions

Because the ultimate we seek in a faith act is something far beyond us, we need, especially in our present-day image-oriented culture, very specific and concrete expressions that will not only visualize the reality we are pursuing but make it really desirable for us at this moment. Symbol and myth both perform this dual function for us. Each in its own way provides the language and the occasion, so that the object of our faith can be known and experienced in a meaningful and dynamic manner. Because these words are understood in notably divergent ways in our society today, we will first clarify what we mean by these terms and then demonstrate how they are present in Lindbergh's *Gift From The Sea*.

As regards the meaning of a faith symbol, we turn once again to Tillich's explanation. He views a symbol as being something (or someone) concrete that not only points towards another reality but participates in the power of that reality. When it fulfills its first function, it may be summing up within itself several assorted ideas whose full meaning we may not always be able to express even to ourself in clear, univocal terms. If a symbol fulfills only this function, it is appropriately called by some a "representational" symbol. When it is also felt to be laden with power, it may evoke intense feelings and personal values regarding the reality that it is pointing to. This second kind of symbol is referred to as a "presentational" symbol. It "presents" power to us. As such, it is both informative and evocative, appealing to our heart as well as our head.

Myth is another concrete and specific way for faith to express itself. It is a term, however, understood in almost diametrically different ways. Many may still regard myth today as a wholly fabricated story. Contemporary theologians, however, view it as being endowed with a deeper meaning. Simply put, a myth is a story with symbols, in the sense of symbol explained above. The primary purpose of the story is not to present us with a strict historical narrative or an "objective" scientific account. Historical facts may indeed be present, but this is incidental. Its main concern is to put us into a vital contact with the spiritual outlook and values prevalent in a community's and our own individual life through the imaginative use of language and story.

The presence of symbols within Gift from the Sea

When Anne Lindbergh chances upon five very different kinds of seashells during her vacation, they act as presentational symbols. They touch her to the quick and elicit a profusion of thoughts, values and feelings concerning herself and her relationships with others. Since we have already discussed in our treatment above on faith the impact that the first shell has had, we will examine now the messages that the other four have imparted to her about her desire for a fuller life and about the critical moments that she discerns to be present in the growth cycle of all relationships.

The second shell that speaks to Lindbergh is the moon shell, so-called because of its "perfect spiral, winding inward to [its] pinpoint center."[6] This highlights for Lindbergh how each of us is in the final analysis alone. She notes how we all fear being alone and continually try to avoid letting it happen. But if we do allow solitude into our life, we may very well find out, as Lindbergh did during her vacation, that life rushes back into the void. She found out paradoxically that, although separated from others, she felt an exhilarating and uplifting sense of being both "melted into the universe"[7] and close to other human beings. Reflecting on this, she comes to the realization that it is "only when one is connected to one's own core [that one] is connected to others...and the core, the inner spring, can best be refound through solitude."[8] She sums up the central idea of the moonshell for her, when she exclaims: "You will remind me that I must try to be alone for part of each year, even a week or a few days; and for part of each day, even for an hour or a few minutes in order to keep my core, my center, my island quality."[9]

The third shell is the double-sunrise, named appropriately because its fragile halves are exactly matched. The shell is "a gift freely offered, freely taken, in mutual trust."[10] It reminds Lindbergh of how the beginning of every relationship is pure and simple, fresh and beautiful. It speaks to her of the enraptured state that we all prize and wish we could maintain forever. Yet as we all know, this perfect unity is quickly invaded. Although it can never be perfectly restored, Anne nevertheless urges us to spend time on occasions in

---

[6]Lindbergh 39.
[7]Lindbergh 43.
[8]Lindbergh 44.
[9]Lindbergh 58.
[10]Lindbergh 64

search of a temporary recovery of this kind of pure relationship. This attempt is healthy as long as we keep firmly in mind that "there is no pattern for a permanent return, only for refreshment."[11]

The fourth shell is an oyster that has small shells clinging to its humped back. It suggests to Lindbergh the middle years of marriage, when a husband and wife are struggling to achieve a place in the world. It is a time for deepening the bonds of marriage and for shedding such "shells" as ambition, material possessions and the ego itself. For Lindbergh, it can serve as an ideal time to pursue a second flowering in our life. For we are now blessed with the opportunity and means to develop and fulfill the neglected sides or aspects of our personality. We can devote ourself now to the intellectual, cultural, and spiritual activities that we may have had no time or even desire for in our earlier years.

The last shell is the rare and beautiful argonauta, named for the fabled ships that sailed in quest of the Golden Fleece. For Lindbergh, the shell symbolizes freedom. Just as a mother argonauta releases her young so that they can live their own life, the same kind of freedom she insists ought to be manifested in an intimate relationship between two fully developed persons. In such a case, each recognizes and respects the unique transcendent value of the other to be his or her own true self and earnestly tries to be the means of releasing this other to achieve his or her fulfillment. The poet expresses this well, when he writes that a person becomes a "world to oneself for another's sake."[12] Such a freeing attitude within a relationship will make "it possible for each to see the other whole and against a wide sky!"[13]

Lindbergh views the daily schedule that she ritualistically follows during the second week of her vacation as having symbolic meaning for her. She sums this up succinctly as my "morning is for mental work . . . [the] afternoon . . . for physical tasks, the out-of-door jobs . . . . But evening is for sharing, for communication."[14] This daily ritual routine helps her to experience a sense of being at one with not only herself and her sister but also with nature and the cosmos itself. We can see this latter kind of at-one-ment expressed in two passages where Lindbergh recounts what she felt while she strolled along the beach with her sister.

We walk up the beach in silence, but in harmony, as the sandpipers ahead of us move like a corps of ballet dancers, keeping time to some interior rhythm inaudible to us. Intimacy is blown away. Emotions are carried out to sea. We are even free of thoughts, at least of their articulation; clean and bare as whitened driftwood; empty as shells, ready to be filled again with the impersonal sea and sky and wind.[15]

---

[11]Lindbergh 74.
[12]Lindbergh 96
[13]Lindbergh 98.
[14]Lindbergh 102.
[15]Lindbergh 101.

The second experience occurs while she and her sister lie flat on the sand at the end of the day:

> We feel stretched, expanded to take in the compass (of the stars). They pour into us until we are filled...up to the brim. This is what one thirsts for, I realize, after the smallness of the day, of work, of details, of intimacy...one thirsts for the magnitude and universality of a night full of stars, pouring into one like a thick tide.[16]

The theological significance of Gift from the Sea

To elaborate on how *Gift From The Sea* has something insightful to affirm about an ecology of the spirit, I want first to present the fourth century Antiochene view of how humans serve as both the image of God and the bond of the universe.[17] It is an ancient tradition that ties together two scriptural views about our human role within the universe: 1) that we humans image God to one another and the world about us, and 2) that we are also the bond of the universe. Let us now consider these in much greater detail.

While the Alexandrian and Augustinian traditions located our "image of God" in the higher "regions" of our rational soul, the Antiocheans looked upon this phrase as being attributable to our whole person as a unique, living composite of body and spirit. They understood this as pertaining above all to Christ, in the sense we have explained a symbol above. For Christ not only points to the reality of God but also shares in a real way in God's power and dignity and reveals these to the world through his bodily nature.

When Scripture speaks of Adam as being made in God's image, the Antiocheans understood this as also referring to humans in a true but secondary sense. Adam foreshadows the coming of Christ who is the primary image, but he is nevertheless a true image in his own right. He not only reveals God's power and beauty to the rest of creation but also shares in God's dominative power as his naming of the animals so convincingly indicates. He is truly God's viceroy on earth, empowered to act decisively in His name. But even beyond this, he serves as the unique, divinely appointed way for all other creatures, material and spiritual, to attain to their transcendent God. According to God's creative intent, we humans truly represent --and present--God's image to all the rest of creation and stand as the sole visible means for them to know and love God.

Closely allied to the Antiochene understanding of how we image God in this world is their view of how we also function as the bond of the universe. According to this view, the universe is an organic whole whose members are

---

[16]Lindbergh 102-03.

[17]For a summary of this view, cf. my article "Man as the Image of God: Its Meaning and Theological Significance in Narsai," *Theological Studies* 42 (September 1981): 458-468. The Antiochene view of image also shows similarities with a number of passages in Irenaeus, cf. David Cairns' *The Image of God in Man* (rev. ed., London, 1973).

either rational or irrational. By our soul, we are akin to the angelic world, and by our body we are united to the corporeal world. We bind both worlds together in the composite physical and spiritual nature of our being.[18] This Antiochene outlook is based on Saint Paul's doctrine of Christ's role as both mediator and recapitulator of the universe. Colossians expresses this emphatically when it proclaims in majestic language that Christ is "the image of the invisible God, the first born of all creation . . . [who] is before all things, and (in whom) all things hold together . . . . For in him all the fullness of God was pleased to dwell, and through him to reconcile to himself all things, whether on earth or in heaven, making peace by the blood of the cross."[19] As is quite evident from what we have already said, the Antiocheans see this as applicable to the symbolic role that Christ and all humans as represented in Adam play within creation. We are symbols of a symbol!

This Antiochene outlook on our nature and role within the universe underscores an aspect of Christian revelation that we tend to overlook. Because of our stress upon faith as an act or state binding us to a personal relationship with God and all others within the life of His church, we often fail to comprehend how a faith life in Christ also entails other horizontal relationships and ramifications. As the Antiocheans have realized, faith connotes a real bond with nature and the cosmos. We are an integral part of a cosmos that is destined to share in Christ's final glory insofar as we assist it through the exercise of our creative power to come to its final fulfillment. God has entrusted us with responsibility for caring for ourself, for other humans, and for the natural world about us, so that we all grow into our full potential as creatures destined for union with Him through Christ.

The Antiochene speculation provides us with what I believe is not only a solid theological basis for a clearer understanding of how we are related in general to nature but also a highly suitable backdrop against which we can see Anne Lindbergh's experiences as having a faith and a religious significance. Her feelings of being an intimate part of both nature and the universe are, from the Antiochene perspective, an intuitive, instinctual awareness of the bond that really exists between us and the world. I think too that we can consider her experiences of union with nature as a stirring foretaste, as it were, of the final atonement--taking this in the English root sense of this word

---

[18] Iso'dad of Merv, a ninth-century "Nestorian" theologian, sums up this viewpoint well when he remarks that Adam "is called image because he is the synthesis of the world, because in him is enclosed and united the entire creation of spiritual and corporeal beings and because he is placed as an image in the city of the world, so that by him the entire creation may show its love towards the Creator." (Ceslas van den Eynde, ed., *Commentaire d'Iso dad de Merv sur l'Ancien Testament* (CSCO 96-97, pp. 50-51) In other words, we humans stand horizontally as the bond of the universe uniting both the spiritual and corporeal worlds within ourselves and also vertically as the image who both represents and presents God in a visible way to these two disparate worlds.

[19] Col 1:15, 17, 19-20.

as an at-one-ment--that Christ will achieve, when he recapitulates all creation and offers it back as a gift to his Father.

Lindbergh's *Gift From The Sea*, therefore, illuminates for us an important theological insight that we may overlook regarding our human relationship to the natural environment in which we live. We may so center our attention on our duty to be responsible stewards of God's creation that we fail to appreciate the deeper ontological relationships existing between us and both nature and the cosmos. Lindbergh was not only able to experience this repeatedly during her two week vacation on a remote island but was also specially gifted with the literary power to spark a similar response in those who contemplate nature. As such, her experiences make us aware of how faith entails more than an enlarging of our vision of life and involves more than being in relationship with other human beings in and through Christ. It is also a means for us to enter into and experience in a real sensible way our existential relationship with the ecological world about us.

Gift from the Sea as a religious myth

From what we have already stated above concerning the symbolic meaning that Lindbergh derives from her shells, I think little has to be said as to why *Gift From The Sea* is indeed a myth. For it is a story recounting Lindbergh's summer vacation on a remote island during which five seashells speak to the meaning of her life. Its purpose is not to provide merely an historical account of what happened, but to relate how the sea exercised a transforming effect upon her life. Her contemplative insights into the symbolic meaning of each of her shells helped her to reach a rhythmic and delicately balanced harmony with herself, others, and nature itself. This enabled her to refind the inner strength she needed to let others feed upon her. It is a story, in other words, of how Lindbergh's faith has been refound and reinvigorated.

Gift From The Sea can also be said--in a very broad but true sense--to be a religious work. While Lindbergh makes only a brief, fleeting reference to God when she reflects upon the times she is able to give herself completely to Him in communion, nevertheless we can interpret from a Christian viewpoint her deep yearnings for personal wholeness as a search for God. As Saint Augustine realized so keenly, every response to our passionate probing for a fuller and more meaningful life is ultimately a religious search for God. If we understand faith in this way, then *Gift From The Sea* stands out as a profoundly stirring mythic account about the deeper meaning of our life, with a clearly discernible religious dimension.

Conclusion

Gift From The Sea contains several messages on how to still our restless hearts. One is especially pertinent to the theme of ecology. It points out to us in a highly affective and effective way that the physical world about us is not merely a creature whose spell-binding beauty is to be wondered at or whose value resides in the innumerable functional ways that it cares for our material well-being. It also possesses a "recreational" value. As the English root of the word "recreation" indicates, it enjoys a power to "re-create" our life in a new fuller, transforming way. As Lindbergh discovered in her own life, to enter into a harmonious dialogue and dance with nature can be a means for both healing and expanding our own inner fractured spirit.

One point, however, needs to be kept foremost in mind. Like any myth, *Gift From The Sea* cannot guarantee that its reading will provoke a faith experience or bring a person a religious sense of at-one-ment with oneself, God, others and nature. As the first word in this title emphasizes so sharply and emphatically, to experience this must come first to us as a gift that we cannot merit or work to achieve on our own. Anne sums this up in a poignant way, when she notes in her first chapter: "the sea does not reward those who are too anxious, too greedy, or too impatient. To dig for treasures reveals not only impatience and greed, but lack of faith. Patience, patience, patience, is what the sea teaches. Patience and faith. One should lie empty, open, choiceless as a beach--waiting for a gift from the sea."[20] Like all religious works of faith, *Gift From The Sea* can spiritually refresh and recreate us, provided that we are humbly open to receive its transforming message patiently and gracefully as a loving gift from our creating God.

---

[20]Lindbergh 17.

NATURE AND GRACE: AN ECOLOGICAL METAPHOR

Sally Kenel

Michael Himes contends that "the development of Christian thought in the Western church has been the story of new ways of formulating the nature-grace relation."[1] It follows then that the ecological concerns of the late twentieth century may warrant a new interpretation of this relation. As early as in 1972, Joseph Sittler attempted such a reformulation; his assertion that viewing the world as an ecosystem provides the occasion for revising the relation of nature and grace has gone largely unheeded.[2] Awareness of the interconnection of all things, however, continues to grow--a perspective with the support of such otherwise diverse theologians as Rosemary Radford Reuther and Pope John Paul II.[3] The relationship between nature and grace is deserving of examination in an ecological context.

We can begin by recalling that Catholic theologians have traditionally described the relationship between nature and grace in contrasting terms. Nature referred to that which made one human rather than animal, angelic, or divine; whereas grace was that free gift of God which raised human beings to another level of existence--the supernatural. The notion of "potentia obedientialis," however, claimed that despite the contrast, it was part of human nature to be open to grace. Such an understanding of nature and grace became problematic, raising such questions as: "Does grace really change human nature, and if so how is human freedom preserved?" and "how is the person able to accept freely the self-communication of God in grace?"[4]

These important questions commonly issue from posing the nature-grace distinction in a way that refers only to *human* nature. On the other hand, nature is also defined, as Walter Burghardt did when describing the various facets of human disunity, as whatever is not human: "by 'nature' I mean all

---

[1] Michael Himes, "This Graced World: Trinity, Grace and Sacraments," *The Church* 1 (1985): 3.

[2] *Essays on Nature and Grace* (Philadelphia: Fortress Press, 1972).

[3] See for example Reuther's essay, "Woman, Body and Nature: Sexism and the Theology of Creation" in *Sexism and Godtalk* (Boston: Beacon Press, 1983) 72-92; and the 1987 encyclical *Sollicitudo Rei Socialis*, especially #34.

[4] Richard McBrien, *Catholicism* Vol. 1 (Minneapolis: Winston Press, 1980) 159.

that is not man or God?"[5] Actually, the change is minor. The notion of nature remains anthropocentric, but this time by exclusion. Moreover, the distinction between the human and the natural here expresses what Lynn White characterizes as a neo-Christian and post-Christian attitude towards nature: "We are superior to nature, contemptuous of it, willing to use it for our slightest whim."[6] We can instead employ a thoroughly inclusive definition of nature--one where nature refers to the whole universe, the totality of creation. Such a concept of nature assumes that reality is an interrelated system, and humanity is one among other unique species.[7]

The implications of changing from an anthropocentric to an ecological world-view are considerable. For Sallie McFague the change requires a revision of theology to include "metaphorical theology," which she defines as "a kind of heuristic construction that in focusing on the imaginative construal of the God-world relationship, attempts to remythologize Christian faith through metaphors and models appropriate for an ecological, nuclear age."[8] Focusing attention on relationship, interdependence, and change rather than substance, hierarchy and immutability, she argues, challenges theologians to experiment and test new metaphors to see if they can more fully illumine contemporary experience, and by their continuity with the Christian scriptures provide a timely expression of faith.[9] An ecological world-view can serve as a challenge to theologians to experiment with new metaphors for the relation between God and the world, and in so doing to revise our understanding of the relationship between nature and God's self-communication, grace.

Accepting this challenge demands appreciation for the heuristic nature of such an endeavor and attention to the limits as well as the potential of metaphors. These limits require that metaphors be used with discretion, since just as metaphors both apply and do not apply, neither can one metaphor depict the whole of reality. To contend, for example, that one image of God is the only valid one smacks of idolatry, while an overemphasis upon God's transcendence over our categories risks confusing the inadequacy of the categories with falsity.

The Metaphor: The World as God's Body

Christian theology has described the relationship between God and the world in many images. An image with strong biblical roots is that of a king and his realm. Many find this model inadequate, and some, like Sallie McFague, judge it dangerous. The danger, as she sees it, lies in the fact that the monarchical model "encourages a sense of distance from the world; it

---

[5]Walter Burghardt, *Towards Reconciliation* (Washington: USCC, 1974) 26.
[6]Lynn White, "The Historical Roots of our Ecological Crisis," *Science* 155 (1967), 1206.
[7]See Sallie McFague, *Models of God* (Philadelphia: Fortress Press, 1987) 8.
[8]McFague 40.
[9]McFague 66.

attends only to the human dimension of the world and it supports attitudes of either domination of the world or passivity toward it."[10] In short, it denies the ecological world view. To offer an alternative model more in keeping with the New Testament stories of Jesus' post-resurrection appearances and their promise of God's continuing presence in the world, McFague experiments with the metaphor of the world as God's body. Since she proposes this model in a metaphorical sense, she insists it be understood that there are areas where the comparison does not hold as well as areas where it does. Thus, in no way is the world to be *defined* as God's body. Despite this restriction, the metaphor immediately raises some difficulties.

An over-identification of the world with God can open this metaphor to the charge of pantheism. It must be remembered, however, that humans both identify with their bodies and recognize they are more than their bodies. The metaphor of the world as God's body implies that God is not the world, nor is the world God. Accordingly, this metaphor intimates a relationship between God and the world which corresponds to the notion of panentheism in process philosophy, which Charles Hartshorne has described as "the view that deity is in some real aspect distinguishable from and independent of any and all relative items, and yet, taken as an actual whole, includes all relative items."[11]

Besides introducing the issue of pantheism, McFague's metaphor also raises questions about the role of humans in this body. Are they merely another organic part? What about freedom and individuality? Here it is important to recall that although embodiedness is an essential part of what it means to be human, there are other dimensions as well--dimensions which indicate that we are a special part of the world. Reflecting on the role of humans in this metaphor, McFague contends:

> We think of ourselves as the *imago dei*, not only possessing bodies but being agents. We view ourselves as embodied spirits in the larger body of the world which influences us and which we influence. That is, we are the part modeled on the model: self:body::God:world. We are agents and God possesses a body: both sides of the model pertain to both God and ourselves. This implies that we are not mere submerged parts of the body of God but relate to God as to another Thou. The presence of God to us in and through God's body is the experience of encounter, not of submersion.[12]

---

[10]McFague indicates no awareness of Frye's "royal metaphor" which he claims indicates that the king represents the unity of society, remarking even that "the king is his people, their existence as a `body'." See Northrop Frye, *The Great Code* (New York: Harcourt Brace Jovanovich, 1983) 87-101.

[11]Charles Hartshorne, *The Divine Relativity: A Social Conception of God* (New Haven: Yale University Press, 1964) 89.

[12]McFague 76.

Thus, the metaphor of the world as God's body can avoid the pitfalls of equating God with the world, and of reducing human beings to one among many organic parts.

In addition, although not the most evident of the biblical descriptions of God's relation to the world, it is found in the Hebrew Scriptures at least elliptically. Consider, for example, this excerpt from the song of Moses:

Thy right hand, O Lord, glorious in power,
Thy right hand, O Lord, shatters the enemy...
At the blast of thy nostrils the waters piled up,
The floods stood up in a heap...
Thou didst stretch out thy hand,
The earth swallowed them up (Ex 15:6-9 RSV).

The metaphor of the world as God's body is a variation of the Christian view that the bread and wine of the vegetable world represent the body and blood of the animal world and specifically the body of Christ, the body which in turn is identified as the church.[13] In other words, while the metaphor of the world as God's body offers a timely ecological approach to the relationship between God and the world, it is an approach which is, at the very least, in continuity with the Christian tradition.

The Metaphor of Embodiment

Since working with metaphors involves moving from the known to the unknown, to understand the world as God's body it helps to understand what it means for human beings to be embodied. Reflection on what it means for a human being to have a body is a prerequisite for reflection on the world as God's body.

In his essay on embodiedness, John Macquarrie lists four major contributions which the body makes to human life:

First, the body is the source of sensations, . . . Second, emotions are closely connected with the body...Third, the body is the seat of certain desires, which arise out of its own bodily processes...Fourth, the body is the basis for our relations with other people.[14]

These four contributions of the body to human life have ramifications for our understanding of God. As the source of sensations, the body is the means by which we interact with others and with our environment. Correspondingly then, the world becomes the means through which God acts and can be acted upon. The connection between emotions and the body leads to an image of a responsive God who can rejoice, suffer, rage over the condition of the

---

[13]Frye 153.
[14]John Macquarrie, *In Search of Humanity* (New York: Crossroad 1983) 55-58.

world. The abuse or destruction of the world as God's body evokes a response of respect for the world. The body as the seat of desire suggests a God who is integrated with the world. Just as bodily desires such as hunger are not merely physical functions but become occasions of interpersonal and social interaction which lead to fulfillment, so too do we see a God whose glory is a fulfillment of the world. Finally, as the human body serves as the ground of human communication, so does the world serve as the medium of divine communication.

Nature and Grace

One insight into a renewed understanding of the nature-grace relationship grows out of the contrast between the monarchical model and the world as God's body. The monarchical model describing the relationship of God and the world considers mainly the human dimension of the world. Elaborating on this limitation, McFague laments that "the monarchical model and an aural tradition fit together naturally, for kings give orders and subjects obey, but the model has no place for creatures who cannot hear and obey."[15] In contrast, employing the metaphor of the world as God's body opens up a much wider frame of relationship in that the world serves as the medium of divine communication. If we stretch this a bit, and say with Marshall McLuhan that the medium is the message[16], then we must conclude that the world is God's self-communication. Or, to put it even more pertinently, nature is grace.

As radical as this statement may seem, it is, in reality, in continuity with traditional Christian theology, reflecting the claim that "if grace is the traditional theological term for the free self-donation of God outside the Trinity, then creation, nature itself, is the first stage of that divine self-gift."[17] Thus, "nature is grace" paraphrases the statement that the external activity of the Trinity is manifest in creation, i.e., as created grace, and affirms the Catholic principal of sacramentality.

While we have just seen that the metaphor of the world as God's body leads to the notion that nature is grace, we must ask whether considering the world as God's body allows one to think of gradations of self-communication or whether it has a leveling effect so that all parts of the universe disclose God to the same degree. Grace Jantzen has considered this question and directs our attention to the analogy between human self-disclosure and God's self-disclosure:

> For example, a letter to a friend will normally be more revelatory of a person than a shopping list he writes, though a detective or a psychiatrist might be able to discern a great deal about the person even from the shopping list. Thus also the Bible could

---

[15]McFague 66.

[16]Marshall McLuhan, *Understanding Media:The Extensions of Man* (New York:McGraw-Hill, 1965) 7.

be taken as more revelatory of God than *The Times*, even though both ultimately depend on him for their existence, and a person who knows how might be able to discern something of the nature of God from a perusal of the latter: at least Christians would not want to rule this out. Although God is present everywhere, certain situations and occurrences bring him more to our attention than others do, as though a person who has been sitting silently in a room suddenly begins to speak.[18]

In this view, the human person complete with intelligence and freedom is among the most revelatory of God's self-disclosures. Our ability to understand and our freedom to choose among a variety of options have bearing both on our being recipients of God's self-communication and being part of this communication. Since we encounter God through the world, we are in the position to understand God's self-disclosures even as we are free to accept or reject them. The same freedom allows us to control our receptivity to God's communications.

Our intelligence and freedom, themselves part of the divine communication, indicate that God's love is so great that in creating us, God was willing to limit the divine exercise of power, to limit divine control over the world. This semi-independence of humans, then, makes the metaphor of the world as God's body more fitting in that we have limited control over the cells forming the human body just as God limits the divine power to control our freedom. In humanity there came into existence a creature who is able to change and develop the world by means of technology, and who consciously can choose either to care for God's body or to destroy it. Although to destroy the world is not to destroy God, the possibility alone puts God at risk in that God's principle medium of self-communication would be destroyed. Thus, our intelligence and our freedom reveal a God whose love "costs him something, a limiting of himself, an expenditure of his power on behalf of our autonomy."[19] Accordingly, human intelligence and human freedom are costly grace, as it were. Here again the metaphor shapes our image of God.

In the world-as-God's-body metaphor grace figures in two ways: nature in general, and humanity as the intelligent and free dimension of nature. In view of the consistent New Testament assertion that the earthly appearance of Jesus is grace,[20] however, any Christian reflection upon grace must also include a Christological dimension. In this way, we come to the question of whether the metaphor of the world as God's body can offer us any insight into the grace of Christ.

Beginning with an examination of the human Jesus, what was said of humans in general holds here also: Jesus is part of the conscious dimension

---

[18]Grace Jantzen, *God's World, God's Body* (Philadelphia: Westminster Press 1984) 98.

[19]Jantzen 153

[20]Edward Schillebeeckx, *Christ: The Experience of Jesus as Lord*, tr. John Bowden (New York: Crossroad, 1983) 466.

of the universe and as such reflects the willingness of God to limit the divine self out of love. In the Scriptures Jesus is commonly depicted as a person who invites the poor, the outcasts, and women into solidarity. He is a teacher who uses such images as the germination of seeds and the interconnectedness of birds and trees to communicate the qualities of the reign of God. Accordingly, we have a Christological approach ("from below") which discloses a human being who lived and preached inclusive love. Our notion of the varying effectiveness of different forms of communication leads to the conclusion that if all humans are grace, then Jesus by virtue of his life and teaching is a special grace.

This conclusion is confirmed when one approaches Christology "from above." Although all human beings can be considered models of the metaphor of the world as God's body, Jesus as God incarnate is the paradigm. The New Testament represents Jesus as the definitive Word of a God who has spoken in various partial ways (Heb 1:1). This Word, however, does not bring us back to a mere "hearing" of God's self-communication. Rather, the Word of God calls for an understanding that is rooted in the whole body, for it is what has been heard, seen, looked at and touched (1Jn 1:1). Jesus, in terms of Christology "from above," is not merely a particularly effective means of God's self-communication, but through the incarnation, the medium truly has become the message.

While Jesus' life and preaching call us to new possibilities and a new way of living, the all-embracing sign of grace is Jesus' love to the point of death, a death which culminates in the resurrection and God's continuing presence in the world.[21] We come full circle. The post-resurrection appearance stories tell of God's abiding presence in the world, and one of the main values of the metaphor of the world as God's body is the light it sheds on this presence.

Evil, Sin and Salvation

Without some reference to evil, both natural and moral, no treatment of the relationship between God and the world is complete. Using the metaphor of the world as God's body has implications for our conception of evil. In the first place, evil cannot be conceived as something totally distinct from God because evil exists in God's body and evil inflicts suffering and pain upon God's body. This is not to say that God causes evil, but neither does the metaphor support the notion that God "conquers" evil. Rather, the metaphor of the world as God's body implies that the pain experienced in the world because of evil is felt by God.[22]

Moreover, although human intelligence and human freedom are part of God's self-communication, they also open the possibility of sin. In terms of

---

[21]Schillebeeckx 466.
[22]McFague 75

God's self-communication, they also open the possibility of sin. In terms of our metaphor, it seems obvious that sin is the refusal to acknowledge that one is part of God's body, and to act as if one were autonomous. It is the refusal to accept one's radical interdependence with all creation.[23] It is the refusal to exercise care and responsibility for the world. In short, sin is the rejection of the grace that is nature.

At the same time, however, we perceive that the total evil in the world is more than the sum of our contributions; there is also the evil over which we have no control. Evolution tells a story of development and extinction, and nature did this long before technology began to transform the environment. Thus, even in the light of the metaphor of the world as God's body, evil remains a mystery.

This ecological concept of evil and sin calls for a corresponding understanding of salvation. Just as the metaphor of the world as God's body makes it inappropriate to speak of sin primarily as personal disobedience against one's God and King, so too does a purely personal understanding of salvation fail to address the complexity of sin. As Sittler contends, "salvation is an ecological word in the sense that it is the restoration of a right relation that has been corrupted."[24] To return to our metaphor, salvation is the restoration of balance and health to God's body.

The ecological understanding of salvation stands in continuity with such New Testament interpretations of salvation as healing (Jas 5:14), cleansing (1Jn 1:7), and reconciliation (Rom 5:11). In these views, Jesus is our "leader to salvation," the model, the one who shows us how to live (Heb 2:10). In accepting the grace of Christ and choosing to live responsibly we engage in the ministry of reconciliation, contribute to the process of salvation and make the world a place of grace (2 Cor 5:18-19). At the same time, "we know that all creation is groaning in labor pains even until now" (Rom 8:22) The contemporary awareness of pollution, of a nuclear holocaust which threatens global annihilation, of the possibilities and limits of technology; all these speak of the continuing need for salvation. Such salvation is one that cannot be achieved in the present and on our own, nor is it one that was totally completed in the past by sacrifice. Rather, the ecological metaphor of the world as God's body calls for a process of salvation which, while rooted in the life, death, resurrection of Jesus, grows through our participation and comes to fruition only when the world is transformed into a new creation.

Conclusion

Contemporary ecological concerns challenge theology to break out of its

---

[23]McFague 77.
[24]Joseph Sittler, "Ecological Commitment as Theological Responsibility," *Zygon* 5 (1970): 177.

value may be judged in terms of such supple criteria as plausibility, illuminating power and timeliness.[25]

The metaphor of the world as God's body is plausible in that it offers a way of viewing the relationship between God and the world that is acceptable as long as one realizes that this metaphor, like all metaphors, both applies and does not apply. Using the metaphor as a guide to reflections on nature and grace attests to its illuminating quality. Moreover, the contention that "nature is grace" to which it leads enables a strong affirmation of the principle of sacramentality. This metaphor, as we have seen, eliminates the dualism between God and the world, and in so doing leads to the dissolution of the nature-grace dualism, an elimination which in turn points to other potential erosions: church-world, individual-social, spiritual-political, eternal-temporal, to name a few. In a world awakening to cosmic interrelatedness this is a timely metaphor which converts Therese of Lisieux's claim that "all is grace"[26] from a spiritual nosegay to a theological concept for an ecological age. Continued creative reflection is nonetheless necessary if the story of the relationship of nature and grace is to be as meaningful for Christians of the present and the future as it has been for those of the past.

---

[25]McFague 132.
[26]Quoted in Schillebeeckx 528.

LIST OF AUTHORS

Paul Santmire has been a leading writer on ecology for twenty years. His latest book is *The Travail of Nature*. He is currently pastor of Grace Lutheran Church in West Hartford, Connecticut.

John F. Haught, professor of theology at Georgetown University in Washington, D.C., is the author of *The Cosmic Adventure* and other works.

Rosemary Ruether is professor of religion at Garrett Theological Seminary in Chicago and a leading American theologian and ecofeminist.

Jay McDaniel teaches at Hendricks College in Arkansas. He is the author of two recent books on ecology, *Of God and Pelicans* and *Earth, Sky, Gods, and Mortals*.

Matthew Fox, noted for his creation-centered spirituality, is the author of *The Coming of the Cosmic Christ*, among many other works.

J. Patout Burns, a noted Augustinian scholar, is professor in the Department of Religion at the University of Florida.

Dennis Hamm, S.J., teaches and writes about scripture in the theology department of Creighton University.

Maureen Tilley teaches early Christian writings in the religion department of Florida State University in Tallahassee.

John Barciauskas, is a reference librarian at the Thomas P. O'Neill Jr. library to Boston College and a student of the works of Eckhart.

James A. Donahue teaches ethics in the theology department at Georgetown University.

William French is a professor of ethics in the theology department of Loyola University in Chicago.

Eugene Bianchi is a professor of religion at Emory University in Atlanta and has recently written two books on the nature of aging as a spiritual journey.

Dorothy Jacko, is chair of the theology department of Seton Hill College in Greensburg, Pennsylvania and teaches about liberation and feminist thought.

William Grosnick teaches and writes on Buddhist thought in the religion department at LaSalle College in Wyncote, Pennsylvania.

Christopher Chapple teaches about Eastern religions in the theology department at Loyola Marymount University of Los Angeles.

Fred McLeod teaches in the theology department at St. Louis University and writes about both patristic and literary materials.

Sally Kenel teaches in the theology department at St. John's University on Long Island, on religion, culture, and literature.